The Science of Words

Cuneiform ("wedge-shaped") writing dates from the fourth millennium B.C. and was used until the first century B.C. by diverse Near Eastern cultures. It preserves the oldest language of which we have written examples (Sumerian), as well as the oldest Indo-European texts known, which are in Old Hittite. This inscription from the fortress of Van (now in eastern Turkey) was carved when that citadel was the royal seat of Urartu, the Assyrian name for Armenia.

THE SCIENCE OF WORDS

George A. Miller

SCIENTIFIC AMERICAN LIBRARY

A division of HPHLP
New York

To Nancy and Donn

"The Great Figure," p. 45, from *Collected Earlier Poems*, © 1938 by William Carlos Williams, reprinted by permission of New Directions Publishing Corporation.

Library of Congress Cataloging-in-Publication Data

Miller, George A. (George Armitage), 1920-
    The science of words / George A. Miller.
        p.   cm.
    Includes bibliographical references and index.
    ISBN 0-7167-5027-9
    ISBN 0-7167-6016-9 (pbk)
    1. Lexicology.   I. Title.
  P326.M55   1991
  413′.028—dc20   90-24023
                                          CIP

ISSN 1040-3213

Printed in the United States of America.

Scientific American Library
A Division of HPHLP
New York

Distributed by W. H. Freeman and Company.
41 Madison Avenue, New York, New York 10010
Houndmills, Basingstoke RG21 6XS, England

First printing 1996, HAW

This book is number 35 of a series.

CONTENTS

Words provide both style and subject in this 1918 watercolor, Einst dem Grau der Nacht enttaucht . . ., *by Paul Klee.*

PREFACE

Although I have lived all my life in a society that is intensely, sometimes morbidly, fascinated with communication, it seems perfectly natural to me that this society should have relatively little interest in language, the principal means of human communication. The practical American attitude is that language is merely a means to an end. The message is what counts; how you say it is of secondary importance. A child of my pragmatic culture, I still take this attitude to be basically correct. But what it took me years to recognize is that I would never understand the end until I knew more about the means.

Because communication is so obviously important it seemed a worthy object of scientific investigation, and that was the task I set for myself as a young psychologist. It was a fortunate choice, and I have never lacked interesting questions to pursue. But the pinch came when I asked about the psychological foundations of human communication. I quickly convinced myself that the structure and functioning of the human mind are intimately related to the human capacity for communication; having gone that far, I could not avoid the conclusion that this intimate relation is a consequence of an innate human capacity for language.

To understand the psychological basis for human communication, therefore, it was obviously necessary to learn more about language. But what I thought at first would be a detour turned out to be a major highway. This book is an account of some of the important stations along that highway—the lexical stations in particular. Why I have chosen the lexical component of language rather than the phonological or syntactic components is a personal question that I am not sure I can answer. Not everything could be included; some focus was necessary. And I find words especially interesting. Every word carries its own surprises and offers its own rewards to the reflective mind. Their amazing variety is a constant delight. I do not believe that I am alone in this—a fascination with words is shared by people in all countries and all walks of life.

But relatively few people have a scientific interest in words. Words are traditionally the province of literary scholars. The idea that there could be a science of words still strikes many people as an oxymoron. A science is expected to provide a systematic and logically defensible explanation of some natural phenomenon. Yet words are surely a natural phenomenon. A science of words assumes merely that scientific methods can be applied to these linguistic units. The story of how such an idea could occur, how it could develop and flower, is as much a part of this book as are the results of the science itself.

The central concern of these pages is with what a scientific approach can tell us about the three-sided character of every word. Each word is the synthesis of a concept, an utterance, and a syntactic role. A person who knows a word knows what it means, knows how to pronounce it, and knows the contexts in which it can be used. These are not three independent kinds of knowledge; they are different views of a single entity.

Yet they are often studied independently. The most tangible of the three is the utterance (or its orthographic associate, the written word). The twentieth century has seen amazing advances in the technology of communication, advances that exploit the physical nature of words. Computer programmers can elicit from a modern speech synthesizer an almost perfect rendition of a human voice, produced without any concern for the meaning or the grammar of the spoken message. A human speaker, in contrast, is largely unconscious of the amazing coordinations involved in producing speech and hears little *but* meanings; only when the sense is garbled will attention be paid to sound or grammar. And a linguistic theorist, trying to characterize what turns words into sentences, is likely to neglect both the sound and the meaning in order to focus on the grammatical contexts in which words can or cannot occur.

Lines of research into all three of these aspects of language contribute to the science of words, and all three are discussed in this book. But the real wonder is the integrity of the word as a linguistic element. How can all that semantic, phonological, and syntactic complexity be assembled in such a small and handy package? Pulling the three threads together in one book may not answer that question, but it will help a reader appreciate the delicate intricacy of this familiar linguistic unit. Science has a way of turning up the unexpected in the most familiar places.

There could not be a science of words if it were not possible to study complicated systems scientifically. Languages are systems. They are highly complex systems of sounds and meanings that have their ultimate reality in the minds of people who know and use them. The scientific way to understand complex systems is not to reduce them to patterns of physical energy exchange, but rather to describe their component parts and to characterize the functional relations within and among those parts. Our language faculty is our innate capacity to acquire and use a special kind of complex system. This book offers an account—a systems account—of one component of this uniquely human kind of complex system.

■   ■   ■

A preface allows authors to confess that they did not do it all alone. My pleasure in having this opportunity to thank those who helped me must be tempered by a recognition that my intellectual debts are far greater than a short preface can accommodate. But any list must include my wife, Katherine Miller, who shares my obsession with words; my assistant, Pamela Wakefield, who made it possible to pile writing on top of other commitments; my colleagues at the Princeton Cognitive Science Laboratory, particularly Christiane Fellbaum, but also Richard Beckwith, Derek Gross, Dan Teibel, and Katherine Miller—the lexigang that has helped me understand what little I do understand of the semantic organization of the mental lexicon; and the many Princeton students, undergraduate and graduate, who spent time with us. I am also indebted to Mark Aronoff, Steven Pinker, and William S-Y. Wang, who were kind enough to read an early draft of the manuscript and to suggest many corrections and improvements, and to Gene Searchinger, who persuaded me that psycholinguistics is something the public should know more about.

I also have institutional debts to acknowledge. Support for my lexical adventures came from the James S. McDonnell Foundation, the Office of Naval Research, and the Army Research Institute—John Bruer, Susan Chipman, and Judith Orasanu provided much more than financial assistance. And Amy Edith Johnson and Jonathan Cobb at Scientific American Books have earned special thanks for coupling my words so artistically to their printing presses. But greatest of all is my debt to Princeton University and to my colleagues in Princeton's Department of Psychology, not merely because they have tolerated my erratic oscillations between psychology and linguistics, but principally because they have created and allowed me to share an environment where serious intellectual work can be attempted.

George A. Miller
January 1991

For this paperback edition, I have made a few changes—correcting minor misprints, adding some new references, and revising in the light of recent work where that is feasible. I am gratified by the respone to the book and pleased that this new paperback edition will make it available to a wider audience.

George A. Miller
October 1995

The Science of Words

▲ Technological advances have provided a set of tools for the study of language as a universal, innate, and definitively human capacity. The strong affinities between the developing sciences of linguistics and anthropology early in this century are represented by the work of Frances Densmore of the Smithsonian Institution, who plays a phonographic record of native American utterances to Mountain Chief, a Blackfoot, who interprets them.

▶ Modern computer displays like this one go beyond the preservation of evidence to facilitate analysis, affording registers of the successive frequencies of the sound waves and the pitch and intensity of speech signals.

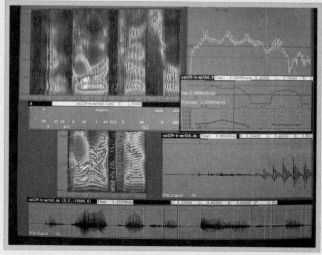

The Scientific Study of Language

The scientific study of language is not a familiar undertaking. Ordinarily when you study a language, you are trying to learn how to speak and understand it. So an important question arises right at the start. Why would anyone want to study language scientifically? Why not simply *use* language and get on with the business of living?

Before trying to answer that question, a distinction must be drawn: namely, the distinction between specific, individual languages and language in general. Language in general is a generic and highly abstract idea; specific languages are instances of language in general, just as specific breeds of dogs are instances of dog in general. A specific language is a particular set of social conventions governing the formation of grammatical utterances and their use in achieving personal goals. People learn particular languages—English, Urdu, Swahili, Japanese—and use them to interact with others in their society. The scientific study of language is the study of language in general, the study of what is common to all languages.

So why would anyone care about language in general? Nobody speaks language in general. It is useless for communication; you cannot order a pizza in language in general. Yet a moment's reflection establishes the central role that language in general plays in all human affairs. People want to know about language in general, not to use it in social interaction, but in the hope of understanding something that is uniquely human about human beings.

There are good reasons to study language scientifically. Language in general is important not only because it distinguishes human beings from all other animals on the earth, but because, directly or indirectly, it makes possible the elaborate organization of civilized society. Because the human capacity for acquiring language is innate—every human group has one—when you investigate language, you are investigating something universal, with a solid base in the biological nature of *Homo sapiens sapiens*. And language in general is interesting because, although everyone knows and uses a specific language, few people understand what they know. Becoming self-consciously aware of what is known unself-consciously carries a special brand of excitement.

A skeptic might resist such claims, of course. "It is not speech," the skeptic might say, "but human intelligence—the amazing human ability to learn and to adapt—that is so extraordinary and unique." And to support that objection the skeptic could point to people who are born deaf and never acquire spoken language, yet communicate splendidly by means of hand gestures. They achieve the same results, and do so almost as expeditiously as their noisier cousins. But what this argument shows is merely that speech and language are different. Systems of hand gestures that are called sign languages—American Sign Language, Danish Sign Language, British Sign Language—are in every sense as much specific languages as are any systems of spoken words. It is true that congenitally deaf people can do quite well without speech, but they cannot get along without language.

One need not be a communications expert to recognize that different signals can carry the same message, so it is tempting to conclude that it is the message, not the signal, that is important. But that overlooks the fact that without a signal there could be no message. The important point is that different kinds of signals—spoken, gestured, written, whatever—can make possible the externalization of thought and perception. A gorilla might be enormously intelligent, but without some system of signals to communicate that intelligence—without language—its remarkable gift would remain unshared. Intelligence alone does not explain the human ability to communicate.

A system of externalizing thought that uses the voice and ear has many advantages over a system that uses the hand and eye. Speech is the biologically given signal system for human communication, and much will be made of spoken words in the pages that follow. But when the voice and ear are not available, the human need to communicate finds other signals to replace them. A theory of language in general should have room for this diversity of signals.

The evolution of language enabled many individuals to think together. The externalization achieved by language is not perfect, of course, but it is

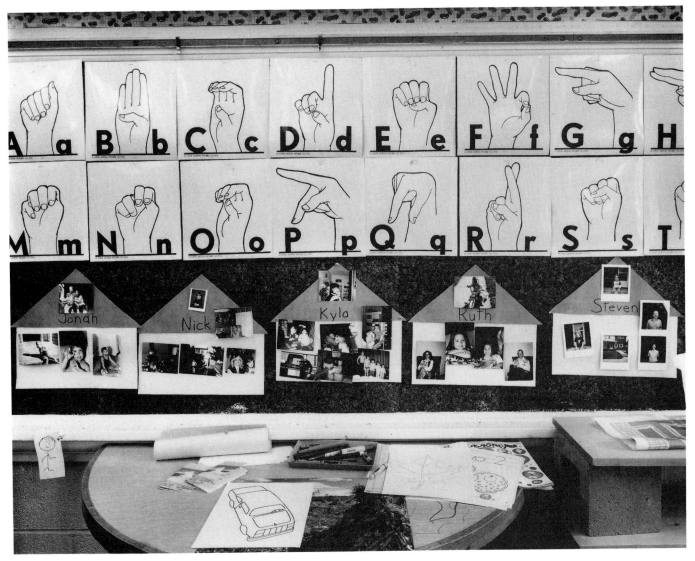

Finger spelling, the one-for-one representation of letters of the alphabet, can be used to spell out proper nouns and rare words. Although the American Manual Alphabet is totally different from American Sign Language, many of these hand configurations are incorporated into American Sign Language to designate English words by the initial letter.

good enough that many people can share, enjoy, and profit from one person's experience. Thus, social units could form and work together in novel ways, cooperating as if they were a single superordinate individual. The survival value of human language was very great.

If language is important, then it should follow that words, the building blocks of language, are also important. Indeed, the very fact that something is a word means that it must have been important to somebody. Or, to put it differently, a word is an idea that some group of people thought was impor-

The Eskimo Vocabulary for Snow

When an idea is important, people are likely to have a word for it. Mountain people will have a word for mountain; people who live on the plains and have never seen a mountain will not have such a word. The more important something is, moreover, the more words there are likely to be. If, for example, a language has many words for different kinds and states of bamboo, an anthropologist knows that bamboo plays a central role in the lives of that people. But it is not necessary to study other cultures to find lexical specialization. Painters have many words for colors, chemists have many words for chemical compounds, horsemen recognize many different kinds of horses. Every professional group develops its own technical jargon for talking about matters of critical concern.

It is remarkable, therefore, that one particular example of lexical specialization has captured the popular imagination and been referred to so often in the press—namely, the Eskimo vocabulary for snow. It is plausible to suppose that snow plays an important role in the lives of the Eskimo, so their language should have several words for it. The interesting question is: Precisely how many different snow words do they have? According to the myth that has grown up, the Eskimo language has hundreds of words for different kinds and grades of snow, an extravagant specialization that is sometimes cited to illustrate how primitive minds categorize reality differently.

Anthropologist Franz Boas (1858–1942).

The anthropologist Laura Martin traced this myth back to a passage in Franz Boas's *Handbook of North American Indians* (1911), where he comments that Eskimo has apparently distinct words for snow: *aput* for snow on the ground, *qana* for falling snow, *piqsirpoq* for drifting snow, and *qimuqsuq* for a snow drift. The number began to grow in 1940 when Benjamin Lee Whorf published a popular article claiming that Eskimo has distinct words for falling snow, snow on the ground, packed snow, slushy snow, wind-driven snow, and other kinds of snow. As interest in the matter spread, the published claims grew vaguer: "Eskimo languages have many words for snow." Thereafter "many" was translated into nine, forty-eight, one hundred, two hundred.

The linguist Geoffrey Pullum advises his readers to fight this Eskimological falsehood. When you hear the claim, he advises, you should stand up and announce that the best dictionary of the Eskimo language gives just two roots: *qanik* for snow in the air and *aput* for snow on the ground. It will not make you the most popular person in the room, but it will strike a blow for truth and the standards of evidence.

Snow in the air, snow on the ground.

tant enough to enter in the lexicon. (This notion of what a word is does not hold up under careful scrutiny, as Chapter 2 takes pains to point out, but it is more vague than wrong.) People who know a word can share that idea with other members of their group, and a shared vocabulary is part of the glue that holds people together and allows them to create a shared culture.

An inescapable fact that will surely impress anyone who carefully considers the operations of the human mind is how much people know. Some people know more than others, of course, but everybody knows a lot. And one thing that everybody knows is a language, which is itself a very large chunk of knowledge. The major part of that large chunk of knowledge consists of knowing the words of the language. It is not the speech sounds or the rules for generating grammatical sentences that require the most extensive learning. It is the vocabulary: thousands of words, each with its own sound, its own spelling, its own meaning, its own role, its own use, its own history.

An intriguing thing about this knowledge is that people know so much that they do not realize they know. In English, for example, Subject-Verb, or Subject-Verb-Object, is a general pattern for grammatical sentences. Subject and Object phrases contain nouns, Verb phrases contain verbs. To conform to this pattern, therefore, people who speak English must know the difference between nouns and verbs. Why, then, is it so difficult to teach this distinction to schoolchildren, who conform to it consistently in their everyday use of language? Apparently there are different ways of knowing. Knowing how to speak grammatically and knowing how to characterize grammatical speech are not the same.

Just as none of the reasons for studying language scientifically depend on any particular language, so none of the reasons for studying words depend on any particular words. What is at issue in a scientific discussion of words is not so much specific words as wordiness: Why are all languages wordy? Why are words a universal design feature of languages? It is words in general, not particular words, that are scientifically important. Humanistic scholars may be interested in individual words in particular documents written in specific languages, but a scientist must search for generalizations and invariants.

A Little History

Curiosity about the origins of language, and about why there are so many different languages, has a long history. The whole idea of studying language in general scientifically grew out of studying specific languages historically.

The desire to learn and understand specific languages is as old as recorded history. In classical Greece every educated man studied grammar and rhetoric, and the scholarly pursuit of those subjects has persisted down to the present day. But correct usage, persuasive oratory, and the accurate preservation of important texts are not the stuff from which the science of linguistics was

Medieval manuscripts were often works of art. This is a page from an illuminated Latin manuscript of the Hours of Alfonso of Aragon, Naples, 1480.

built. Foundations for linguistic science had to await comparative studies of different languages.

The scientific study of language began just two hundred years ago with systematic attempts to trace historical relations among languages. Medieval scholars studied Latin, of course, and with the Renaissance came knowledge of ancient Greek. But it was not until the eighteenth century that the rediscovery of the ancient Sanskrit language of India made the comparison of languages an active field of study. Sir William Jones, who learned Sanskrit as Chief Justice of Bengal, wrote that no one who was familiar with Sanskrit, Greek, and Latin "could examine all three without believing them to have sprung from some common source, which, perhaps, no longer exists." Sir William's observation, made in 1786, stirred many imaginations and identified an ideal starting point for comparing languages and tracing their historical changes.

Two questions became salient. First, what was the lost "common source" from which Sanskrit, Greek, and Latin had sprung? Second, what other languages had sprung from the same source?

The initial demonstration that Sanskrit, Greek, and Latin are related was easy. But reconstructing their common source was not easy. Many scholars had to follow Jones's lead before the details became clear. The most important approach is to compare the attested languages, looking for shared features. This comparative method is based on the assumption that if two languages share a special feature, they probably inherited it from a common ancestor. Comparative reconstruction always starts with vocabulary, where resemblances are particularly striking. Lists of similarities were drawn up, and from them the phonology and vocabulary of the ancestral language were inferred. For example, the words for numbers from one to ten show how similar the three languages are, and how different they are from Japanese, which is not related.

At first it was thought that Greek and Latin were descended from Sanskrit, but after extensive discussion and debate over the accumulating evidence it was finally agreed that all three are descended from some mother language, called Proto-Indo-European (PIE), a language spoken before the invention of writing and now lost forever.

How do linguists decide such things? It is generally accepted that languages change, of course: Old English changed into Middle English and then into Modern English; Latin changed into Italian, French, Spanish. Those changes are well documented in the written record. But what do linguists do when the evidence is less compelling?

Suppose, for example, that someone wanted to say that Italian is not really the sister of Spanish, but its mother. The challenge would be to prove that all the changes that were introduced in going from Latin to Italian are also present in Spanish, and also to find other innovations in Spanish that have not

Sir William Jones (1746–1794) was appointed to the Supreme Court of Justice in Calcutta as one of the three Judges of the British Crown in 1783. A year after he arrived in India, Jones founded the Asiatick Society of Bengal and became its first president. His famous statement about the common source of Greek, Latin, and Sanskrit was made in a speech to the Society in February 1786. Jones was not the first scholar to notice these similarities, but the impact of his startling claim was reinforced by his widely recognized stature in social and political life.

Although Jones was a jurist by profession, he was a philologist at heart and had a classical scholar's command of Greek and Latin. But Sanskrit was the ancient religious and literary language of India; before Jones could become one of the first Europeans to learn it, he had to overcome the reluctance of the Brahmin gurus to share the language of the holy Vedas with someone who was not a Hindu. To help others learn Sanskrit and to check his conclusions, Jones proposed a system for transcribing it into the Roman alphabet. He recognized the importance of phonetic comparisons, but the science he needed to formulate such questions did not yet exist.

Numbers from One to Ten in Five Languages

English	Latin	Greek	Sanskrit	Japanese
one	unus	heis	ekas	hitotsu
two	duo	duo	dva	futatsu
three	tres	treis	tryas	mittsu
four	quattuor	tettares	catvaras	yottsu
five	quinque	pente	panca	itsutsu
six	sex	heks	sat	muttsu
seven	septem	hepta	sapta	nanatsu
eight	octo	okto	asta	yattsu
nine	novem	ennea	nava	kokonotsu
ten	decem	deka	dasa	to

occurred in Italian. That case cannot be made, of course, but if it could, linguists would declare that an early form of Italian was an older stage of modern Spanish. The point of this counterfactual example, however, is that all such judgments are comparative, not absolute. There are no absolute linguistic properties that are primitive, primordial, or imperfect and that will therefore mark one language as older than another. A line of linguistic descent is not some simple "given." It must be inferred indirectly as a special kind of relatedness.

By comparative arguments, therefore, scholars decided that Greek, Latin, and Sanskrit were sister languages descended from a common ancestral language. The more languages there were to be compared, of course, the more reliable such inferences were judged to be. So the first question led naturally to the second: What other languages were descended from PIE? The same kinds of comparisons that were used to reconstruct PIE from languages now dead were also used to establish common ancestors of living languages. The large family of modern languages that descended from this lost PIE—including Kurdish, Persian, Urdu, Hindi, modern Greek, French, Spanish, Italian, Portuguese, German, Dutch, Norwegian, Swedish, Russian, Ukrainian, Bulgarian, and many others in addition to English—are called Indo-European languages. Tracing out relations among these different and widely distributed languages became an exciting intellectual adventure, and the implications for European prehistory are still debated by archeologists.

One of the first fruits of this budding science of language were the *sound laws*, which resulted from attempts to establish that modern Germanic languages (including English) belong to the Indo-European family. Proto-Germanic, an early form of German that might have split off from PIE sometime prior to 1000 B.C., can be reconstructed from early records of Gothic, Old English, Old High German, and Old Norse, written between A.D. 200 and 1200. Scholars such as Rasmus Rask noted that many words in these early Germanic languages bear a systematic relation to words in Latin if you assume that the voiceless stops in Latin [p, t, k] became voiceless fricatives in Germanic [f, θ, h], as in the initial sounds of these:

> Latin *pater* → Old Norse *fathir* (with voiced *th*, ð)
> Latin *tres* → Old Norse *thrir* (with voiceless *th*, θ)
> Latin *cornu* → Old High German *horn*

Rask's observations were summarized by Jakob Grimm in 1822 in what is usually called, somewhat unfairly, Grimm's Law. It summarized these systematic sound shifts and established that the Germanic languages do belong in the Indo-European family. However, the changes were so drastic and the number of important German words that have no known Indo-European source was so large that something more than ordinary linguistic evolution must have been going on. Some scholars have speculated that Proto-Germanic

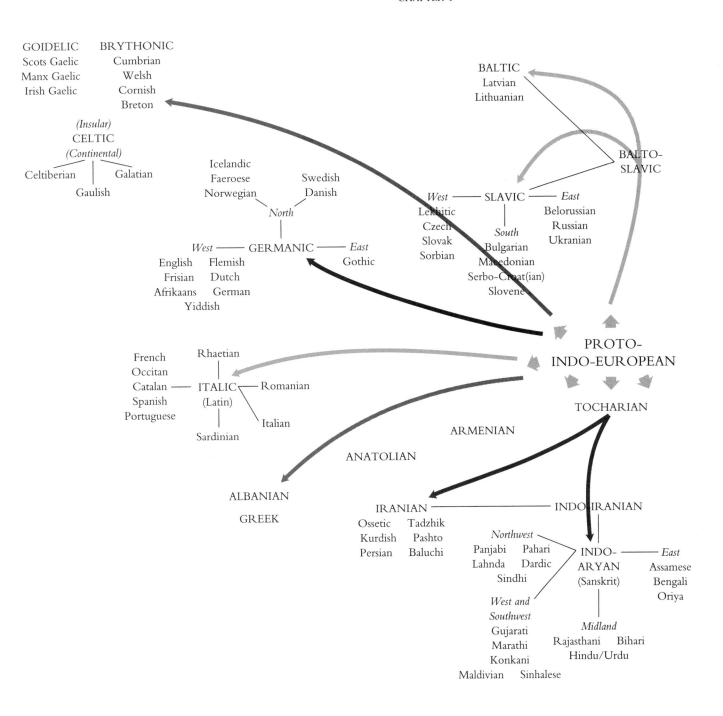

The Indo-European family tree of languages.

In 1811 Rasmus Christian Rask (1787–1832), a Danish scholar and philologist, published a historical grammar of Icelandic; like most of his writings, it did not receive the attention it deserved, because it was written in Danish. Whereas other early linguists tried to document linguistic changes by comparing the written texts of dead languages, Rask was able to make meaningful comparisons of Germanic languages. And because he dealt with living languages, Rask was the first to realize that letters can be misleading and that it is the sounds that provide the best evidence for linguistic evolution. Although Jacob Grimm (1785–1863), a German linguist and folklorist, is usually given credit for discovering the sound laws that firmly established Germanic as a member of the Indo-European family of languages, Rask was the first scholar to have recognized and systematically applied the principle of regular sound change, in both historical and comparative language analysis. Karl Verner, another Dane, further elaborated the Germanic sound laws in 1875.

developed when some people who spoke a non-Indo-European language rich in voiceless fricatives came in contact with speakers of PIE.

It was immediately recognized that there were exceptions to Grimm's Law. For example, according to the Law, the PIE voiceless stop *t* in *pater* should have become the voiceless fricative *th*-sound (θ, as in English *thin*), but instead became the voiced *th*-sound ($\eth$, as in Modern English *father*). The *t* in Latin *frater*, on the other hand, was replaced by the voiceless θ in the Gothic *brothar*, as Grimm's Law specified. In view of such contradictions, Grimm's Law was assumed to describe merely a general tendency.

In 1875, however, many of the exceptions were explained by Verner's Law, which said that if the PIE voiceless stop is not initial, or is not immediately followed by a stressed vowel, then it becomes a voiced fricative in the Germanic languages. In other words, the Danish linguist Karl Verner (1846–1896) discovered that a whole series of noninitial consonant shifts in Proto-Germanic depended on which syllable was accented. When it was realized that German has *t* in *vater*, but *d* in *bruder*, because the two words had a different accentuation three or four thousand years ago, it served not only to heighten respect for the linguistic science that was able to demonstrate such truths, but also to increase the feeling that the world of spoken sounds is subject to laws as strict as those of natural science.

This strategy—to account for sound changes as dependent on the contexts in which the sounds had originally occurred—was so successful that one enthusiastic group, the Neogrammarians (nicknamed the "young grammarians"), claimed that linguistics had become a precise science and that there

Jacob Grimm   *Karl Verner*

Gothic, c. 350

8 Jah hairdjos wesun in pamma samin landa, pairhwakandans jah witandans wahtwom nahts ufaro hairdai seinai.

9 Ip aggilus fraujins anaqam ins, jah wulpus fraujins biskain ins, jah ohtedun agisa mikilamma.

10 Jah qap du im sa aggilus: Ni ogeip; unte sai, spillo izwis faheid mikila, sei wairpip allai managein,

11 Patei gabaurans ist izwis himma daga nasjands, saei ist Xristus frauja, in baurg Daweidis.

12 Jah pata izwis taikns; bigitid barn biwundan, jah galagid in uzetin.

13 Jah anaks warp mip pamma aggilau managei harjis himinakundis, hazjandane gup, jah qipandane:

14 Wulpus in hauhistjam gupa, jah ana airpai gawairpi in mannam godis wiljins.

For *q* read "*qu*".

Old English (West Saxon Dialect), End of Tenth Century

8 And heirdas wæron on þām ilcan rīce, waciende and nihtwæccan healdende ofer heora heorda.

9 Þā stōd dryhtnes engel wiþ hī, and godes beorhtnes him ymbescān; and hī him micelum ege ādrēdon.

10 And sē engel him tōcwæþ: Nelle gē ēow ādrǣdan, sōplice nū, ic ēow bodie micelne gefēan, sē biþ eallum folce,

11 forþām tōdæg ēow is hælend ācenned, sē is dryhten Christ, on Davides ceastre.

12 And þis tācen ēow biþ: gē gemētaþ ān cild hrœglum bewunden, and on binne ālēd.

13 And þā wæs fǣringa geworden mid þām engle micelnes heofonlices werodes, god heriendra and þus cwependra:

14 Gode sī wuldor on hēahnesse, and on eorpan sibb mannum gōdes willan.

Spelling regularized and marks of length added.

Middle English, Wyclif, 1389

8 And schepherdis weren in the same cuntre, wakinge and kepinge the watchis of the nyzt on her flok.

9 And loo, the aungel of the Lord stood by sydis hem, and the clerenesse of God schynede aboute hem; and thei dredden with greet drede.

10 And the aungel seide to hem: Nyle ze drede; lo, sothli I euangelise to zou a grete ioye, that schal be to al peple.

11 For a sauyour is borun to day to vs, that is Crist the Lord, in the cite of Dauith.

12 And this a tokene to zou; ze schulen fynde a zong child wlappid in clothis, and put in a cracche.

13 And sudenly ther is maad with the aungel a multitude of heuenly knyzthod, heriynge God, and seyinge,

14 Glorie be in the hizeste thingis to God, and in erthe pees be to men of good wille.

Modern English evolved from early Germanic languages. Here for comparison are three versions of Luke 2 : 8–14. The Gothic was translated from Greek, the Old English from Latin. The Middle English version is from the Wyclif Bible, which was the first complete translation of the Latin Vulgate into English.

could be NO exceptions to the sound laws. They did not think of sound changes as more or less haphazard events affecting some words but not others. Instead, they believed that a sound change was simply a change in the way speakers produced the speech sound (or a series of speech sounds), and so would affect that sound (or series of sounds) anywhere it happened to occur. When some apparent exception was noted, it was assumed that the relevant contexts had not been properly analyzed; a correct analysis would show it to be regular after all. This attitude led to acrimonious debate over endless details of the pronunciation of different languages, most of which were no longer spoken by any living people.

Ferdinand de Saussure (1857–1913) never wrote a book, but in 1906, on the retirement of another professor, the University of Geneva asked Saussure to teach the course in general linguistics. Between 1907 and 1911 he three times gave the series of lectures that were to become the Cours de linguistique générale. *But Saussure suddenly fell ill and died in 1913, and so the* Cours *was compiled and edited from the notebooks of the students who had attended his lectures. The students' judgment that Saussure's ideas were too important to lose has been fully justified by subsequent events, for this book was destined to reshape the field and earn Saussure the title, "founder of modern linguistics."*

The distinction between diachronic and synchronic linguistics was but one of the fundamental principles Saussure introduced. Saussure defined language as a system of arbitrary signs, where a sign is both an auditory word-image, the signifiant *(signifier), and a concept, the* signifié *(signified). He defined linguistics as the study of* la langue, *the formal system of a language, not the study of* la parole, *the actual speech. By insisting on these basic distinctions and drawing out their implications, Saussure gave all linguists a new and clearer conception of the task of scientific linguistics.*

In 1878 the Swiss linguist Ferdinand de Saussure, then only twenty-two years old, published a *Memoir* on the PIE vowel system in which he tried to explain the irregular behavior of certain sounds in the daughter languages. After a highly technical analysis, Saussure proposed that PIE must have had another speech sound, whose pronunciation he could not determine by formal analysis. This hypothetical speech sound had been lost in the daughter languages, but not before leaving traces on the sounds that had preceded or followed it. Saussure's hypothesis, which came to be known as the "laryngeal theory" because it was thought that the lost sound might have had a laryngeal pronunciation, solved a number of problems in the development of various Indo-European languages. It remained purely hypothetical, however, for almost fifty years, until cuneiform Hittite had been discovered and deciphered. In 1927 it was demonstrated that ancient Hittite still had laryngeal consonants, written *h* or *hh*, in just those places where Saussure had claimed that the lost sound must have been in PIE. By purely formal analysis, Saussure had discovered the laryngeal consonants of PIE—and the validity of Neogrammarian principles had been upheld.

By necessity, these linguists dealt with written texts. As the new science emerged, however, the sound laws focused attention on pronunciation and on the need for more precise descriptions of speech sounds. Toward the end of the nineteenth century, the foundations were laid for phonology, the description of systems of speech sounds used in different languages. It was probably inevitable that attempts would be made to apply this tool for describing spoken languages to the many languages of the world that had no accumulated literatures because they had never been written down. Thus a bond was forged between the young science of linguistics and the young science of anthropology. An anthropologist in the field must know how to deal with the language of whatever exotic people he or she wishes to study. Training in linguistics became part of the technical education of every professional anthropologist.

As a consequence of this extension of linguistic methods to the study of languages that had no literary heritage, the original definition of linguistic science as the study of historical change in language had to be amended. The exotic languages that interested anthropologists obviously had histories, but no one would ever know what they were. Even without knowing its history, however, there is much of interest that can be said about a language. So two ways of studying language gradually sorted themselves out. The traditional study of linguistic change came to be called historical linguistics. The newer approach—which took a cross-sectional slice of a language, treating each language as a complex symbolic system existing within a limited period of time— came to be known simply as linguistics.

It was Ferdinand de Saussure who first insisted on the importance of this distinction between two different approaches to the study of language. To Saussure, historical or diachronic facts about language must be derived from nonhistorical or synchronic facts, or from a long succession of synchronic facts. As he defined the terms, synchronic linguistics is concerned with the

A ritual against the plague is preserved in the Anatolian languages Hittite and Luwian on this tablet, dating from about 1400 B.C., which was found in modern Turkey. Although the Anatolian language group, now extinct, was spoken in Asia Minor as much as four millennia ago, it was not until 1915, after Saussure's death, that Hittite, its main language, was shown to be Indo-European.

logical and psychological relations that organize coexisting language elements as a system in the minds of language users, whereas diachronic linguistics is concerned with relations that organize successive language elements, but are not present in the minds of any language users and so do not form a system. By giving priority to the synchronic approach, Saussure defined the central task of linguistic science.

By the 1930s synchronic linguistics had established itself as a respectable scientific discipline, related to but independent of diachronic linguistics and the humanistic study of written languages and their literatures. Synchronic descriptions of a language treated three major domains: pronunciation, grammar, and vocabulary. The new science of phonology handled pronunciation; it provided systems of phonetic writing in which to transcribe and analyze spoken utterances. Long utterances transcribed in this way were analyzed into constituent parts—words, phrases, clauses—and a theory of syntax was used to write rules for forming grammatical phrases and sentences. Finally, the accumulation of an alphabetical list of words and their meanings provided information needed to reveal morphology, the rules for forming words.

In this way, linguistic anthropologists were able to record and preserve many languages that had never been written down before. They could learn the language, could reduce it to writing, and could return from the field with a large collection of recorded utterances—a corpus—to analyze at their leisure. (Today, of course, tape recorders relieve them of the tedium of phonetic transcription in the field.) By limiting their generalizations to the actual corpus of utterances that they had recorded, these linguistic anthropologists always had solid empirical evidence to fall back on.

As part of their basic training, therefore, linguistic anthropologists mastered a synchronic theory of language in general, but primarily as an aid in learning specific languages. Linguistic theory served largely as a guide for drawing generalizations about some particular language on the basis of finite samples of recorded speech in that language.

Not until the 1950s did a linguist present a persuasive alternative to this anthropological approach. Then Noam Chomsky put forward the argument that language, properly conceived, is not a collection of texts that someone has written or a corpus of utterances that someone has transcribed. A language is something that people know, something that children learn and adults use. Any particular corpus can contain but a small sample of the infinite variety of sentences that a speaker of the language could produce and understand. In short, Chomsky redefined the subject matter of linguistics. No longer would synchronic linguistics be limited to the study of recorded instances. The subject matter of linguistics for Chomsky was the competence of language users, not their performance. Performances are merely the evidence from which their shared competence can be inferred.

Chomsky placed grammar at the center of his new formulation and named his new approach to it "generative grammar." A generative grammar consists of explicit rules that assign structural descriptions to sentences. An

Linguistic anthropologists have always used the best available technology to preserve the sound of unwritten languages, and in 1924 that meant making dictaphone records. Here J. P. Harrington is shown in the Smithsonian Institution with three native Americans, recording the speech and songs of the Cunan language of Panama.

ideal generative grammar would describe all and only the grammatical sentences of a particular language, and so could be considered a (highly abstract) description of what a person must know in order to speak and understand that language.

Describing abilities is a responsibility of psychology, so Chomsky's redefinition effectively made linguistics a branch of cognitive psychology. In recent years, linguistics and psychology have forged a bond as strong and as valuable to both as was the earlier bond between linguistics and anthropology. This book is a product of that new conception of linguistic science.

Psycholinguistics

To psychologists, these new ideas became known as psycholinguistics. Even before experimental psychology emerged from philosophy late in the nineteenth century, the central role of language in the minds of human beings was generally acknowledged. But few practitioners of the young science of psychology knew enough linguistics to design and execute studies that could reveal the role of language in controlling people's attention, memory, imagery, thought, or behavior.

The earliest attempts by psychologists to incorporate language into their experiments concentrated heavily on words. Human learning was studied by asking people to memorize lists of words, or to remember pairs of words; vocabulary size was found to be a good indicator of mental age; human intelligence was measured with vocabulary tests, and every high school graduate was expected to know the most frequently used words; the acuity of hearing and the effects of acoustic interference were assessed by asking people to write down the words they could hear; aberrant human emotions were diagnosed with word association tests; reading ability was calibrated in terms of words per minute. In these and other ways psychologists demonstrated their appreciation of the importance of language, even though the only unit of language they found comfortable to work with was the word.

Psycholinguistics, dedicated to understanding both the psychological foundations of language and the linguistic foundations of psychology, was initially populated by psychologists and anthropologists who had discovered their shared interest in synchronic descriptions of language. Psychologists brought to this new science their experimental techniques and their extensive studies of words; anthropologists brought to it their comparative methods and their broader perspective on what a language can be and do. Together they quickly discovered the great psychological complexity of human languages, and many psychologists who had initially assumed that speech must be some kind of conditioned reflex were forced to revise their opinions. But what to substitute for existing theories of conditioning and learning was far from clear. Psycholinguists were ready for the kind of theory that Chomsky soon provided.

Chomsky developed the conception of generative grammar to describe people's linguistic competence, and it held obvious implications for psychology. How is it possible, he asked, that people can know as much as they do when their contacts with the world are so personal and limited? In particular, how can children learn a language so readily when their exposure to its subtleties is so brief and impoverished? Chomsky's answer was that the capacity for language is part of the genetic endowment of all human beings, and that this innate competence can be characterized in terms of explicit principles governing the kinds of linguistic constructions that are possible—that is to say, in terms of generative grammar. His generative theory not only reformulated what psycholinguistic experiments should be investigating, but it suggested mechanisms of language comprehension and language acquisition that were novel and exciting.

One effect of Chomsky's ideas was to redirect psycholinguistic research toward grammar and away from vocabulary. The claim was accepted that the indefinite variety of grammatical sentences a language user is competent to utter and understand can only be described (and, presumably, can only be learned) in terms of generative rules. What those rules are, how children acquire them, how those rules organize adult language, what happens when brain injuries limit them—these were new and challenging questions that suddenly seemed open to investigation. Words, by comparison, were uninteresting. It was assumed that the number of words must be limited, that words are subject to too many exceptions to support any interesting system of rules, and that there is nothing a child can do but memorize them. Psycholinguistic research on words almost disappeared.

Excessive interest in words was followed by excessive neglect, so it was probably inevitable that these basic building blocks of language would again come into favor. Psycholinguists began to recognize that words are linguistic universals just as surely as sentences are, that their number is not limited in most languages, and that learning them is anything but a tedious exercise in rote memorization. Even generative grammarians revived their interest in words as they came to realize that many of the syntactic rules they studied could just as well be stated as features of words and so regarded as lexical knowledge.

For example, a generative grammar for English must have a rule stating:

R1. Sentences have a noun phrase as the subject followed by a verb phrase as the predicate.

That rule is needed to account for such sentences as *The woman wept*. Note that *The gun wept* also follows this rule, but it is not an acceptable sentence. In the lexical entry for *weep*, therefore, it is necessary to specify that this particular verb requires an animate, perhaps even a human, noun phrase in the subject position. But if the lexical entry for *weep* already specifies that it must take a noun phrase as its subject, R1 is simply redundant and can be discarded. The grammatical rule has been caught in the lexical entry.

The need to treat morphology also drew attention back to words. Initial accounts of generative grammar drew heavily on English examples—and English, of course, relies largely on word order to signal the grammatical roles of various noun phrases. No doubt as a consequence of this emphasis on word order, the inflectional morphology of English has grown progressively simpler over the centuries; plural, possessive, and tense inflections are about all that is left. It was probably an advantage that the early versions of generative grammar did not need to struggle too much with the intricacies of inflectional morphology, but eventually such matters must be faced; in many languages, the morphology is more complex than the syntax. To extend the theory to account for rules of word formation as well as rules of sentence formation, a closer examination of words was unavoidable.

In recent years, therefore, there has been a revival of scientific interest in words, both in linguistics and in psycholinguistics. This book, a product of that revival, attempts to bring together existing scientific knowledge of words. The approach is synchronic, not diachronic. That is to say, the concern here is not with where words come from or how they change, but rather with the much less familiar science of words as living components of the reader's own mental life.

Overview

Clearly, the study of words is part of the study of language, and so falls directly into the province of linguistic science. Any serious discussion of words must rely heavily on linguistic generalizations and hypotheses. But words are too important to leave to linguists. Words concern everyone. And because everyone is interested in them, words have been studied from many perspectives. A variety of approaches are assembled in this book in the hope that they will combine to yield a more comprehensive appreciation of this ubiquitous and essential unit of language. But, since selection is unavoidable, in these pages a synchronic view of words is favored over diachronic accounts of their histories.

The discussion should begin with a definition of "word." Of course, everyone knows what words are—and it is fortunate that they do because, as Chapter 2 will show, a good definition is hard to find. Part of the difficulty arises from the fact that words lead a double life. On the one hand, words are simply physical things or events—noises, gestures, marks; on the other hand, they express meanings. To know a word is to know (at least) two different kinds of things: First, it is to be able to produce and recognize physical tokens representing the word; second, it is to understand the meanings that those tokens can be used to communicate. The basic structure of lexical knowledge, therefore, is a mapping between two sets: the set of word forms and the set of word meanings.

That cognitive structure provides the organization for this book. Chapters 3 through 7 delve into the word forms themselves: written and spoken. These linguistic units are characterized by formal properties and relations—formal in the sense that they pertain to the forms of words, not their meanings. Since these forms are the most tangible manifestations of linguistic competence, they have been described and analyzed with great precision, yet there is much we still do not understand about them. But we do know that they control important aspects of human language.

Given that background, Chapter 8 turns to the system of word meanings—the lexical concepts that word forms can be used to express. These are intangible linguistic units whose physical instantiations are still unknown, but whose properties and relations can be inferred from the use that is made of them. The story is complicated, however, by the fact that a word's meaning interacts in complex ways with the grammatical role that it plays. In English and other Indo-European languages, words in different syntactic categories express different kinds of meanings; Chapters 9 through 11 discuss the semantic structures of nouns, verbs, and modifiers.

A final chapter pulls together some of these ideas in terms of what is known about the way words are learned—about the growth of vocabulary in children and adults.

■   ■   ■

A book much larger than this would be required to treat everything that is worth reporting about words. Nevertheless, this short trip through the lexical component of language should illustrate some interesting facts about language in general—and about the human minds that find such knowledge so very useful.

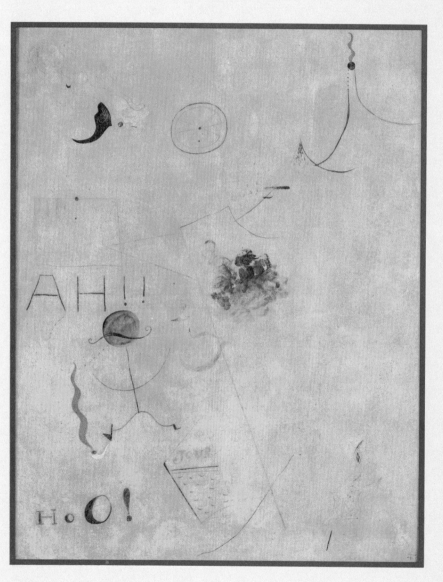

◀ *How do we discriminate the crucial formal elements of language? Juan Miró's 1924 painting* Le Renversement *incorporates monosyllables that may—like* jour; *in English,* day—*or may not—like the interjections* ah *and* hoo—*find their way into dictionaries.*

▼ *A single word in the Nootka language, spoken by natives of the Pacific Northwest, can approximate a whole English sentence:* Inikwihl'minik'isit *means roughly* several small fires were burning in the house. *How, then, do we define "a word"?*

Units of Analysis

anguage is so familiar that people seldom question why it is the way it is. How else could it be? To someone who has not thought about it, it is far from obvious that natural languages are extraordinarily and (apparently) unnecessarily complex, not at all what anyone would invent if given a free choice. To appreciate the peculiarities of natural language, it is necessary to contemplate alternative language systems. That is, to see natural language as a special case drawn from a broad spectrum of alternative possibilities, it is necessary to have a theory of language in general. And the construction of a theory of language in general is the constitutive problem of linguistic science. The question, "How else could language be?" is one of the keys that opens the door to a science of language.

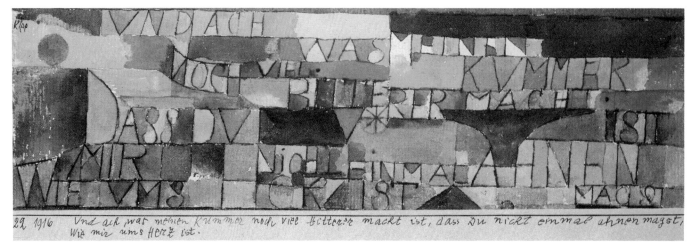

Paul Klee had his own way to express the stringiness of language.

Consider an obvious feature of human language: Speech proceeds by concatenation, by linking speech sounds together in long streams. People do not bark isolated sounds back and forth. When a person starts to talk, the flow of sound goes on for a while—sometimes for a long while. Why? Why are words formed from strings of sounds? Why are sentences formed from strings of words? In short, why is language so stringy?

A General Design Principle

A powerful design principle underlies efficient communication systems. A firm grasp of that principle should make it easier to understand what goes on behind the linguistic scenes. The principle is this:

P1. The number N of different strings of length λ formed from a repertoire (an alphabet or vocabulary) of A alternative units is

$$N = A^\lambda$$

P1 can be called the exponential principle; it explains the advantages of stringy languages.

Imagine a language in which $\lambda = 1$. That is to say, imagine a language in which all signals are one unit long. In that case, the number of different signals N is simply equal to A, the number of alternative units available. And suppose, to keep things as simple as possible, that $A = 2$, like the dit and dah of Morse code. When $\lambda = 1$, the two units are used in isolation, one at a time, in which case the language is able to communicate only two different messages: perhaps dit = "by land" and dah = "by sea." If the users of this binary system had to cope with an air attack, they would be stymied.

The exponential principle shows how to generate many more different signals. Suppose the two units could be concatenated in pairs to form strings of length $\lambda = 2$. Then it would be possible to set up the following convention:

dit	E
dah	T
dit dit	I
dit dah	A
dah dit	N
dah dah	M

If everyone agreed that it was to the advantage of all to observe this convention, it would be possible to transmit signals conveying any one of the six messages: E, T, I, A, N, or M. To transmit E or T, use a string with a single unit; to transmit I, use a string with two units, dit dit; to transmit A, dit dah; and so on. Note that N, the number of different signals available when 2 units are used in strings of length 2, is $2^2 = 4$. And the total number of different signals available is $2 + 4 = 6$.

Since people want to send more than six different messages, a practical communication system must increase the number of possible signals it can carry. The grand thing about concatenation is that the number of signals available grows exponentially as a function of string length:

λ	N	ΣN
1	2	2
2	4	6
3	8	14
4	16	30
5	32	62
6	64	126

where ΣN is the cumulative sum of N. Even with λ as small as 6, the exponential principle yields 64 different language signals 6 units long, or a total of 126 signals shorter than 7 units

To take numbers closer to those involved in natural languages, let $A = 40$ for the approximately 40 different speech sounds of English. Then the number of available signals grows extremely rapidly as λ increases. If you could speak the 40 sounds of English in any order, you could have a repertoire of more than four billion different messages, with no utterance longer than six sounds.

(That is 10,000 times as many words as are in the unabridged *Webster's Third New International Dictionary*.)

Of course, concatenation is not the only way that the stock of word forms in a language can be increased. In tonal languages, syllables must be pronounced with different pitch contours. The Beijing dialect of Chinese, for example, has four tones—level, rising, falling-rising, and falling—which increases the number of available monosyllables by a factor of four. The same syllable means different things depending on which tone is used. For example, *mā* (with the level tone) can mean *mother, má* (rising tone) can mean *hemp, mǎ* (falling-rising tone) can mean *horse,* and *mà* (falling tone) can mean *scold.* In the Beijing dialect, these tones are significant, just as voicing (vibrating the vocal cords during the articulation of a speech sound) is significant in English. Voicing, however, is a feature of individual speech sounds, whereas tones are features of whole syllables. Tones simply increase A, the size of the repertoire.

Not all of the possible concatenations are usable, however. No one can pronounce all the conceivable strings of speech sounds, much less associate meanings with all of them. Linguistic signals are not like numbers; any string of digits is a meaningful number, but not every string of speech sounds conveys a meaningful message. This hypothetical language would seem more plausible if it were constrained by a simple rule, a rule that would limit the variety of signals that could be used as messages. Assume, for example, that consonants and vowels must alternate. Then, given 25 different consonants and 15 different vowels, a string of length 6, $CVCVCV$, could occur in $25 \times 15 \times 25 \times 15 \times 25 \times 15 = 52,734,375$ different ways. That is to say, if vowels and consonants alternate to make the strings pronounceable, and if four billion different signals are really needed, then strings 8 or 9 sounds long will be required to produce as many different sounds as are produced with unrestricted strings of length 6. For that reason, a pronounceable system is redundant—pronounceable strings are longer than theoretically necessary. But notice that this redundancy carries a compensating benefit: If you should ever receive a signal having two consonants or two vowels in a row, you would recognize immediately that an error had occurred.

Because linguistic rules generally have the effect of introducing this limited kind of predictability, natural languages are said to be redundant. They are even more redundant than the simple example just considered. The communications theorist Claude Shannon has estimated that English messages are more than twice as long as they theoretically need to be. This book, for example, could be reduced to half its present size if it made the most efficient possible use of the Roman alphabet. But to remove this redundancy would be a false economy. The redundancy provides a margin of safety for linguistic strings that is not available for numerical strings. Change a digit in a long number and you have another perfectly good number: The change cannot be detected. Change a sound in a long utterance and the chances are good that the change will be apparent: For example, *Come to breekfast* contains an obvious and easily correctable error. The exponential principle not only yields an enormous vari-

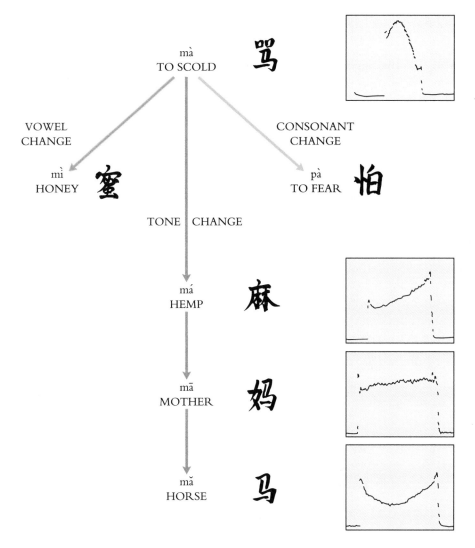

The meaning of a Chinese word depends on its tone. The standard dialect of Chinese has four tones: falling (mà), rising (má), level (mā), and falling-rising (mǎ). The oscillograph traces at the right show the fundamental frequency of the speaker's voice as each word was spoken.

mà
TO SCOLD

VOWEL
CHANGE

CONSONANT
CHANGE

mì
HONEY

pà
TO FEAR

TONE   CHANGE

má
HEMP

mā
MOTHER

mǎ
HORSE

ety of strings that can be used as signals, but even allows room for some error detection and correction.

Thus, the stringiness of languages is explained in terms of the exponential principle. So far, however, the explanation has been couched in terms of artificial examples—toy languages that you can design however you like. So far, it has not even been specified whether the signals correspond to words or sentences. To see how the principle is exploited in natural languages, it is necessary to look more carefully at the linguistic units that natural languages string together.

Linguistic Units

When you listen to speech in an unfamiliar language, it sounds like a modulated but continuing flow of sound. It is a curious fact that, if you know the language, you cannot hear it that way. Speech in a familiar language is perceived as chopped up into discrete units: into sounds, words, phrases, and so forth. The ability to produce and to recognize those units is the best evidence that someone knows the language.

The segment of principal interest in this book, of course, is the word; but before going too far with this unit of analysis, an obvious question needs to be asked. Everyone knows that the familiar Indo-European languages have words, but do all languages have words? If scientists want to study language in general, choosing words as the unit presupposes that language in general has words. But is that true? Clearly, the question would be easier to answer if there were a definition of "word" good enough that you could recognize a word anywhere you saw one. Crafting such a definition, however, turns out to be surprisingly difficult.

Take a non-Indo-European language as a test case. Nootka is a Wakashan language spoken by a group of American Indian tribes living on Vancouver Island and in the Flattery Cape region of northwestern Washington. Little is known of the origins of Nootka, but it clearly developed independently from English. Linguists are confident that Nootka is not related to English because there is no historical record of interaction between these two languages, because they have no words in common, and because the rules for generating comprehensible utterances in Nootka are very different from those in Indo-European languages. Like most American Indian languages, but unlike English, the rules of word formation in Nootka are highly elaborate—so elaborate, in fact, that one Nootka word might seem to include information that must be introduced by many separate words in English.

For example, the Nootka word *inikw-ihl* can be translated roughly as *fire in the house*—*inikw-* means *fire* or *burn*, and the suffix *-ihl* means *in the house*. If the suffix *-'minih* is added, it becomes plural; *inikwihl-'minih* means *fires in the house*. The diminutive suffix *-'is* can then be added; *inikwihl'minih-'is* means *little fires in the house*. Then the tense suffix *-it* can be added. The final result is *inikwihl'minih'isit*, a single Nootka word, consisting of the radical *inikw-* and a string of grammatical elements, that means something like *several small fires were burning in the house,* which is an eight-word English sentence. After only a little exposure to Nootka, one begins to imagine languages in which every sentence is a single, elaborately derived word—in which case any distinction between words and sentences would disappear. How could you tell whether there is a unit of linguistic analysis in Nootka that corresponds to the word unit in English?

Early in the twentieth century this question was considered by a distinguished linguistic anthropologist, Edward Sapir, and the examples given here are quoted from his works. Sapir studied these native Americans and learned their language. In defense of his claim for the psychological reality of words in Nootka, Sapir commented: "No more convincing test could be desired than this, that the naïve Indian, quite unaccustomed to the concept of the written word, has nevertheless no serious difficulty in dictating a text to a linguistic student word by word; he tends, of course to run his words together as in actual speech, but if he is called to a halt and made to understand what is desired, he can readily isolate the words as such, repeating them as units. He regularly refuses, on the other hand, to isolate the radical or grammatical element, on the ground that it 'makes no sense.' " Sapir taught young Nootkas to write their own language according to the system of phonetic notation that he used. They were taught merely how to render the individual sounds accurately. They had some difficulty learning to break up a word into its constituent sounds, but no difficulty whatever in isolating the words, which they did with spontaneous and complete accuracy, precisely as Sapir himself would have isolated them. "What, then," Sapir asks, "is the objective criterion of the word? The speaker and hearer feel the word, let us grant, but how shall we justify their feeling?"

The question is as challenging today as when he asked it in 1921. Yet both Nootka and English, as well as every other human language we know about, are spoken in sentences that are composed of words consisting of strings of speech sounds. Apparently, sounds, words, and sentences are natural building blocks for spoken communication. Since they are found in all human languages, sounds, words, and sentences are basic elements for describing language; they are universal units of linguistic analysis.

In other words, the exponential principle is so effective that human languages use it twice. It is first used to provide a vocabulary of some thousands of different words. Then it is used again to string those words together in an unlimited variety of different sentences. It is not clear why two levels of patterning are needed—we can easily imagine languages that do not distinguish between words and sentences—but the use of two levels of patterning is one of the most distinctive design features of natural languages.

So, granted that all languages have units of intermediate length that correspond to words, how, precisely, is this unit to be defined so that you can recognize it whenever you encounter it?

What Is a Word?

It comes as a surprise to most people that something as familiar as "word" does not have a simple, straightforward definition. Every native speaker of a language—that is to say, everyone—has an intuitive appreciation of what words are. Reducing those intuitions to precise definitions is not easy, but

Edward Sapir (1884–1939) is best remembered for his sensitive appreciation of the role language plays in shaping all aspects of a culture. "Human beings," he wrote, "do not live in the objective world alone, nor alone in the world of social activity as ordinarily understood, but are very much at the mercy of the particular language which has become the medium of expression for their society. It is quite an illusion to imagine that one adjusts to reality essentially without the use of language and that language is merely an incidental means of solving specific problems of communication or reflection. The fact of the matter is that the 'real world' is to a large extent unconsciously built up on the language habits of the group. No two languages are ever sufficiently similar to be considered as representing the same social reality. The worlds in which different societies live are distinct worlds, not merely the same world with different labels attached."

because the word is such a basic linguistic concept, every serious student of language faces this challenge.

Words as Concepts

Sapir, for example, observed that "our first impulse, no doubt, would have been to define the word as the symbolic, linguistic counterpart of a single concept. We now know that such a definition is impossible." One problem with such a definition is that "concept" is even more difficult to define than "word." What may be said in a single word and appear to be a single concept in one language (Latin *dico*, for example) can require more than one word in another language (English *I say*). As a counterexample to the notion of one-word:one-concept, Sapir cited a Nootka verb meaning *I have been accustomed to eat twenty round objects while engaged in . . . ,* where a single word expresses concepts that require almost a whole sentence in English. "Word" cannot be defined in terms of single concepts, ideas, or meanings. "The word," Sapir concluded, "is merely a form."

Words as Strings of Letters

If words are merely forms, then what is required is a formal definition—a definition that makes it possible to recognize words even when their meanings are unknown. Here is a candidate:

> **D1.** A word is any sequence of letters printed between spaces, with no spaces intervening.

Armed with this definition, even someone who knew no English could look at this page and, on purely formal grounds, recognize all the words on it.

But D1 will not do. What is wrong with it? Ignore the fact that, according to D1, asdfg could be mistaken for a word. Ignore, even, the fact that prior to about A.D. 1000, words were not distinguished by spaces in European orthographies. A more serious defect is that D1 defines words only for written languages—indeed, only for alphabetically written languages. The fact that a language has never been reduced to writing does not mean that it has no words. People who cannot read or write still know what a word is.

In linguistics, writing is considered derivative from and secondary to speech; many distinguished linguists have gone out of their way to emphasize the primacy of spoken over written language. Their reasons are simple. For one thing, every human society has some form of spoken language, but not all have a system of writing. For another, every normal child acquires spoken language by simply playing the language game, but not everyone learns to

This eighth-century Latin manuscript was carefully inscribed, but without spaces to mark word boundaries.

read and write. In short, spoken language evolved biologically, whereas written language was a cultural invention. A definition of word that ignored spoken language could hardly be considered satisfactory.

Words as Morphemes

An alternative definition of word, intended to hold for spoken as well as for written language, reads as follows:

> **D2.** A word is a minimal free form.

There are problems with D2, too, but the definition must be unpacked before it can be criticized.

First, a *linguistic form* is usually defined as any meaningful unit of language. (A linguistic analyst does not have to know its meaning; it is merely necessary to establish that native speakers of the language know its meaning.) A linguistic form that cannot be divided into smaller linguistic forms is a simple form, or *morpheme*. That is to say, a morpheme is the smallest individually meaningful unit. "Smallest" means that the meaning of a morpheme cannot be derived from the meanings of any components into which it might be divided. For example, the spoken unit *carpus* is a morpheme: It contains two syllables, but it is a single morpheme. Consider how *carpus* might be segmented into smaller morphemes: Either *carp* and *us*, or *car* and *pus*, are separate morphemes with their own distinct meanings, but those meanings cannot be combined to yield the meaning of *carpus*. That is to say, no part of *carpus* can be uttered alone without having a meaning that is different from the meaning of *carpus*. Note that this stipulation implies that anything inserted into a morpheme also changes its meaning; for example, *carpwristus* or *carjointpus* are not English words, they are meaningless. (Note also that it is not necessary to know what carpus means in order to follow this argument.)

Second, a *free form* is a form that does not have to be attached to some other form, but can be used alone. Free morphemes contrast with bound morphemes, like the English prefix *un-* in *unhappy*, or the past tense inflection *-d,* which cannot occur meaningfully in isolation.

And, third, a *minimal free form* is a free form that can be uttered alone as a sentence. For example, the utterance of the minimum free morpheme, "Carpus," is an acceptable answer to "What did the professor call your wrist?"

D2 is an improvement over D1, yet marginal cases still cause trouble: The English word *the*, for example, can hardly be uttered alone as an acceptable sentence; *je* is a French word despite the fact that it can be used only in conjunction with a verb; and so on. D2 also leaves one wondering about the status of polymorphemic words. There are compounds like *Boston-to-Chicago* that act like words (you cannot break into them, as in *He took the Boston-, where he lives, -to-Chicago flight*), although they contain more than one morpheme.

Definitions always leak at the margins, where experts delight in posing counterexamples for their peers to ponder. Fortunately, the typical cases are clear enough that a little fuzziness around the edges does not interfere with the larger picture.

Instead of starting with the connected flow of language and searching for formal rules to segment it into natural units, assume that everyone knows, intuitively, what a word is. Then the discussion can jump directly to the *lexicon*, the collection of words that constitute the vocabulary of a language.

The Lexicon

When one undertakes to learn a new language with the help of teachers and textbooks, the task is usually divided up, along traditional lines, into pronunciation, vocabulary, and grammar. It is necessary to learn how to pronounce the new language—even closely related languages usually have some unfamiliar sounds. It is necessary to learn the meanings of words in the new language, a task that may go on for years and years. And it is necessary to learn rules for combining words into acceptable, comprehensible phrases and sentences. These three learning tasks are usually pursued independently but in parallel, and a person is not a competent speaker of a new language until all three aspects have been mastered.

These three parts are sometimes called components of a language; every language has a phonetic component, a lexical component, and a syntactic component. But the components are not independent; one component is of little use without the other two. A fundamental task of linguistic science, therefore, is to understand how these components relate to one another. For example, a compositional theory might try to pull together all three components by assuming that the units of the syntactic component are composed of strings from the lexical component, and that the units of the lexical component are composed of strings of units from the phonetic component. Or, at the opposite extreme, the components might be treated separately: Each component is assumed to be a unique perspective from which to view linguistic competence, and each requires a separate theory that borrows little or nothing from the other two.

Fortunately, such questions need not be settled here. The present task is more limited—here attention is focused on the lexical component. That should make the job easier. But close inspection of the lexicon reveals that it must make extensive reference to the phonetic and the syntactic components. Even if it were possible to construct separate theories for each component of language, they could not be unrelated. No reasonable theory of the phonetic component could avoid rules of pronunciation that apply only to words; no reasonable theory of the lexical component could avoid rules that apply only to words in a particular syntactic category. The borrowings among the three theories can be minimized, but they cannot be eliminated entirely. Single-minded concentration on the lexicon does not represent a license to ignore phonetics and syntax.

The simplest notion of a lexicon holds that it is a collection of words, with associated information about each word. As more and more information is added about each word, the lexicon rapidly becomes a major repository of knowledge. Some of that knowledge is phonetic, some syntactic, some semantic. The simplest way to appreciate how these different kinds of information come together is to examine an ordinary dictionary entry. Consider the following example, borrowed from *The American Heritage Dictionary of the English Language* (Boston: American Heritage and Houghton Mifflin, 1975), William Morris, Editor:

> **word** (wûrd) *n.* **1.** *Abbr.* **wd.** A sound or a combination of sounds, or its representation in writing or printing, that symbolizes and communicates a meaning and may consist of a single morpheme or of a combination of morphemes. **2.** Something that is said; an utterance, remark, or comment: *May I say a word about that?* **3.** *Plural.* A discourse or talk; speech. **4.** *Plural.* The text of a vocal music composition; lyrics. **5.** An assurance or promise; sworn intention: *a man of his word.* **6. a.** A command or direction; an order: *executed at the general's word.* **b.** A verbal signal; a password or watchword. **7. a.** News: *the latest word.* **b.** Rumor: *Word has it she's married.* **8. a.** *Plural.* A dispute or argument; a quarrel. **b.** A quarrelsome remark or conversation: *Words were exchanged between umpire and batter.* **9.** *Capital* **W. a.** The Logos. **b.** The Scriptures or Gospel: *The Word of God.* —**at a word.** In immediate response. —**by word of mouth.** Orally; by speech. —**have no words for.** To be unable to describe or talk about. —**in a word.** In most precise form; in short: *You are, in a word, a fool.* —**in so many words.** Precisely as stated; exactly. —**take at one's word.** To be convinced of another's sincerity and to act in accordance with his statement. —**word for word.** In the same words. —*tr. v.* **worded, wording, words.** To express in words. [Middle English *word*, Old English *word.*]

There is, first, phonetic information: spelling, which is the information most often sought from a dictionary, and the standard pronunciation, spelled in a phonetic alphabet that must be learned separately. Syntactic information is given by an abbreviated but important notation, *n.*, for the syntactic category, or part of speech, but also by multiple illustrations of how the word is used in conjunction with other words. Semantic information about meaning is given by phrases and paraphrases: Nine different senses are distinguished, where only the first is the sense being discussed here. The run-on entry for *word* as a transitive verb illustrates the kind of information about inflectional morphology that is given in dictionaries. Finally, the etymological note says it is a four-letter Anglo-Saxon word that has been around a long time.

Printed Lexicons, and How They Grew

Nobody invented the dictionary. Modern dictionaries, now so taken for granted that alternatives are hard to imagine, evolved to their present form over many centuries. They grew by a process of collaborative competition—each new dictionary took full advantage of earlier dictionaries and was similarly incorporated into later works.

The origins of lexicography are lost to history, but it seems that lexicographic labors of one kind or another are almost as old as writing itself. It is known, for example, that lists of difficult words were drawn up by the ancient Greeks, and the Chinese compiled wordbooks as early as the second century. Such lists were not dictionaries, however; a dictionary should be organized so that a user can find particular words easily and rapidly.

For languages written alphabetically, a systematic alphabetical ordering is required. Although numbers order themselves in a natural way, the principles of alphabetization were not discovered until the thirteenth century. Then, in the preface to the Latin *Catholicon*, an influential encyclopedic dictionary, it is explained that

amo	precedes	*bibo*
abeo	precedes	*adeo*
amatus	precedes	*amor*
imprudens	precedes	*impudens*
iusticia	precedes	*iustus*
polisintheton	precedes	*polissensus*

"and so in like manner." The principle is obvious, but hardly natural. As late as 1604, in the first dictionary of English, *A Table Alphabeticall,* many words are out of order in the first few pages, but the second half is nearly perfect. The compiler, Robert Cawdrey, was learning how to alphabetize as he worked.

The *Catholicon* was the first dictionary to be printed—in 1460. But as more and more authors began to write in their local vernacular, a variety of dictionaries appeared: for Dutch in 1511, for Russian in 1596, for French in 1606, for Spanish in 1611. By and large, these works concentrated on the hard words. For example, Cawdrey, a schoolmaster, described his list of 2,500 entries as "hard usuall English wordes, borrowed from the Hebrew, Greek, Latine, or French, &c." Ladies were considered a special audience, since they had fewer educational opportunities than men.

In England, the design of a proper dictionary continued to evolve for more than a century after Cawdrey's contribution. The first English lexicographer to include common as well as difficult words was John Kersey, whose *New English Dictionary* appeared in 1702 and remained in print for seventy years. Nathan Bailey's *Dictionarium Britannicum,* published in 1730, contained most of the features—spelling, pronunciation, etymology, definitions, illustrations—that are expected in modern dictionaries.

By 1730, therefore, the general shape of dictionaries had been set. The task for subsequent lexicographers was to improve the content: to standardize spelling, devise better guides to pronunciation, provide historically accurate etymologies, and polish the definitions of alternative senses. Those refinements, especially those affecting pronunciation and etymology, had to await the development of linguistic scholarship in the nineteenth century.

The question, however, is not what a conventional dictionary contains, but what is in the heads of language users. Do people have all that information about *word* in their mental lexicons? Apparently they do. Setting aside the etymology, there is little or nothing in the above entry that an educated English-speaking person would not know (and even the etymology may be known implicitly). Indeed, it provides an interesting perspective on the capacity of human memory to look at a 1,500-page dictionary and realize how much of that information resides in the long-term memory of an educated adult.

How similar is a hand-held dictionary to the dictionary in people's heads? Could the hand-held dictionary possibly serve as an extremely detailed and exhaustive linguistic theory about the contents and organization of the mental lexicon? Lexicographers may have some of the contents about right, but the organization of the mental lexicon is surely different from the alphabetical listing of entries in a standard hand-held dictionary. People tend to associate words that rhyme, or that have similar meanings, or that are frequently used together. Dictionaries ignore all that. By putting together words that are spelled alike, an alphabetical organization scatters related words haphazardly through the list. Still another difference between printed and mental dictionaries follows from the fact that a dictionary must use words to define words; a person has in addition a vast resource of images, experiences, and special knowledge to use in representing meanings and relations between meanings.

Dictionaries are valuable scholarly tools that people take for granted. No one would want to be deprived of them. But they were conceived as reference books, not as theories of the mental lexicon—the psychological validity of a lexical entry is nothing that a serious lexicographer would fret about. It cannot be assumed that, because dictionaries and grammars are written as separate volumes, the mental lexicon is a distinct component of a language user's competence, unrelated to the grammar. Nor is there any reason to assume that the mental lexicon is organized into discrete lexical entries just because that organization is convenient for lexicographers. Finally, it should not be assumed that the mental lexicon contains only linguistic information just because dictionaries are so frequently distinguished from encyclopedias. There is much that is not yet understood about the lexical knowledge of competent language users, but it seems unlikely that the lexicon can be walled off from the other components of language, or even from the language users' other, nonlinguistic knowledge.

The Lexical Matrix

Insofar as dictionaries can be thought of as alphabetical lists of word forms and their associated word meanings, lexicographers draw a basic distinction between forms and meanings. The question must be asked, therefore, whether that distinction is valid for the mental lexicon, too. Psychological evidence suggests that it is. For example, psychometricians—psychologists who, among other things, are responsible for constructing and interpreting mental tests—have developed a method called factor analysis for teasing out component abilities, or factors, that contribute to success on various tests. When tasks requiring verbal intelligence are included in a test battery, it is a consistent observation that two different factors are involved. L. L. Thurstone (1887–1955), the father of factor analysis in America, named these factors V and W: V for verbal meaning and W for word fluency. Factor V is important for success on tests requiring you to solve such analogies as *tree : plant :: horse : ——— ,* to think of synonyms or antonyms, or to understand proverbs and quotations. Factor W is important on tests of spelling, solving anagrams, or thinking of words that begin and end with particular letters. Factor V apparently reflects an ability to appreciate relations between word meanings—to deal with what Ferdinand de Saussure called concepts or "signifieds"—whereas Factor W reflects skill in manipulating word forms—Saussure's sound-images or "signifiers." Thus, the psychometric analysis supports claims that the lexicographers' distinction between meanings and forms has psychological validity.

In drawing this basic distinction, however, Saussure was insistent that a word is not two different things, but rather is "a two-sided psychological entity." The conceptual problem is not so much to understand the distinction as it is to see how form and meaning can combine in a single mental unit. Indeed, explaining how form and meaning are related is the central problem for all linguistic theory. Explaining the bonding of word forms and word meanings is the lexical version of the general linguistic problem.

What can be saved from the lexicographers' art is the picture of a word as an association between an objective (pronounceable or writable) form or token and a cluster of lexicalized concepts or meanings that the form can be used to express in appropriate contexts. Since every language user masters thousands of these associations, discovering the organization of the mental lexicon is a matter of tracing out not only (1) the lexical relations between the word forms and the word meanings, but also (2) the phonological, morphological, and syntactic relations between the word forms themselves, and (3) the semantic relations between the word meanings. These tasks may seem less nebulous if the relation between word forms and word meanings is formulated as a matrix.

A hand-held dictionary is simply a mapping of meanings onto forms; it can be conveniently represented as a *lexical matrix*. Imagine a huge matrix with all the words in a language along the top of the matrix and all the different meanings those words can express down the side. If a particular meaning can be expressed by a word, then the cell in that row and column contains an entry; otherwise it contains nothing. The entry itself can provide phonetic and syntactic information, examples of usage, even a picture—whatever the lexi-

Meanings	Forms				
	F1	F2	F3	F4 . . .	Fn
M1	E				
M2	E	E			
M3	E		E		
M4				E	
.					
.					
.					
Mm					. . . E

In this lexical matrix the columns represent words and the rows represent meanings. An E in a cell of the matrix signifies that the word in that column can be used to express the meaning in that row.

cographer deems important enough (and has room enough) to include. The accompanying table illustrates the general idea.

Any printed dictionary can be represented as a lexical matrix: add a separate column for every word form and a separate row for every word meaning. Then the matrix becomes a dictionary printed on a single sheet (a very large sheet) of paper.

Entering such a matrix consists of searching down some column or across some row. That is to say, a lexical matrix can be entered either with a word form or with a word meaning. If you enter it with a meaning and search along a row, as you might do when searching for words, you find all the word forms that can express that meaning. When two different word forms express the same meaning, they are said to be *synonyms*. In the lexical matrix table, for example, F1 and F2 are synonyms (or partial synonyms) because both can be used, in appropriate contexts, to express the meaning M2. Thus, F1 might be the word form *file* and F2 the word form *line,* in which case M2 would be the concept that these words express when referring to a row of people or things arranged one behind the other.

On the other hand, if you enter the matrix with a word form and search down a column, as you might do when trying to interpret a sentence, you find all the different meanings that that form can express. When a word form is used to express more than one meaning, it is said to be *polysemous*. In the matrix table, for example, F1 is polysemous because it can be used, in appropriate contexts, to express meaning M1, M2, or M3. If F1 is the word form *file*, then M1 could be the concept of a folder to hold papers, and M2 could be that of a row of people or things arranged one behind the other, and M3 could be that of a tool with cutting ridges. Thus, two major complications of lexical organization, synonymy and polysemy, are seen as complementary aspects of a single abstract structure.

In a lexical matrix, relations between word forms and word meanings are represented as a many:many mapping; a form may express many meanings, and a meaning may be expressed by many forms. But the matrix itself is largely empty. The structure of the lexicon is given by relations among the forms and relations among the meanings.

Formal relations among the forms themselves are relations among columns of the matrix; semantic relations among meanings are relations among rows of the matrix. That is to say, a lexical matrix can be viewed as a large collection of word forms, each with associations to other word forms and to the meanings that they can express. Or it can be seen as a large collection of lexicalized concepts, each with associations to other concepts and to the word forms that express them. The important point is that, although these two perspectives can be made to appear very different, in fact both are looking at the same basic knowledge structure.

This general framework will serve to organize the following chapters, beginning with the word forms and the formal relations among them.

■ ■ ■

This discussion has been greatly simplified. Many difficult issues have been left in need of further analysis. But it should give a glimpse into the complexity underlying something that seems blazingly simple to anyone who speaks and understands a natural language. The linguistic units that are so easily recognized as words not only occupy a central position in the hierarchy of human linguistic abilities, they are as subtle and complex as they are necessary.

► *The links between literacy and historical culture are dramatized in this late nineteenth-century print by Kobayashi Kiyochika, depicting a war correspondent taking notes during a battle of the Satsuma Rebellion (1877–1878) on the Japanese island of Kyushu.*

▼ *Japanese orthography, mixing phonological and nonphonological elements, is both flexible and conservative. As these handwritten prayer/wish notes at a Tokyo temple suggest, modern Japan regularly employs the Roman alphabet, Arabic numerals, and international pictograms (here, heart shapes), as well as three distinctively Japanese writing systems: kanji logograms, derived from Chinese, and the hiragana and katakana syllabic scripts.*

The Written Word

ike Molière's Monsieur Jordan, who learned that for forty years he had been speaking prose without knowing it, you may be surprised to learn that for two chapters you have been reading metalanguage. Metalanguage is language used to discuss language; the language under discussion is object language. It is a distinction that philosophers enjoy, especially when metalanguage and object language are the same—printed English, in this instance.

Many different systems of writing are used in different parts of the world. For example, Mongolian is written in vertical columns; (A) represents successive segments of the Mongolian version of Once upon a time, countless past ages ago. *Arabic is written from right to left in descending curlicues; (B) is Arabic for* star of dawn.

To discuss word forms and types, it is necessary to be able to refer to them, to be able to indicate which particular vocalizations or inscriptions are being talked about. By all odds the most convenient way to do that in a book of this sort is by the use of alphabetic writing—anyone who has read this far is necessarily familiar with printed representations of English words. Thus, printed words in these pages will lead a double life: on the one hand, being used metalinguistically to communicate the message and, on the other hand, being mentioned as objects of that communication. To avoid confusion, words being used will be printed in roman font and words being talked about will be printed in italics. For example, in "The word *word* contains four letters," *word* is first used and then referred to.

This distinction is reasonably obvious and should cause no confusion. What may not be so obvious, however, is that designating words by the use of alphabetic writing is the product of some five millennia of linguistic analysis and represents one particular theory about the nature of human speech—a theory that, however familiar, is almost surely wrong.

Alphabetic writing is so useful for so many purposes that its status as a theory of speech is easily overlooked. An alternative perspective regards writing as parallel to, but different from, speech; instead of saying that the theory of speech underlying alphabetic writing is incorrect, it argues that written language is a separate cultural product similar to, but independent of, spoken language. In a language like Chinese, this view of writing as an independent system makes sense. The Chinese dialects are mutually unintelligible; people from different regions cannot understand one another, but they can all read the same characters—they just don't utter the same noises when they read those characters aloud. The shared use of written characters has been the glue that holds the Chinese dialects together. This view, that writing is a mode of expression independent of speech, may even be necessary in critical and literary discussions of writing. But from the point of view of this book—that is to say, from the perspective of linguistic science—Chinese characters will be taken to be the embodiment of a theory that is even worse than the alphabetic theory.

Most linguists insist that written language is secondary and derivative from spoken language. Their point is that many people around the world command a spoken language, yet are unacquainted with reading and writing. The reverse situation, writing without speech, is unheard of. Spoken language evolved, but writing is a human invention. The historical fact is that writing was invented not once, but several times: in different societies, and based on different analyses of the spoken language that writing was intended to represent.

The relations between written and spoken words may seem trivially obvious to anyone who uses an alphabetic writing system, but that is merely one of several ways that different societies have found to reduce the spoken word to a more permanent visual form.

Orthography

An orthography is any method of mapping the sounds of a language onto a set of written symbols. To someone familiar with a language, spoken utterances are not heard as continuously varying vocalizations, but as strings of recognizable words and sounds. So it is natural to think of speech as divisible into discrete segments and to assume that those segments can be represented graphically by distinctive marks.

Orthographies differ both in the graphic characters they use and in the speech segments that the characters are mapped onto. The variety of characters that have been used can be appreciated by inspecting an array of several different orthographies. Such a display is a reminder that orthographies are arbitrary and that many different schemes have grown up around the world. But even that does not fully reveal the diversity that actually exists: It says nothing about the number of different graphic characters available to a writer or about the linguistic units that they represent. It may not even indicate that some orthographies are written from right to left and others from the top down.

A first reaction to this variety is usually annoyance. It is bad enough that languages must sound so different; why must they also look so different? In time, this culture shock may be replaced by a desire to rationalize orthography. Since it doesn't really matter what kind of squiggles are inscribed on the page, why can't the United Nations or somebody standardize them? It should promote international understanding, and the economies that could be realized in international communications are obvious. Economic arguments begin to fade, however, when it is realized that all of the contents of all the libraries of the world would have to be transcribed into the new orthography.

Moreover, not everyone agrees that the choice of graphic representations is irrelevant. Language and culture are inextricably intertwined, and theories of language are not easily cleansed of cultural presuppositions. Consequently, the analysis of language that is embodied in an orthographic technology can represent far more than the sounds of the words. The point can be illustrated by a story. When A. L. Becker was a young linguistic anthropologist doing fieldwork in Burma, he undertook to learn Burmese from a kindly old scholar. He would ask the names of things, his teacher would pronounce them, and he would write them down in a phonetic notation that he had learned in America. His Burmese teacher, seeing him transcribe phonetically, objected strongly and insisted that he learn and use Burmese script. The young American maintained that the writing system made no difference; he believed that his phonetic transcription was language-neutral. But since he really believed that it made no difference, he learned Burmese orthography to appease his teacher.

Burmese script is nonlinear—a symbol for one sound is placed at the center and other sounds in the word are arranged around it. Since he could not do linguistics without segmenting the stream of speech, Becker had to rewrite it phonetically behind his teacher's back. Not until a decade later, in Bali, did

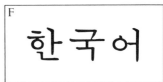

Hebrew is also written from right to left, but with discrete letters that carry markings; (C) is the Hebrew word for where. *Hindi letters can be written out of phonetic order; (D) is the word* hindî, *but it is written, in effect,* ihdnî. *Thai has vowels surrounding consonants; (E) is the Thai word for* month. *Korean uses a syllabary; (F) is the Korean way of writing* Korean language. *Chinese is written with thousands of different characters; (G) shows two ways of writing* Chinese language.

A wall in China's Sichuan province.

A Burmese inscription.

he realize how much difference the writing system made. Both Burmese and Balinese scripts incorporate a nonlinear feature. In Balinese, he learned, all knowledge is arranged around one figure: a center with four or more points around it. In addition to the points of the compass, there are overlaid on this configuration the parts of the body, days of the week, stages of life, colors, illnesses, places, professions, and much else—all the categories of knowledge, in fact. The arrangement was a mnemonic device for all traditional learning, a metaphor holding the world together, just as linear, sequential writing is a metaphor for Western notions of causality and history.

Even within a linear, sequential view of language, however, there is still room for alternative theories. They have to do not with the nature of the graphic symbols themselves, but with the speech segment that a graphic symbol is intended to represent. At least three different linear systems of orthography must be distinguished.

Linguistic unit	Type of orthography
Word or morpheme	Logographic characters
Syllable	Syllabary
Phoneme	Alphabet

Sake casks at Japan's Kasoga shrine.

A writing system based on phrasal units is conceivable—some systems of stenography have single symbols to represent a few locutions that are used frequently in business correspondence. But a comprehensive system of phrase-ography would not be practical. The number of different phrases would be so large (thanks to the exponential principle) that the creation of individual symbols to represent each one would be out of the question. The writing systems that developed historically have been logographic, syllabic, alphabetic, or some mixture of these. Syllabic and alphabetic scripts are phonetic—they provide characters to represent the sounds of the language.

Chinese is a relatively pure case: It is written entirely in logographs that map onto speech at the level of morphemes. Since there are many different morphemes, it is necessary to learn thousands of different characters to become literate in Chinese. But even Chinese mixes the levels, because the characters contain phonetic as well as morphemic information. Modern Japanese, on the other hand, is written in a great mixture of logographic characters, called kanji, that were originally borrowed from the Chinese, and syllabic symbols, called kana (and even, in some texts, romaji, the alphabetic representation used for Japanese words in this sentence). There are two types of kana symbols: Hiragana is used to write the grammatical affixes and function words (which have grammatical significance rather than full lexical meaning, and which are not used in Chinese), and katakana is used mainly to write words borrowed from other languages. Japanese could be written entirely in the kana syllabary, but since the morphology of spoken Japanese is very simple, there are relatively few different syllables. Consequently, transcription entirely in kana script results in many homonyms—words that have the same sound and spelling, but different meanings. To reduce potential ambiguity, many of the ancient Chinese logographs have been retained as kanji characters.

The fact that logographic and syllabic characters can be so freely mixed together in Japanese orthography might suggest that there are no important differences between them. Yet they cannot be learned the same way, and there is neurological evidence to indicate that logographic characters may be psychologically simpler. It has been found that Japanese who have suffered brain injuries that interfere with their ability to read are better able to read the logographic (kanji) characters than they are to read the syllabic (kana) characters.

Since the Arabic numerals are now internationally recognized logographic characters—most people understand 1-2-3, even if they pronounce it differently—the same comparison can be made with people who are accustomed to an alphabetic orthography. Patients who experience great difficulty in reading alphabetically written words can often read six-digit numbers fluently. In other words, these patients, diagnosed as having "alexia without agraphia" (see Chapter 7), are more likely to understand a symbol that is arbitrarily associated with a word than they are to understand strings of symbols that must be deciphered phonetically.

Modern English is written in an alphabetic system, where each letter is supposed to represent a phoneme, although some logographs (in addition to numerals) are widely used: &, =, $, and ♥, for example, represent the words *and, equal, dollar,* and *love.* English has no syllabic symbols; the nearest approximations would be A and I, which are morphemes as well as letters of the alphabet. But the orthography of English is not as simple as this description might imply. Spelling rules are complicated by the fact that they try to respect phonetics and morphology at the same time. For example, if *sign* were spelled phonetically, it would probably be something like *sain,* but then its morphological relation to *signal, signature,* and *significant* would be lost. Where English has a choice in how a word can be spelled, the spelling that preserves morphological relations is usually chosen.

From such considerations it becomes obvious that the orthography of any living language will be far from ideal for the purposes of scientific linguistics.

The Origins of Writing

Although it is accurate to call writing an invention, it is an invention without an inventor. No one sat down one day and said, "I think I will invent writing." It grew organically out of practical needs. Innumerable nameless geniuses must have contributed to it; over thousands of years it was reinvented,

Charles Demuth painted this homage to his friend William Carlos Williams in response to a poem published by the writer and physician in 1921:

The Great Figure

Among the rain
and lights
I saw the figure 5
in gold
on a red
firetruck
moving
tense
unheeded
to gong clangs
siren howls
and wheels rumbling
through the dark city.

revised, and improved in many different ways at different places. In the course of that history, many different systems were developed as the theories of language on which they were based slowly evolved.

   The archeological record suggests that the earliest attempts at writing—pre-writing or proto-writing, as it is sometimes called—began with larger, meaningful linguistic units and only gradually evolved toward the nonmeaningful symbols of the alphabet. The available evidence strongly suggests that writing did not originate as a representation of speech, but instead grew out of an interest in pictures and pictorial representations. Why ancient peoples created such representations can never be known, but that has not prevented otherwise sober scholars from speculating. Certainly, some of the pictures have a more definite communicative intent than do others.

Consider an example. In southern Alaska, native American hunters drew on a piece of wood the figure below: (A) a canoe, (B) a figure with arms extended sideways to represent the idea of nothing, (C) another figure with hand raised to mouth to represent eating, and (D) a hut. The total can be interpreted to mean, Nothing to eat in the hut; that is to say, the hunters had not found game.

Do such drawings qualify as writing? It is true that they seem to tell a story, but the story is not in any particular language. The figures are stereotyped, suggesting a communicative intent on the part of the artist, but they are not conventionalized. That is to say, they are not part of some fixed list of symbols agreed to in advance by all users of the writing system. Such drawings are more artistic than linguistic. But a connection between them and true writing is apparent. It is as if the earliest theory of language analyzed it into a sequence of visual images and sought to represent those images by drawing pictures of them.

According to I. J. Gelb, whose classic *A Study of Writing* (Chicago: University of Chicago Press, 1963) is a challenging introduction to these questions, the first appearance of phonetic elements in this kind of picture-writing was in the representation of proper names. A native American whose name meant Big Bear, for example, could be referred to by a picture—sometimes called a pictogram or an ideogram—of a big bear. But the early Sumerians, in southern Mesopotamia, favored names like Enlil-Has-Given-Life, which are difficult to express so simply. To solve this problem, they were forced to develop symbols to represent the sound of the name. And so the theory that language is a sequence of images began to give way to the theory that language consists of a sequence of spoken syllables.

Scholars argue about the date, but most agree that the phonetization of writing began about 3000 B.C. The best documented example is Sumerian,

This example of picture-writing, found in Alaska and first published in 1893, had originally been stuck into the ground on a trail where it would be discovered by the writer's fellow tribesmen.

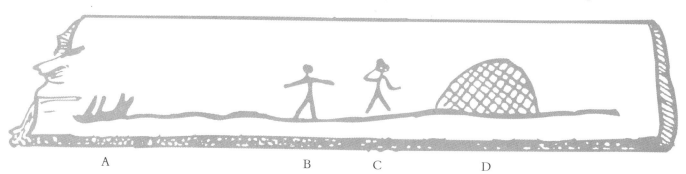

A   B   C   D

Petroglyphs from Newspaper Rock in Canyonlands National Park, Utah.

which began with logographs for objects, numbers, and personal names, then added signs to express the sounds of words that could not be easily pictured. The result was a logo-syllabic writing system: The signs that were used phonetically were also meaningful words. "Once introduced," Gelb writes, "the principle of phonetization spread rapidly. With it entire new horizons were opened to the expression of all linguistic forms, no matter how abstract, by means of written symbols."

But establishing such a system is not a simple undertaking. Meaningful correspondences between the symbols and the spoken words had to be established, particular symbols with definite syllabic values had to be chosen, the form of the symbol had to be standardized, and everybody had to memorize the symbols and their values. Sumerian writing did not have symbols for every possible syllable. To economize on the number of symbols that had to be agreed to, syllables that had a similar sound were often represented by the same symbol.

When did speech sounds replace syllables as the appropriate segments for orthographic transcription? The importance of this advance in linguistic analysis seems to have been unforeseen, an incidental (if not accidental) development probably begun by the Phoenicians and completed by the Greeks.

The Roman alphabet, with which this book is written, was derived from the Greek alphabet, and the Greek alphabet was derived from the version of

Evolution of Modern Alphabets from Phoenician Origins

Phoenician	Old Hebrew	Early Greek	Classical Greek	Etruscan	Early Latin	Modern Roman	Greek Form	Greek Name	Cyrillic	Hebrew Form	Hebrew Name	Arabic Form	Arabic Name
𐤀		Δ	A	A	A	Aa	Αα	alpha	Аа	א	'aleph, 'alef	ا	'alif
			B		B	Bb	Ββ	beta	Бб	ב	bēth	ب	bā
			Γ			Cc	Γγ	gamma	Вв	ג	gimel	ت	tā
		Δ	Δ		D	Dd	Δδ	delta	Гг	ד	dāleth	ث	thā
			E			Ee	Εε	epsilon	Дд	ה	hē	ج	jīm
			Φ			Ff	Ζζ	zēta	Ее	ו	vav, waw	ح	hā
						Gg	Ηη	ēta	Ёё	ז	zayin	خ	khā
		B	H		H	Hh	Θθ	thēta	Жж	ח	heth	د	dāi
		I	I	I	I	Ii	Ιι	iota	Зз	ט	teth	ذ	dhāi
						Jj			Ии Йй	י	yod, yodh	ر	rā
		K	K		K	Kk	Κκ	kappa	Кк	כ	kāph	ز	zāy
			Λ		L	Ll	Λλ	lambda	Лл	ל	lāmedh	س	sin
		M	M		M	Mm	Μμ	mu	Мм	מ	mēm	ش	shin
		N	N		N	Nn	Νν	nu	Нн	נ	nūn	ص	sād
		O	O	O	O	Oo	Ξξ	xi	Оо	ס	samekh	ض	dād
			Π			Pp	Οο	omicron	Пп	ע	'ayin	ط	tā
		Φ	Q	Q	Q	Qq	Ππ	pi	Рр	פ	pē	ظ	zā
		P	P		R	Rr	Ρρ	rhō	Сс	צ	sade, sadhe	ع	'ayn
		Σ	Σ			Ss	Σσς	sigma	Тт	ק	qōph	غ	ghayn
		T	T		T	Tt	Ττ	tau	Уу	ר	rēsh	ف	fā
		Υ	Υ	V	V	Uu	Υυ	upsilon	Фф	שׂ	sin	ق	qāf
						Vv	Φφ	phi	Хх	שׁ	shin	ك	kāf
						Ww	Χχ	chi, khi	Цц	ת	tāv, tāw	ل	lām
		X	Ξ		X	Xx	Ψψ	psi	Чч			م	mim
						Yy	Ωω	omega	Шш			ن	nūn
		I	Z			Zz			Щщ			ه	hā
									Ъъ			و	wāw
									Ьь			ي	yā
									Ыы				
									Ээ				
									Юю				
									Яя				

The development of early alphabets in relation to different modern alphabets.

the Semitic alphabet that the Greeks had learned from the Phoenicians. Where the Phoenicians got it has been a matter for scholarly debate, but there is evidence that it had its origins in the early picture-writing of the ancient Egyptians. The Egyptian hieroglyphic system presumably developed the same way the Sumerian system did, beginning with rebuslike signs to represent personal names and rapidly developing into a logo-syllabic system. The Egyptians carried the principle of economy further than the Sumerians did, developing separate symbols for all the consonants, but no symbols for vowels. For the Egyptians, these were auxiliary symbols, used mostly to indicate word-initial consonants in ambiguous contexts. Because Egyptian had no word-initial vowels, no vowel symbols were developed. Their syllabary contained about twenty-four nonsemantic symbols standing for an initial consonant followed by any vowel (that is, the same symbol would be used to write the syllables *ma, me,* or *mu*), and about eighty symbols standing for pairs of consonants plus any pair of vowels. The Egyptians came close to an alphabetic system, but they continued to use their syllabary along with the older symbols, both logographic and syllabic.

The next step in this development was probably the Semitic script. There is no record of Semitic picture-writing, so presumably the Semites borrowed the idea of writing from some other people. The evidence that they borrowed it from the Egyptians is that they used a small set of symbols for initial consonants followed by any vowel. Like the Egyptians, they lacked word-initial vowels, so they did not develop symbols to represent vowels; but unlike the

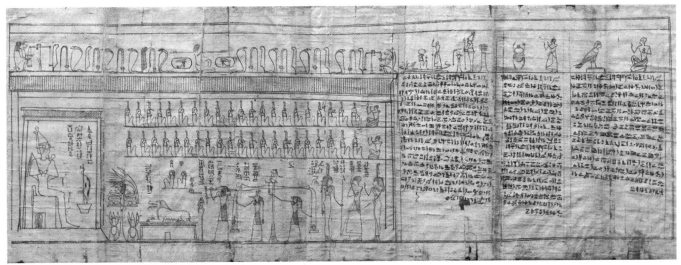

Egyptian hieroglyphics from a twenty-first dynasty papyrus of the Book of the Dead.

A prototype of the British linguists of the last century, Sir Henry Creswicke Rawlinson (1810–1895) laid the foundations of modern Assyriology as an adjunct to his career as an army officer and an official of the East India Company. Stationed in Persia, Rawlinson scaled a sheer 500-foot rock face at Behistun (now Bisitun, Iran) to transcribe the trilingual cuneiform inscription carved there more than two millennia earlier by Darius the Great, King of Persia. Rawlinson eventually deciphered, interpreted, and published the inscription, which was in Old Persian (an Indo-European language), Akkadian (a Semitic language of the Babylonians), and Elamite (a language isolate).

Egyptians, they used no logographs and no phonetic symbols with two or more consonants. Some of their symbols resembled a cursive form of hieroglyphic writing developed by the Egyptians, but that resemblance could have been accidental. In any case, they gave their symbols Semitic names, using words whose initial sound (always a consonant) had the appropriate sound. Whether or not the resulting system of writing should be called alphabetic is one of those fine points of definition that only experts are qualified to debate. But it was not a fully alphabetic system because they had no letter-symbols for vowels. The Semitic practice of consonantal writing, writing without vowels, is still preserved in modern Hebrew script. The result is a bit harder to read than if the vowels were present, but much more efficient—a simple experiment can demonstrate the principle for those unfamiliar with Hebrew and Arabic script:

CMPRD T NGLSH RTHGRPHY,
HBRW SCRPT S STRKNGLY LW N RDNDNCY.

There is little doubt that Greeks borrowed this system of writing from the Phoenician Semites—in 776 B.C., according to Greek tradition. The Greeks preserved the forms, the names, and the order of the Phoenician symbols; they even called the system Phoenician writing. The Phoenician names ʾāleph, bêth, gīmel, dāleth—which meant ox, house, camel, and door to Phoenicians—were meaningless to the Greeks, who modified them to alpha, beta, gamma, delta in accordance with Greek phonology. The principal contribution of the Greeks was to use some of the symbols to represent vowel phonemes. For example, in the Semitic alphabet the first symbol, named ʾāleph, stood for a weak consonant that did not occur in Greek, so when Greeks pronounced it they omitted the weak initial consonant, thereby exposing the initial vowel *a*. Similarly, when in some Greek dialects the initial consonant expressed by the Semitic symbol named hēth was lost, the Greeks called it eta, and so the symbol H, η acquired the phonemic value $\bar{e}$.

With the addition of symbols for the vowels, and the final disconnection of the name of the symbol from its sound, alphabetic writing as it is known today had arrived. In the light of history, the Greek contribution can be seen as one among many innovations made during the thousands of years that writing was developing.

How did it happen that alphabetic writing spread so rapidly throughout the Western world? The Romans were responsible for that. They borrowed the Greek alphabet, adapted it to Latin, and carried it with them to the remotest corners of the Roman Empire.

It is not surprising that words dominated the earliest attempts to write, and that only gradually did logo-syllabic writing give way to syllabic writing, and syllabic writing give way in turn to alphabetic writing. As Sapir said, "The speaker and hearer feel the words." But attempts to represent that feeling

A Roman inscription honoring Caesar, 2 B.C. This is the form of alphabetic writing that the Roman legions carried throughout their empire.

graphically proved awkward and in many parts of the world gave way to attempts to represent the sounds instead. The history of alphabetic writing can be characterized as moving progressively closer to spoken language, with each advance signaling an improvement in linguistic analysis. Eventually, the exponential principle wins out: In order to have enough different written word forms, writers have to generate them the same way speakers do, by concatenation.

The Phonetic Alphabet

Speech analysis did not end with the ancient Greeks. On the assumption that advances in linguistic theory should be reflected in advances in orthography, one would expect to find advances in the technology of writing still occurring. And that is indeed the case.

Modern concern with problems of orthography reached a peak in the nineteenth century as the sound laws became a major focus for work in historical linguistics. The spelling conventions observed in ancient documents that provided evidence for the sound shifts were not sufficient to settle important issues concerning pronunciation. In a perfect alphabetic orthography, every written symbol would correspond to a particular phoneme, and every phoneme would have its own written symbol. Some orthographies, like Spanish, come closer to that ideal than others, but no existing system of alphabetic writing was considered adequate to the needs of linguistic science.

The Discovery of Linear B

Each Greek city-state had its own calendar, but Hellenistic scholars in Alexandria were able to establish a fairly satisfactory chronology because the Greeks came together every four years for their Olympiads. From records available to them in the third century B.C., the Alexandrians designated a date corresponding to 776 B.C. on the Gregorian calendar as the year of the first Olympiad—and also as the year that the Greeks adopted the Phoenician alphabet. Thus, Greek history (in the sense of "history" as a written record) begins in 776 B.C. All that preceded that date, including whatever basis there was for events recounted by Homer in the *Iliad* and the *Odyssey,* are part of the prehistory of Greece.

In 1876 the German archeologist Heinrich Schliemann, taking the Homeric poems as his guide, discovered a grave circle at Mycenae, in the northeastern corner of the Peloponnesian peninsula. The wealth and artistry uncovered there proved that the prehistoric Greeks had achieved a high level of civilization. When the Englishman Arthur Evans saw the treasures that Schliemann had recovered, he reasoned that such wealth and craftsmanship could not have been achieved by illiterate people. Yet

Sir Arthur Evans.

no inscriptions had been found on their buildings, and Mycenae was violently destroyed three hundred years before the Greeks adopted alphabetic writing.

This puzzle led Evans to search for prehistoric writing, and in 1900, at Knossos on the island of Crete, he uncovered clay tablets with writing on them. Evans was able to distinguish three different scripts on the tablets. The oldest consists of pictorial signs that reminded him of Egyptian script, so he named it hieroglyphic, although there was no evidence that it was

borrowed from Egypt. In the second script, the pictures are mere outlines and the writing goes from left to right; Evans named it Linear A. The third and latest script, Linear B, seems to have replaced Linear A, probably in the fifteenth century B.C. Photographs of a few tablets were published, but Evans became distracted by the larger task of recording his discoveries in the ancient palaces at Knossos, which, according to Homer, had been the capital of a vast and legendary empire.

To decipher an unknown language written in an unknown script is as near an impossibility as any task that a scholar might be tempted to undertake. Many guesses were advanced, but without a large supply of texts it was impossible even to test their plausibility. Publication of the inscriptions Evans had found was delayed until 1952, but in 1939 Carl Blegen, an American archeologist working at Pylos, on the mainland of Greece, found hundreds of Linear B tablets—a discovery that provided the large source of texts that was needed for serious attempts to decipher Linear B.

First, what kind of script is Linear B? There are only three ways to commit language to writing. Logographic scripts provide no clue to the pronunciation of the words they represent, but syllabic and alphabetic scripts do represent speech sounds. Linear B texts contained some reasonably obvious logographic characters: Some were pictures of men, women, horses, pigs, spears, and so forth, and some were clearly numerals. But many others suggested no obvious pictorial interpretations. Were they logographs that had been abbreviated into unrecognizability? Or were they arbitrary characters with phonological significance? The number of different characters provides the clue. An alphabetic script needs relatively few distinct characters; a logographic script needs thousands. Linear B texts contain eighty-nine different characters: too many for alphabetic writing, too few for logographic. Scholars felt confident that they were dealing with a syllabary.

The more difficult question was the identity of the language. The first step along a path to the answer was taken in the 1940s by an American, Alice E. Kober, who asked whether the language was inflected. If it was an inflected language, which seemed highly probable, then words occurring in similar contexts should have similar terminal characters. After patient and methodical work, she isolated characters that represented terminal inflections for three different cases of nouns and established that the language respected gender. Miss Kober died in 1950 at the age of 43, too soon to participate in the final insight for which she had prepared the way.

A sample of the writing that Evans called Linear A.

The Decipherment of Linear B

The solution to the puzzle of the Linear B tablets was finally achieved by an Englishman, Michael Ventris, who applied Alice Kober's methods to the larger body of evidence that was becoming available. Ventris had guessed as early as 1940 that the language was Etruscan, since the Etruscans were supposed to have lived around the Aegean prior to migrating to Italy. In 1951 Ventris returned to the problem and worked on it continuously for eighteen months, during which time he kept detailed notes of his progress.

On the assumption that the syllables were all of a simple open, consonant-vowel type, Ventris worked with a two-dimensional syllabic grid, with vowels heading the columns, consonants heading the rows, and Linear B characters entered in the cells. The use of syllabic grids was not new; what Kober and Ventris contributed was the idea of using a grid without deciding in advance which vowels or consonants a particular set of syllables might have in common. For example, suppose the texts contain two polysyllabic words that are identical except for the last character; in that case, it is highly likely that the two different terminal characters both start with the same consonant. If the same contrast is found for other polysyllabic words, the likelihood is increased. Ventris's early grids were weak on vowels; because he believed the language was Etruscan, he was reluctant at first to think that terminal vowels might differentiate gender.

As his methodical combinatory work proceeded, Ventris repeatedly attempted to relate his results to Etruscan words and suffixes. By June 1952, however, his grid was complete enough to enable him to recognize several Greek words. These could have been borrowed words, of course, so he set out to disprove the possibility that the language of Linear B was Greek. But every test indicated that the Greek solution was correct. It was archaic Greek, of course, related to Classical Greek as Old English is related to Modern English; but it was inescapably Greek. Together with John Chadwick, a specialist in Greek dialects, Ventris published the evidence for his claims.

Even then much work remained to be done, testing and extending Ventris's initial insight. Not all Greek syllables are the simple consonant-vowel type, so the representation of the spoken language in this script could not have been perfect; a description of the rules of transcription used by the scribes forms an important part of the solution. At present seventy-

A sample of the writing that Evans called Linear B.

three Linear B characters have known values; for another sixteen rare characters, values have not yet been established.

Many words in the texts still have not been interpreted, and critics of Ventris's decipherment (there are always critics) point out that its correctness has not been proved. Real proof is probably impossible. Several hundred years intervened between the palace administrators who wrote Linear B and the Ionic Greek of the epic poet Homer, time enough for words to change or disappear. But where the tablets and Homer can be compared point for point, there are some puzzling discrepancies. Perhaps critics emphasize those differences because they find it difficult to believe that the Greeks, who perfected the Semitic system of alphabetic writing, had a syllabic system hundreds of years earlier.

It is amusing to speculate that if the centers of the ancient empires on Crete and the mainland of Greece had not been violently destroyed between 1400 and 1100 B.C., later Greeks would have had little need for alphabetic systems of writing, and this book would probably have been written and printed in a syllabic orthography derived from Linear B.

a	e	i	o	u
da	de	di	do	du
ja	je		jo	
ka	ke	ki	ko	ku
ma	me	mi	mo	mu
na	ne	ni	no	nu
pa	pe	pi	po	pu
qa	qe	qi	qo	
ra	re	ri	ro	ru
sa	se	si	so	su
ta	te	ti	to	tu
wa	we	wi	wo	
za	ze		zo	

initial ai   initial au   rai   ha

p^h u   nwa   pte   tja

twe   two   dwe   dwo

rjo   rja

These are the seventy-three characters of Linear B with known phonetic values. Each character represents a syllable. There are a few other characters that seem to belong to the Linear B system, but they occur so infrequently that their values are still not established.

The complexities are all too easily illustrated with English orthography. Words like *colonel* and *kernel* are pronounced the same way and spelled differently, whereas words like *lead* (the metal) and *lead* (the verb) are spelled the same way and pronounced differently. A verse by Charles Follen Adams makes the point:

An Orthographic Lament

If an S and an I and an O and U
With an X at the end spell Su;
And an E and a Y and an E spell I,
  Pray what is a speller to do?
Then, if also an S and an I and a G
  And an HED spell side,
There's nothing much left for a speller to do
  But to go commit siouxeyesighed.

Many a child trying to learn the rules of English spelling must have shared Adams's despair. Spanish, by comparison, is better behaved. People who know only the rules of pronunciation can read a Spanish text aloud well enough that Spaniards can understand it, even though the readers have no idea what they are saying. A similar experiment with English would end in disaster.

English orthography is a quasiregular system: A set of rules can be formulated that will apply most of the time, but there are unpredictable exceptions to every rule. The existence of rules can be demonstrated by asking people to pronounce nonwords. For example, people who speak and read English will pronounce VOME, TIVE, and LOES to rhyme with *home, strive,* and *toes,* respectively, indicating that *come, give,* and *does* are irregular. From that demonstration it is usually concluded that a person who can correctly pronounce both irregular words and nonwords must have mastered two separate pronunciation systems. A list of irregular words must be consulted because they cannot be pronounced by rule; rules must be consulted to determine the pronunciation of nonwords because they are not included on any word list. There is even evidence that brain injuries can affect one of those systems and spare the other. Certainly it is true that both regular and irregular pronunciations must be learned, but precisely how independent those two kinds of learning are is still a question for debate.

The simple solution would be to get rid of the irregularities. Various authorities have argued in favor of spelling reforms that would bring English orthography into line with accepted pronunciation. Because the history of alphabetic writing has been the story of how the advantages of sound-letter correspondences were discovered, the idea of deliberately extrapolating from this history to the ultimate perfect system is very attractive. But why limit this extrapolation to English? While you are about it, why not construct an alpha-

Agraphia

Some brain injuries result in a condition known as agraphia, a pathological loss of the ability to write. Writing difficulties can be a secondary effect of more serious injuries, of course, but there are attested cases of specific agraphia—where the symptoms are restricted to the writing process—in patients whose languages had an alphabetic orthography. It may seem curious that a person able to read would have difficulties writing, but that was the condition of these specific agraphics. If they were asked to write words from dictation, consistent errors of spelling would occur. It could be shown that the trouble was not a motor incapacity—they could, for example, copy a text from lower-case to uppercase. Nor was it a memory problem—after writing or failing to write a word, they could always repeat aloud the word they had been asked to write. And it was not a perceptual or a comprehension deficit—they could read fluently and could give synonyms for the words they were trying to write.

Two patterns of agraphic behavior offer an instructive contrast. In the form known as lexical agraphia, the patient can write words with regular spellings, but makes mistakes with irregular words by regularizing their spelling: "subtle" elicited *suttle*, for example; in the case of a French patient, "église" elicited *aiglise*. A lexical agraphic also spells plausible nonwords like *pake* just as normal subjects would. In the contrasting form known as phonological agraphia, on the other hand, the patient can spell frequently used words correctly, but may make a few mistakes with the less frequent words—almost always in the form of writing some

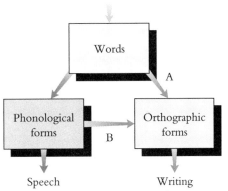

This model represents two paths normally available to people when they write: the direct path through a visual image of the orthographic form and the indirect path through an auditory image of the phonological form plus sound-to-letter rules. A lesion that interrupts the system at A results in lexical agraphia; a lesion that disrupts the sound-to-letter rules at B results in phonological agraphia.

other word: "ascend" elicited *ascent,* for example. A phonological agraphic, however, cannot spell nonwords and cannot segment simple words like *cat* into the corresponding speech sounds. One patient who showed this pattern of difficulties would say that he could not write *amenable* because he did not understand it; when the meaning suddenly occurred to him a little later, he was able to write it.

Apparently, normal people have visual word-images as part of their lexical representation of words, and those images guide their writing of familiar words. When that method is not adequate, they can resort to a system of phonological rules for segmenting the spoken word and pairing sounds to letters. The lexical agraphic has apparently lost the visual word-images from lexical memory, but still has access to the phonological system. Such cases, where one system is lost while the other is preserved, are interpreted as evidence that the two systems are independent—in technical terminology, "dissociated." A phonological agraphic, who has apparently lost the phonological rules but retains visual word-images, provides further evidence for dissociation. In such cases, the two systems are said to be doubly dissociated.

Alexander Melville Bell (1819–1905).

bet in which *any* language can be written? Instead of the many different orthographies that have evolved haphazardly out of the accidents of history, why not a single international alphabet that everyone can share? Almost certainly it was such optimistic anticipations of the resulting benefits that led to the creation of the International Phonetic Alphabet.

As the quantitative study of speech developed during the nineteenth century, a number of phoneticians became involved in classifying speech sounds and developing notational systems for recording them accurately in written form. One of those pioneers in America was Melville Bell, a speech therapist who developed a notational system to help his deaf students learn to articulate intelligible speech. Bell's symbols bore no relation to the Roman alphabet, but instead were abstracted from drawings of the positions and movements of the articulatory organs during speech. (The Korean alphabet, Han'gŭl, was designed with a similar idea in the fifteenth century. Han'gŭl characters have a systematic structure correlated with the phonetic features of Korean: They distinguish vowels from consonants, they reflect the position of the tongue and the place of articulation, and so on.) Bell described his system in a book, *Visible Speech: The Science of Universal Alphabetics,* published in 1867. It con-

Four years after the publication of his father's book, Visible Speech, *Alexander Graham Bell (top row, right), the "teacher of the teachers," was photographed with his staff and students at the Pemberton Avenue School for the Deaf, Boston.*

tains a systematic account of the different activities that each articulator is capable of, a discussion of the various sounds that result from combinations of activities of specific articulators, and a graphic system for representing those activities. His son, Alexander Graham Bell, helped him to demonstrate the accuracy of his notation. At public lectures Melville Bell would ask someone from the audience, preferably someone who spoke an unfamiliar dialect, to come to the stage and say a few words of his or her own choosing, which Bell would write down. Alexander, who had been out of hearing range, would then be called to read aloud what his father had written. Alexander's imitation and the original speaker's pronunciation were then compared.

In Europe, a group of phoneticians joined together to form the International Phonetic Association in 1886. One active member of the group was Henry Sweet, the inspiration for Henry Higgins in George Bernard Shaw's *Pygmalion*. These workers drew up the International Phonetic Alphabet (IPA), which was designed to be applicable to all languages. The IPA did not try to depict the articulatory positions; it retained the familiar letters of the Roman alphabet, but supplemented them with many other symbols and with a variety of modifying marks. The features of speech sounds that were used to define phonetic categories for the IPA were the product of many years of patient analysis, and are still used by phoneticians today. Unfortunately, however, the IPA was an alphabet.

The IPA is the ultimate embodiment of the segmental theory of speech. Symbols of the phonetic alphabet designate segments into which the flow of speech is assumed to be divided, as if speech sounds were as independent and self-contained as letters of a printed alphabet. Although the IPA was little more than a self-conscious extrapolation of the theory that had been evolving slowly for 5,000 years, attempts to base a phonetic science on it finally uncovered its deficiencies.

To understand the limitations of alphabetic scripts, it is necessary to understand the dynamic process of speaking that the alphabetic characters are supposed to represent. The theory underlying the IPA can be summarized in terms of the features that are used to distinguish different categories of speech sounds. A first distinction was drawn between vowels and consonants. Then vowels were characterized by tongue positions (high-low and front-back) and lip rounding; consonants were characterized by place (from bilabial back to glottal) and manner of articulation (plosive, nasal, fricative, and so forth; see Chapter 4). The resulting categories are arranged hierarchically in the figure on the next page.

The hierarchy of features in the figure represents the theory underlying the IPA, not the IPA itself. It is a theory of the limits of human linguistic phonetic capabilities. In order to produce the IPA, this figure must be supplemented by certain conventions. There is a convention that says there is an either-or choice between the italicized features, whereas all the boldface features must be selected. That is to say, from **Segment** there is a choice between

The words visible speech *written in the phonetic alphabet developed by Melville Bell, 1867.*

The features used in the International Pho-
netic Alphabet to categorize speech sounds
are arranged here as a hierarchy.

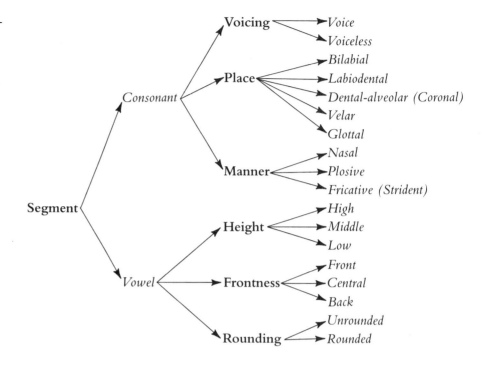

Consonant or *Vowel;* from *Consonant,* however, all three of **Voicing, Place,** and **Manner** must be selected, since every consonant has a value of all three of those features; from **Place** there is a choice among several places of articulation. For example, if the **Segment** is a *Consonant,* and if the values of **Voicing, Place,** and **Manner** are *Voiced, Bilabial,* and *Nasal,* respectively, then the IPA symbol is *m* (the initial consonant in *mat*).

In the years since it was proposed, a number of problems with this theory have been discovered. For one thing, the IPA lacks any way to deal with sounds that have more than one place of articulation. Apparently the framers of the IPA were not familiar with such speech sounds. A more serious problem is that segments are either consonants or vowels, as if consonants and vowels had no features in common. Thus, voicing and nasality are not admitted as features of vowels (although nasality can be indicated by special markers).

But the worst trouble with the IPA is that no way is provided to account for the fact that consonants are regularly modified by the vowels that accompany them, a phenomenon known as co-articulation. Compare the English words *keep* and *coop,* for example. Both are pronounced with an initial voiceless, velar, plosive consonant. Under close analysis, these two consonants are recognized to be consistently different. Pronounce the initial sounds to yourself: Unless you listen closely you will not notice the difference, because it has no significance, but when you listen for it, it is unmistakable. The phenomenon is not limited to English: Whenever velars are followed by front vowels, their articulation is advanced—simply because both sounds are being produced by the same mouth. The problem that this poses for the IPA is that, having carried segmentation as far as it would go, the IPA lacks any way to account for this kind of interaction between adjacent segments in the same syllable. In this and many similar instances, strings of IPA symbols cannot give an accurate representation of what speakers actually say. The segmental assumption was carried too far.

In spite of its shortcomings, however, the IPA helped to standardize phonetic notations and so played an important role in the development of scientific linguistics; it will undoubtedly be revised to bring it more into line with current linguistic thinking. Because it is an alphabet, the IPA necessarily gives special prominence to speech sounds, whereas the most fundamental insight gained during the last century has been the realization that it is the features (voicing, place, manner, height, frontness, rounding) rather than the sounds themselves that are the basic building blocks of spoken language. But that thought must wait for the discussion of the spoken word in Chapter 4.

Simplified Spelling

Meanwhile, where does this leave the question of spelling reform in English? Even if the IPA is not adequate for the needs of science, would it not be better to spell words in an alphabet designed to represent just those features of speech that native speakers of English distinguish? It has been argued that an alphabet of about forty letters, each representing a single phoneme of English, would be easier for children to learn to read and write, because the written language would be much closer to the spoken language. Although such proposals sound reasonable, they have never been widely accepted, perhaps because libraries are already filled with books written in the existing orthography, because printing machines would have to be changed, and (most likely) because people are unwilling to learn new spelling habits. Writing has a conservative influence on language—it works to resist change, not to promote sudden reforms.

Moreover, not all linguists deplore conventional English orthography. Some argue that it is actually close to an optimal system for representing what a speaker must know about the pronunciation of English words—knowledge that is not predictable by phonological rules. Simplified spelling might help people who do not know English to read printed words aloud more or less correctly. But the price of that advantage would be to penalize people who do know English; they would have to convert the simplified spelling back into something resembling the present orthography in order to understand what they were reading.

For example, consider how the plurals of *rope, robe,* and *rose* are formed. People who speak English already know (tacitly, at least) that *ropes* ends with a

Efforts to reform English spelling have a long history. As early as the thirteenth century, a monk named Ormin tried it. Ormin's proposals for reform were ignored, but when his manuscript turned up six hundred years later, it proved to be a mine of information about Middle English pronunciation. Probably the most famous modern advocate of simplified spelling was George Bernard Shaw (1856–1950), whose will left prize money for a competition that was won by Kingsley Read in 1959. The Shavian system has 48 characters unrelated in appearance to any existing alphabet. The sentence He paused for a moment and a wild feeling of pity came over him *looks like this in Shavian orthography:*

ꕗ ꕙꕚ꓿ ꓜ ꓫ ꕛꕜꕝ ꕞ ꓫ ꕟꕠ ꓜꕡꕢ ꓫ ꓜꕣ꓿ ꕤꕥ ꕦꕧ ꕨꕩ.

Not all writing resists change. Graffiti on a subway car in the South Bronx declare their place of origin: Tuff City.

voiceless sibilant *-s*, that *robes* ends with a voiced sibilant *-z*, and that *roses* ends with a syllable containing a neutralized vowel and the voiced sibilant *-ɨz*. For people who know English, therefore, it is not necessary to represent these different pronunciations by different spellings; the plural can be written simply by adding *-s*. In a simplified orthography, however, these plurals might be written *rowps, rowbz,* and *rowzɨz,* which could be pronounced correctly by someone who knew nothing more than the rules governing this spelling system. But people who speak English know that all three endings, when added to nouns, mean "more than one." To understand what they were reading, therefore, they would have to convert *-s*, *-z*, and *-ɨz* back into the underlying concept of plurality. If this argument is correct, then learning to read and write conventional English orthography must heighten a person's awareness of significant regularities in the language—regularities that hold for phonetically divergent dialects and are resistant to historical change, but that are far from obvious in the patterns of sounds that are actually uttered.

In any case, it should be clear by now that a close phonetic transcription of sound segments does not provide a complete description of the physiological processes or the acoustic results of speaking. Phonetic transcriptions represent speech sounds by discrete, invariant letters. The process of speaking is not a series of staccato jumps from one fixed position to the next, and the stream of speech cannot be cut up into discrete sounds.

■   ■   ■

The evolution of speech made it possible to externalize thought, but it was the invention of writing that made it possible to preserve externalized thought—with consequences for the human race more important than all the battles ever fought. The written word has its own validity, but there are good reasons behind linguists' claims for the primacy of the spoken word.

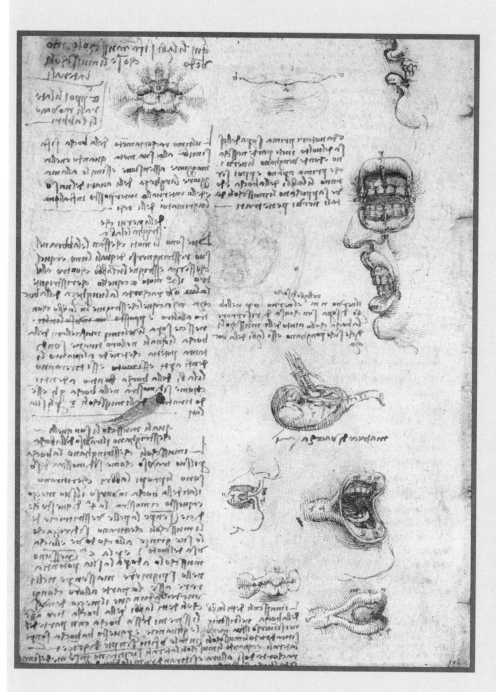

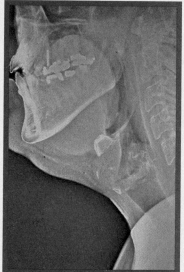

◀ *Human anatomy is one foundation of the neurophysiology and acoustics of spoken language, which characterizes every known community of Homo sapiens. Among Leonardo da Vinci's drawings in an anatomical manuscript of c. 1506–1509 are these nine studies of the mouth and lips, with notes on their musculature.*

▼ *Today, X rays afford a detailed view of the vocal organs; here, a speaker pronounces an [i] vowel.*

The Spoken Word

Everyone knows that human beings are innately prepared to acquire language, and that the spoken word is one of biology's masterpieces. But when this curtain of grand generalities is lifted, what lies behind it? A cautious scientist will find little more there than a question. A question as simple as it is difficult to answer.

What is the biological basis for spoken language? In part, it is anatomical: The vocal tract of human beings is specially adapted to produce a rich and rapidly modifiable variety of sounds. But it is also neurophysiological: For human language to work, language users must command highly complex motor and perceptual skills. They must have at their immediate disposal a large collection of neural patterns capable of controlling the articulatory gestures of word production. And they must have access to a correspondingly large collection of neural patterns capable of discriminating the sound of one word from another.

Alexander Graham Bell with Helen Keller and Annie Sullivan.

Neurologists are confident that such mechanisms exist. They even know, approximately, where in the brain they are located and what can happen to speech when they are damaged. But the details are still poorly understood. Much of what is known (or believed) about the biological basis of human language has been learned indirectly, by inferring what the mechanism must be from observations of the functions it performs. To understand the neurophysiological bases of language, a scientist must begin with what the mechanism produces: with the spoken words themselves.

It is essential, therefore, to have precise information about the actions of the speech organs and about the acoustic consequences of those actions. Alphabetic writing, for all its virtues, does not provide a representation of spoken words adequate for the needs of scientific linguistics. Until the twentieth century the human ear and the human hand were the best instruments available for making permanent records of human speech. But then technology intervened. The invention of the telephone by Alexander Graham Bell (1847–1922) in 1875 was a critical first step, but it was really Lee De Forest (1873–1961) who sparked a revolution with his 1906 adaptation of the thermionic vacuum tube to serve as an amplifier. Today, with the help of digital tape recorders and computers, speech sounds can be recorded and their physical properties specified with great precision.

It turns out, however, that although such information about spoken word forms is necessary, it is not sufficient. The relations among movements of the speech organs, the acoustic properties of speech, and how speech is perceived are immensely complex. Different articulatory gestures can have similar acoustic results. Utterances like *rider* and *writer*, whose physical properties are similar, are treated as totally different by the people who use them; other utterances, such as *rider* spoken by a female child or an adult male, have different physical properties but are treated as identical. In addition to specifying how words are spoken, it is also necessary to specify how they are understood. Speaking and understanding are reciprocal processes that together link sound and meaning.

How do listeners categorize the utterances they hear? The formal relation of identity holds between two words that are assigned to the same category, even though they may be distinguishably different physiological and acoustical events. For example, the acoustic properties of *hello* when uttered by two different people can be very different, yet they are said to be two utterances of the same word form (two tokens of the same type). A formal relation between utterances is a relation that depends on form, not meaning. Rhyme is a simple example. The English words *boys* and *noise* sound alike and are said to rhyme with one another. But *boys* and *boys* also sound alike and rhyme with one another—they are not merely related by rhyme, they are related by identity. In both *Boys will be boys* and *Boys will make noise* the beginning and ending words are similar, but in the first sentence there are two word tokens of the same type, whereas in the second all the words are different. The trick is to learn which differences between words are significant and which are not.

Because the differences are so obvious in a familiar language, it is easy to overlook how subtle the physical cues can be. Consider the set of English words *nut, not, neat,* and *newt,* which might occur together in a sentence like *The nut's not neat, Newt.* All four words begin the same way and end the same way; the significant differences are in the vowels. If a speaker could not articulate those differences, or a hearer could not distinguish them, the sentence would become gibberish: *The nut's nut nut, nut.* People who speak English hear the distinctions so clearly that it is hard to believe that the four words are not completely different, yet there are only small differences in tongue position for each word. But those small differences are critically important. Without the ability to generate and discriminate such small differences precisely and rapidly, speech would be very difficult, if not impossible.

Although tongues and ears are different organs and the motoric neural activity controlling articulation is totally different from the perceptual neural activity arising from the ear, speech production and speech perception are—must be—closely coordinated. The two are necessarily related because speakers hear their own vocalizations; if speakers did not hear themselves, they would find it extremely difficult to develop the kind of precision required to generate discriminably different words.

The Source-Filter Theory

The complex processes that are required to utter a word provide the subject matter for a field of research called speech science. The historical origins of speech science lie in the middle of the eighteenth century, but its modern development began in the 1930s and accelerated with the increasing availability of sophisticated electronic technology. Modern speech science is a fascinating combination of muscular and neural physiology, physical acoustics, linguistics, and psychology. Physiology is used to describe how the sounds of speech are produced, acoustics is used to analyze the sounds themselves, and linguistics and psychology are used to determine what aspects of those sounds are important for linguistic communication.

Speech is sometimes called an overlaid function: It depends on breathing, and the basic function of breathing is to get oxygen; vocalization is a kind of biological afterthought. In quiet breathing, about 40 percent of the time is spent inhaling and 60 percent exhaling, but when you speak the ratio is more like 20 to 80 percent. As you vocalize, air is expelled in a controlled way through the larynx and the vocal tract—the throat (pharynx), mouth, teeth, lips, and, for some sounds, the nose. Records of breathing during speech show that there are two components: a relatively slow, controlled component due to the contraction of the abdominal muscles as air is expelled and, superimposed on the slow component, a series of shorter pulses as the intercostal muscles (muscles between the ribs) contract in quick strokes that force air upward

Tracings of changes in chest girth during quiet breathing, speaking, and singing. A downward deflection represents inspiration; an upward deflection, expiration. D is the duration of a complete respiratory cycle; I is the inspiratory portion of the cycle.

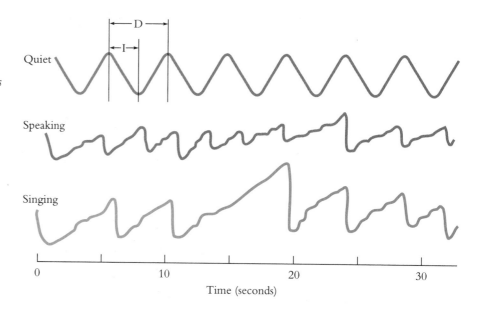

during each syllable. In English, each syllable contains a vowel, so vowels and consonants tend to alternate regularly in the flow of speech. The syllable's power is in its vowel; consonants are simply different ways to turn a vowel on or off.

The flow of air gives rise to sound as a result of constrictions in the vocal tract. The loudest source of sound is in the larynx (the so-called voice box, or Adam's apple), where the vocal folds or cords (infoldings of mucous membrane) can be brought together with just the right tension to vibrate—to release a rapid series of puffs of air into the vocal tract. This rapid series of puffs is the laryngeal tone, the basic source of a speaker's voice. It is a complex sound, with a fundamental frequency of vibration given by the number of puffs of air per second, and a complex series of overtones at frequencies that are multiples of the fundamental. The laryngeal tone is not heard directly, however. What is heard is the voice after it has passed through the vocal tract—the throat, mouth, and nose. These cavities act as filters (resonators that reinforce some frequencies of vibration and attenuate others). The sound that comes out of the mouth depends on the sizes and shapes of these resonators, which change continuously as speech proceeds. (Of course, not all speech sounds involve this laryngeal tone. Those that do are called voiced sounds.)

The source-filter theory of speech production was proposed in 1848 by the German physiologist Johannes Müller (1801–1858), and it is still the basic concept that guides research on the vocalizations of human beings and other animals. The vibration of the vocal folds is taken to be the source; the vocal tract is viewed as an acoustic tube that, depending on its shape and length, filters the source in different ways.

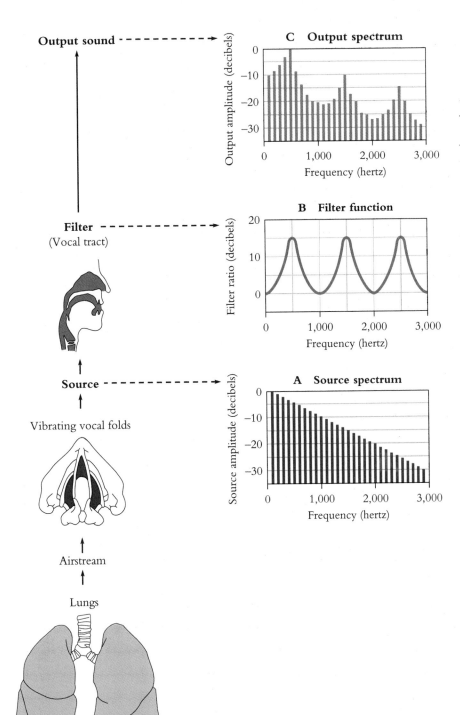

Output sound

C Output spectrum

Filter
(Vocal tract)

B Filter function

Source

Vibrating vocal folds

A Source spectrum

Airstream

Lungs

The lungs supply the power for speaking, the vocal folds act as an oscillator, and the vocal tract is a resonator. According to the source-filter theory, the source is the laryngeal tone produced when the vibrating vocal folds interrupt the airstream from the lungs. The acoustic spectrum for a source with a fundamental frequency of 100 Hz (A) shows the amplitude decreasing uniformly with frequency. The vocal tract is a filter that modifies the source spectrum in a predictable way. For the vowel [ʌ], for example, the filter function (B) has resonant peaks at 500, 1,500, and 2,500 Hz. When the source passes through this filter, the output spectrum (C) has peaks, or formants, at those frequencies.

Early Speaking Machines

*T*he idea of building a machine that could synthesize recognizable speech is quite old; the earliest documented success was more than two hundred years ago. In 1779 the Imperial Academy of St. Petersburg offered its annual prize to the person who could explain the difference between five vowel sounds and construct an apparatus to produce them artificially. The German physicist Christian Kratzenstein (1723–1795) won the prize by constructing acoustic resonators in a shape similar to the human vocal tract, then activating them with a vibrating reed.

In 1791 a Hungarian, Wolfgang von Kempelen (1734–1804), a skilled mechanician with a good ear for speech sounds, built a com-plete and surprisingly successful speaking machine by manipulating mechanical elements to simulate the essential parts of the human vocal system. His speaking machine was widely publicized, but not taken seriously—probably because von Kempelen had earlier claimed to have built a mechanical chess-playing machine whose "mechanism" turned out to be a concealed midget. The speaking machine was legitimate, however. Bellows supplied air to a reed that excited a leather resonator, which could be varied manually to pro-duce different vowels; consonants were simulated by four separate constricted passages that were con-trolled by the fingers of the other hand. In 1835 Sir Charles Wheat-stone (1802–1875) demonstrated a machine that he built from von Kempelen's description.

Von Kempelen's efforts may have had a more far-reaching in-fluence than is generally appreci-ated. As a boy in Edinburgh, Al-exander Graham Bell (1847–1922) saw Wheatstone's reproduction of von Kempelen's machine. Alexan-der, with his brother's assistance, was inspired to construct his own speaking machine, molding the vocal tract with gutta-percha in-side a cast of the human skull. Compared to the sophisticated electronic speech synthesizers of today, these early mechanical ef-forts seem clumsy and amusing. But they laid the foundation on which all later workers built.

A schematic representation of the shapes used by Kratzenstein in 1779 to synthesize vowel sounds. The resonator for I was activated by blowing across the opening, the others by inserting a vibrating reed into the aperture.

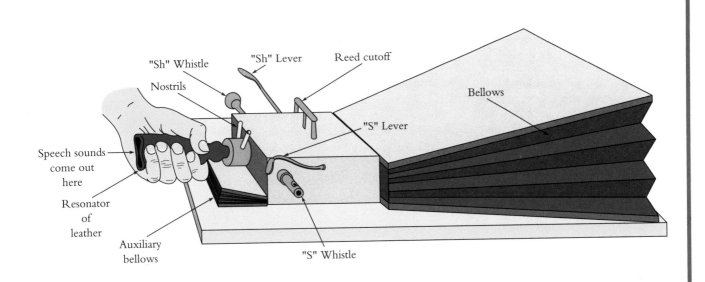

"Sh" Whistle

"Sh" Lever

Reed cutoff

Nostrils

Bellows

"S" Lever

Speech sounds
come out
here

Resonator
of
leather

Auxiliary
bellows

"S" Whistle

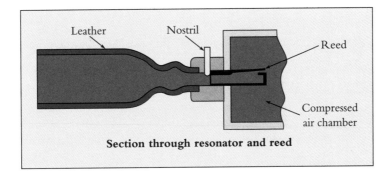

Leather

Nostril

Reed

Compressed
air chamber

Section through resonator and reed

*A drawing of the speaking machine built by Wheatstone on the basis of
a description of von Kempelen's machine.*

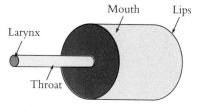

A simple two-tube model illustrates the vocal-tract configuration for the vowel [a]. Although the throat tube has only one-tenth the cross-sectional area of the mouth tube, both will resonate at frequencies corresponding to quarter wavelengths. If both are 8.5 centimeters long, therefore, both will resonate at the same frequency (about 1,000 Hz). Because of coupling (interaction between the tubes), however, one resonance will be slightly higher than the other. Small variations in the lengths of the tubes will merely change which tube gives the lower resonance and which tube gives the higher, a change that will not affect the sound of the vowel. Consequently, the filtering characteristic of the tubes is very stable.

Facing page: *Drawings made from X-ray pictures can be used to estimate cross-sectional areas of the vocal tract, and those estimates can then be used to compute the filter function of the tract. The configurations of the tract for the vowels [i] as in feet, [a] as in father, and [u] as in food are shown from top to bottom. Corresponding models of the vocal tract appear in the central column, and the acoustic output spectrum for each vowel is given at the right.*

The theory is most easily illustrated for vowel sounds, which are produced without the articulatory obstructions in the vocal tract that are characteristic of consonants. Consider the neutral vowel in *nut*, which phoneticians represent by the symbol [ʌ]. Assume that a man has said *nut* and that the fundamental frequency of his voice was 100 Hz (hertz, or cycles per second—middle C on the piano is 262 Hz). The laryngeal tone, if it were unmodified by the vocal tract, would consist of this fundamental frequency plus harmonic overtones at 200 Hz, 300 Hz, 400 Hz, and so on. Most of the sound energy would be in the fundamental; the higher the frequency of an overtone, the less sound energy it would have. This pattern is called the acoustic spectrum of the laryngeal tone. If the laryngeal tone were produced at some other frequency—call it x Hz—the shape of the spectrum would be the same, but the overtones would occur at $2x$ Hz, $3x$ Hz, $4x$ Hz, and so on.

From X-ray pictures it is possible to determine the shape of the vocal tract between the larynx and the lips while the vowel in *nut* is being produced. In this case the tract can be approximated reasonably well by a uniform tube 17 centimeters long and open at one end. The lowest resonant frequency of such a tube can be calculated from its quarter wavelength. Because 17 centimeters is one-quarter the length of a sound wave that is 68 centimeters long, and because the velocity of sound in air at sea level is approximately 33,500 centimeters per second, the lowest resonant frequency will be 33,500/68, or about 500 Hz. Therefore, an overtone at 500 Hz will have just the right wavelength to be reinforced (to resonate) in this tube, and overtones below or above 500 Hz will be relatively weaker as a consequence of passing through it. At about 1,000 Hz a tube of this length will not resonate, and these frequencies will be attenuated, or partially filtered out. At 1,500 Hz, however, there is another resonant frequency, corresponding to the three-quarter wavelength, and at 2,500 Hz there is a third resonant frequency, corresponding to the five-quarter wavelength. Thus, the filtering produced by such a tube can be simply calculated; the resulting filter function has peaks at 500, 1,500 and 2,500 Hz.

When the laryngeal tone is filtered by such a tube, the resulting resonant peaks are imposed on the acoustic spectrum of the tone. In fact, this filtered spectrum can be produced artificially—either mechanically, with an appropriate sound source and an actual open tube 17 centimeters long, or electronically, by simulating such an acoustic system with a computer. The artificially generated spectrum is similar acoustically to the spoken spectrum, and it sounds to the ear like the vowel [ʌ]. It is this general shape of the spectrum that listeners use to identify which vowel has been spoken.

Because the resonant frequencies of the vocal tract are so important for the recognition of vowels, they have been given a special name: They are called formants. The first formant of [ʌ] is at 500 Hz, the second formant is at 1,500 Hz, and the third formant is at 2,500 Hz. It is these formant frequencies, not the fundamental frequency of the voice, that determine the character of the spoken sound and so reveal the speaker's articulatory gesture to a hearer.

Cross section of vocal tract   **Model of vocal tract**   **Acoustic spectrum**

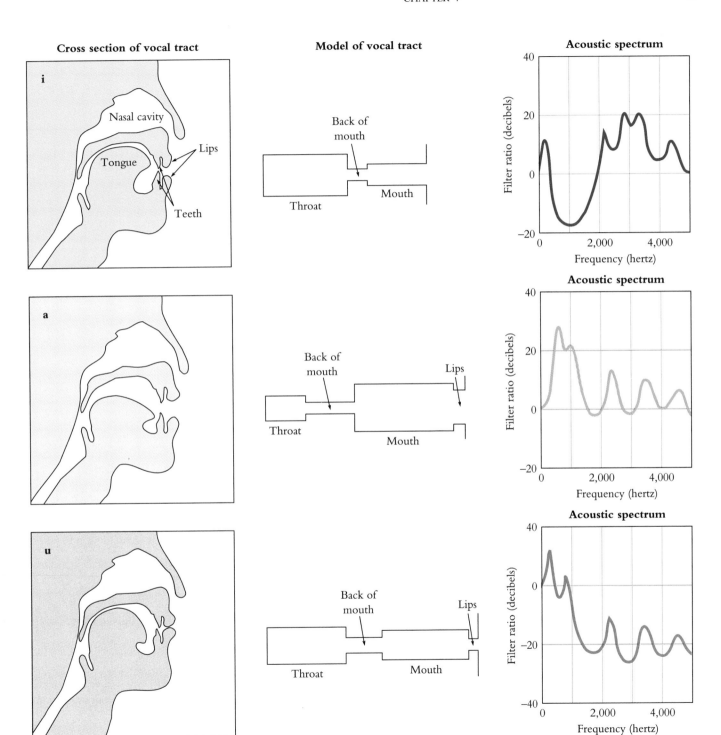

The Descent of the Larynx

From X rays and casts of the vocal tracts of apes, it is apparent that the larynx in these primates is high (directly back of the mouth) and their throat cavity is small. This anatomical arrangement limits the variety of vowel sounds that apes can produce, but it has the advantage that food and drink are less likely to pass through the larynx and into their lungs. On the assumption that human beings are descended from ancestors having this kind of high larynx—and some scientists have argued that the Neanderthal people were so constructed—then at some time in the evolution of human beings the larynx must have descended into its present position, creating an enlarged throat with a corresponding increase in the versatility of the vocal-tract filter. But the cost is that now, to avoid choking, people must have a highly elaborate swallowing reflex—which doesn't always work properly.

Newborn children resemble apes in having high larynxes, small throats, and a limited variety of vowels in their early cries. The descent of the infant's larynx during the first year of life is assumed to be an example of ontogeny recapitulating phylogeny—that is, the development of the infant is assumed to follow the same course as the evolutionary development of the infant's ancestors. Figuratively speaking, it is as if Mother Nature doesn't trust you to have a large throat until you are old enough to take voluntary control of it.

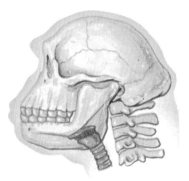

Gorilla

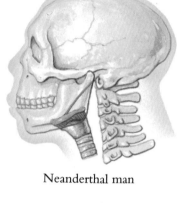

Neanderthal man

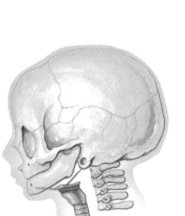

Human infant

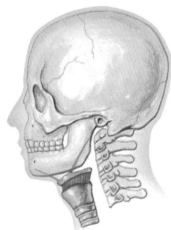

Human adult

Reconstruction of the larynx in relation to the skull of Neanderthal man suggests that this relation is more similar to that in a great ape or a newborn infant than it is to that in a modern adult male. In the ape and infant, the larynx is high and the throat is relatively small, limiting the range of vowel sounds that can be produced.

The vowel [ʌ] is called a neutral vowel because the resonators are in their more or less natural shapes; [ʌ] is what comes out when nothing is done to alter the resting position of the open vocal tract. It can be thought of as a point of origin from which other vowels deviate—by changing the shape of the vocal tract to make it resonate at different frequencies. For example, when a speaker says *not*, the vowel [a] is produced by moving the tongue down and back in the mouth, which enlarges the mouth cavity and constricts the throat cavity. (When people are told, "Lower your tongue," they have no idea what to do, so when a physician wants to see their throats, he or she tells them to "Say ah.") The vowel [i] in *neat* is produced by just the opposite maneuver of the tongue. For *neat* the tongue is moved forward and up, thus enlarging the throat cavity and constricting the mouth cavity. The vowel [u] in *newt* is also produced with a high tongue position, but with the tongue drawn back and with the open end of the vocal tract reduced by constricting the lips. The vowels in *not, neat,* and *newt* are the most extreme departures from the neutral position that you are able to produce by moving your tongue and lips. All other English vowels and diphthongs are intermediate between these extremes.

From an analysis of the shapes of the vocal cavities it is possible to estimate formant frequencies, and computers can be programmed to synthesize remarkably lifelike imitations of all the different vowels. But when these vowels must be combined with consonants to form spoken syllables and words, the story becomes more complicated.

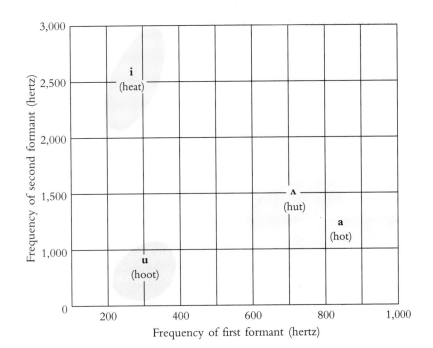

The first two formant frequencies of the extreme vowels [i], [a], and [u] are shown relative to the central vowel [ʌ].

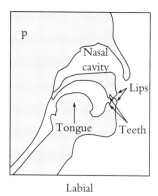

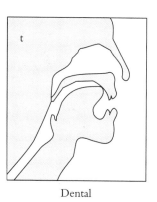

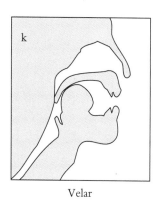

Vocal-tract configurations for labial, dental, and velar points of articulation that are used to produce the plosive consonants [p], [t], and [k].

The Major Articulators

Vowels are not the only way that words can differ. Consonants are, if anything, even more discriminating. Consider the initial sounds of *pill, till,* and *kill,* for example. In terms of the descriptive features introduced for the International Phonetic Alphabet, these three initial segments are all voiceless plosive consonants. They differ only in the feature called place of articulation—*pill* begins with a bilabial plosive, *till* with a dental-alveolar plosive, and *kill* with a velar plosive. In all three, the vocal tract is obstructed and air pressure builds up behind the articulators, then is released in a plosive burst. The only difference is where the obstruction occurs: at the lips for [p], between the blade of the tongue and the gum ridge for [t], or between the body of the tongue and the velum for [k].

Similar accounts of the movements of the articulators could be given for the other consonants—tracing out such details is the sort of thing phoneticians love to argue about. The interest here, however, is more in understanding how the anatomy and physiology of the speech organs shape the words that result. And for that purpose, it helps to focus on the fact that all speech sounds are produced by the action of six anatomical structures: the larynx; the soft palate (velum); the lips; and the root, body, and blade of the tongue. The articulators differ in the variety of configurations they can assume: The soft palate is either open (for nasal sounds) or closed (for nonnasal sounds), whereas the tongue body can take a wide range of positions. A grouping of these articulators that is intended to suggest how they work together in the production of speech is shown in the figure at right.

An important point about this figure is that each articulator implements its own features. That is to say, the feature that phoneticians call labial can be implemented only by the lips; the feature called dental-alveolar (or coronal) can be implemented only by the tongue blade; nasality can be implemented only by the soft palate; and so on. Because the features that are used to characterize speech sounds are so articulator-bound, the figure could be taken as an alternative organization for a new phonetic alphabet, one that, unlike the IPA, would make explicit the roles of the various articulators.

In the act of speaking, these articulators must move rapidly and synchronously to produce 120 to 150 words per minute. Accomplishing this feat intelligibly is probably one of the most complex motor skills most people ever master. One of the problems that must be solved in order to do it is timing. Since the articulators are situated at different distances from the brain, the center that coordinates them must send out its commands to each articulator at slightly different times. First, a command must go to the intercostal muscles to produce a pulse of air to power a syllable; then, for each speech sound in the syllable, an appropriate message is sent first to the larynx, next to the soft palate, and last to the tongue and lips. If the commands are all properly delayed, they will all arrive together and produce the intended vocalization. Establishing these fixed timing patterns is an important part of learning to speak.

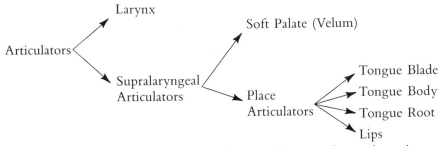

A classification of the major articulators on the basis of the ways they work together.

If the figure above is viewed as a kind of circuit diagram for the neural control of speech, then each arc between the nodes can be thought of as having a binary, on-off switch. In that case, the intention to utter a particular speech sound would correspond to a specific pattern of switches on and off in the circuit. To produce a [b], for example, the switches in the lines to both the Larynx and the Supralaryngeal Articulators would be on; the switch for the Soft Palate would be off (closed); the Place Articulators would be on; the Lips would be on; and the Tongue Blade, Body, and Root would all be off. When a switch is off, all switches beyond it (to the right in the figure) are effectively off as well—no commands can reach them. When a switch is off, the articulator that it controls receives no instructions; presumably, it stays where it was or moves to its neutral position.

One descriptive feature that this figure does not accommodate, however, is what the IPA calls manner of articulation. For example, no way is provided to distinguish between sounds like [t] and [s], which are both voiceless consonants involving the blade of the tongue, but one is produced with a burst whereas the other can be continued until the speaker runs out of breath. Since this feature can be implemented by any of the articulators, it clearly has a different status from that of the articulator-bound features just discussed. Neural control must do more than select which articulators are to be active; it must also specify what manner of action they must take.

Phones and Phonemes

The first lessons in phonetics are devoted to descriptions of different kinds of articulatory positions, often described as if they were fixed and invariant. In fact, however, there is great variability among speech sounds, so much so that it becomes necessary to ask what it means to say that two speech sounds are the same.

The human vocal tract, showing the anatomical relations of the larynx and supralaryngeal articulators.

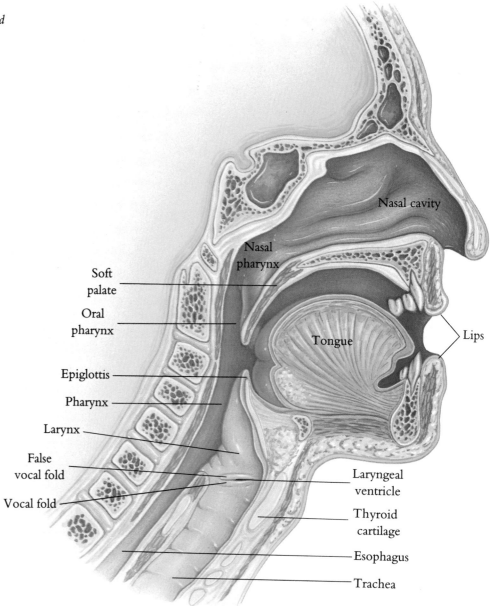

Nasal cavity

Nasal pharynx

Soft palate

Oral pharynx

Tongue

Lips

Epiglottis

Pharynx

Larynx

False vocal fold

Vocal fold

Laryngeal ventricle

Thyroid cartilage

Esophagus

Trachea

Consider, for example, the initial and final consonants in the English word *peep*. A detailed analysis of the articulatory processes and their acoustic results would show beyond question that these two consonants are different. The initial consonant is accompanied by a small but audible outflow of air, called aspiration, before the vocal cords come together and the laryngeal tone begins for the vowel. The final consonant is not aspirated when it occurs in the normal flow of speech. (Put the back of your hand near your lips and say, "Don't peep now"; you should feel the puff of air for the first p but not for the second.) Two symbols are needed to represent this difference: Use $[p^h]$ for the aspirated form and $[p^=]$ for the unaspirated. Then you can transcribe the pronunciation of *peep* as $[p^h ip^=]$.

These two different acoustic events are heard as identical by people who speak English. In English speech, the aspirated $[p^h]$ occurs only in syllable-initial positions, and the unaspirated $[p^=]$ occurs in all others. There is no pair of words in English, like $[p^h i]$ and $[p^= i]$, that differ only with respect to the occurrence or nonoccurence of aspiration. Consequently, this difference is not distinctive in English: No confusion of meaning results when they are lumped together as the same sound. In Chinese, however, aspiration is distinctive; aspirated and unaspirated forms are heard as different words.

It has been estimated that there are less than thirty features of speech that can be used to differentiate words. Each language uses about ten to fifteen of them; no language uses them all. The features used by any particular language are called distinctive features for that language. When a distinctive feature changes, the meaning changes.

The distinctive feature is a unit of linguistic analysis even smaller than an individual speech sound. For example, the English words *crumble* and *crumple* are identical in every respect except that the [b] of *crumble* is voiced and the [p] of *crumple* is unvoiced; that is to say, the vocal cords vibrate while [b] is produced, but they do not vibrate while [p] is produced. Since speakers of English treat these two utterances as different words with different meanings, we know that this difference in voicing must be a distinctive feature for English. If voicing were not a distinctive feature of English, then *crumble* and *crumple* would be merely two pronunciations of the same word.

Up to this point, the expression "speech sound" has been used in a loose way, on the assumption that anyone familiar with alphabetic writing would have a general idea what a speech sound is. But letters and sounds can be very different. And the set of speech sounds in one language is never the same as the set in another language. For greater precision, therefore, most phonologists draw a distinction between two meanings of "speech sound." When the attempt is to describe the precise acoustic or physiological nature of a speech sound, with no consideration of its meaning or of the language in which it occurs, it is called a phone, and the science of phones is called phonetics. On the other hand, when the description is limited to a single language, the speech sounds that are distinguished by speakers of that language are called phonemes, and the science of phonemes is called phonemics. Using this terminology, one would say that $[p^h]$ and $[p^=]$ are different phones, although in English they are the same phoneme, whereas in Chinese they are different phonemes. Square brackets are used for phones, slanting lines for phonemes. Thus, in English, the phones $[p^h]$ and $[p^=]$ are allophones of the phoneme /p/.

You have now seen one example of a feature, aspiration, that is not distinctive in English—it does not serve to distinguish one word from another. And you have seen one example of a feature, voicing, that is distinctive. Consider voicing in greater detail. Many pairs of minimally different English words are distinguishable only on the basis of the presence or absence of voicing. Although this difference is obvious to anyone who speaks English, it is the result of a relatively small difference in the manner of production. Whether you say /ba/ or /pa/, for example, depends on when your vocal cords start vibrating. In both cases, the flow of air is stopped momentarily and pressure builds up behind the lips. For /ba/, the voice-onset time (the point in time when the vocal cords begin to vibrate) coincides with the release of the stop consonant, whereas for /pa/, the voice-onset time usually lags behind the release of the stop consonant about one-tenth of a second. If the voice-onset time in synthetic speech is varied in small increments, the percentage of listeners who report hearing /pa/ rather than /ba/ will increase rapidly when the onset of voicing lags by more than 0.02 second.

Other languages rely on other distinctions. For example, it is also possible for the onset of voicing to precede the stop release: In Spanish and Dutch the distinctive difference is between coincident and advanced voice onset. The Thai language uses all three: Advanced, coincident, and delayed voice onsets correspond to three different phonemes in Thai. All languages in which voicing is distinctive use coincident onset; they differ in whether coincidence is contrasted with advanced or delayed onset or both.

If the voice-onset time (the time the vocal folds begin to vibrate) precedes or coincides with the release of a plosive consonant, speakers of English will hear the consonant as voiced. If the onset lags behind the release by more than 0.02 second, the consonant will be heard as voiceless. If the voice-onset time is varied over a wide range, the crossover occurs at about +0.02 second, where [b] turns into [p]. Small differences in onset time are not noticed unless they fall at the category boundary.

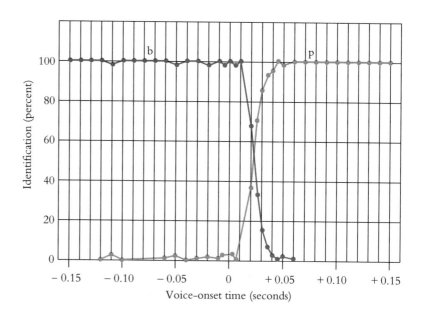

These differences are subtle, in the sense that an adult who has learned to use one set of voice-onset times finds it difficult to produce another set when he or she tries to learn another language. There is some evidence that the difficulty is perceptual; the foreigner cannot hear the distinction he or she would like to imitate. Up to puberty, children have little trouble with this kind of learning, but then the relevant parts of the brain seem to become less adaptable, perhaps as a consequence of hormonal effects on the nervous system. Such observations suggest that there may be a critical period for learning the sound patterns of a language.

Speech Perception: One System or Two?

Congenitally deaf children have great difficulty learning to speak, and even traumatically deafened adults encounter problems in maintaining their intelligibility. Speaking is a highly complex motor skill, and hearing yourself is an important link in controlling it. Without direct auditory feedback, the ability to synchronize the rapid, coordinated movements of the speech muscles is both difficult to acquire and difficult to maintain. Speech production and speech perception are intimately related—the sounds you can produce are the sounds you can discriminate. So closely are the two processes associated that many linguists and psychologists have assumed that, at some central place in the brain, the two must use the same phonological control system.

Is there a single phonological input-output system? Or are there two separate systems that, as a consequence of auditory feedback, have learned to work closely together? Parsimony argues for a single system, but anatomy for two. Both opinions have good arguments in their favor, and it is not clear what kind of evidence would settle the question one way or the other. The evidence that has been most hotly debated has concerned the production and perception of phonemes.

Advocates of a single-system theory understand that there are obvious differences between talking and listening, but they consider those differences to be superficial. In their view, speech production and speech perception are different sides of the same coin. The heart of the argument is that there is something about speech that is special: For other input-output systems (seeing and pointing, for example), the stimuli and the responses are different; for speech they are the same. And because speech is special, there must be a special mode of hearing, probably innate, that is tuned to human speech and perceives it differently from other sounds.

Speaking consists of making articulatory gestures that modulate a flow of sound. Advocates of a single system argue that it is those articulatory gestures that carry the information. They are the basic phonetic units. What a listener wants to perceive are not the sounds per se. Rather, the listener uses the sounds as evidence from which to infer the motor gestures that caused them. That is to say, what a listener really perceives are the neural patterns that control a speaker's utterances. Therefore, since production and perception are both regulated by the same neural representations, a single system serves them both.

To support this conclusion, proponents point to the general failure over many years to define the distinctive features of speech in purely acoustic or auditory terms. There are consistent acoustic consequences of the articulatory gestures, but the way speech is actually used—rapidly, by different speakers, in noisy locations—makes it impossible to establish a one-to-one mapping between acoustic properties and phonemes. If distinctive acoustic features were invariably associated with each phoneme, it would be a relatively simple matter to program a computer to recognize and transcribe human speech, yet that technology has proved to be unexpectedly difficult. One interpretation of this history is that the distinctive features of speech that people listen for are not acoustic. They are something else.

In 1976 H. McGurk and J. MacDonald published an article in *Nature* that provided striking evidence that this nonacoustic "something else" might be the articulatory gesture. In their experiments people would hear someone say /ba/ at the same time they saw someone articulate /va/ silently. What they reported hearing, very clearly, was /va/. Subjects in this experiment did not suspect that their percept was partly auditory and partly visual, because to them it was neither—the perceived event was the articulatory gesture itself. According to single-system theorists, what is so special about human speech is that its messages are encoded in articulatory movements; the evidence used to infer those gestures is normally auditory, but visual evidence can also be used. It is the gesture that is important for perception, and the gesture is also what is important for producing speech.

Why do dual-system theorists resist such arguments? They think that there is nothing that single-system advocates describe that cannot be explained equally well by postulating two systems that have learned to work closely together. And other kinds of evidence seem to demand two separate systems, one for speaking words and another for hearing words. Consider, for example, experimental situations requiring divided attention. When people try to perform simultaneously two demanding listening tasks, or two demanding speaking tasks, they have great difficulty. But they can perform the listening task almost as well while they are speaking as while they are silent. Neither the input nor the output system can do two things at once, but simultaneous input and output interfere relatively little with one another. Such results are hard to explain if you believe that input and output are both processed by the same system.

Another kind of evidence comes from people who have suffered brain injuries resulting in language impairments. These patients, who suffer from aphasia, can have a disruption in speech that is not paralleled by a disruption in hearing, or vice versa. For example, some aphasics have been observed to discriminate normally between voiced and voiceless plosive consonants (between /d/ and /t/, say), although their own speech shows abnormal voice-onset times. And one aphasic patient showed the reverse pattern: normal voice-onset times in speaking, but not in perception. Such differences would be expected if there were two systems, input and output, that could be injured or spared independently. Moreover, there is a class of patients, called conduction aphasics, whose principal symptom is that they are unable to repeat correctly a word or phrase that they have just heard. When asked to repeat they often find it so difficult that they prefer to write, yet they may use that same word or phrase spontaneously in their own speech.

A single-system theorist might reply that such evidence is obtained only under highly unusual or abnormal circumstances. Certainly it is true that, under ordinary conditions, a normal person behaves as though there is a single phonetic system. Whether there is one system or two, the relation between spoken words and heard words is normally so close as to be effectively the relation of identity. The question is still under debate.

The Shapes of Syllables

Characterizing how phonemes are produced and perceived is a necessary part of any theory of the spoken word, but it is far from sufficient. Phonemes must be combined to form words, so in addition to having its own set of phonemes with their own distinctive features, each language also has its own rules for stringing phonemes together into syllables. The MIT linguist Morris Halle likes to show people that they know those rules by asking them which of the following ten are English words.

ptak   thole   hlad   plast   sram   mgla   vlas   flitch   dnom   rtut

People who know—speak and write—English recognize that *thole, plast,* and *flitch* could be English words (even when they have no idea what they might mean), whereas the rest could not be. That is to say, when people learn English, they learn something about the structure of possible words in English.

Like most of what people know about their native language, this knowledge is implicit: People can follow the rules even though they cannot state them. The rules for forming admissible syllables, however, seem to be learned at an extremely deep level. Even when injuries to the brain result in "jargon aphasia," a condition in which the victim can speak fluently but is largely unintelligible because the speech is dense with nonwords, nearly all of the neologisms that are generated still conform to the conventional rules of syllable formation.

Restrictions on the acceptable sequences of phonemes must be stated within syllables; between one syllable and the next, any sequence of phonemes can occur. A well-formed word is always a sequence of well-formed syllables. But within a syllable, each language has its own rules. The internal structure of a syllable can be shown graphically, with X representing the individual phonemes in the syllable. The onset of a syllable includes any initial consonants; there may be none, of course. A vowel or diphthong nucleus and any terminal consonants are defined as the "rime" of the syllable. Some languages have syllables without vowels, in which case the structure is a simple consonant string.

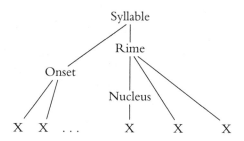

In some languages the rules for forming syllables are relatively simple. In Japanese, for example, all syllables are (C) V (N), where C is a consonant, V is a vowel, N is a nasal phoneme, and parentheses indicate that the phoneme is optional. English rules are much more complicated and allow strings of three or four consonants, as in *glimpsed* or *spree* or *sixths*. *Glimpsed* is a remarkably complex syllable.

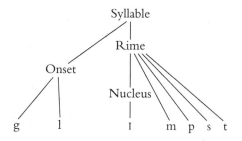

Spree illustrates a restriction on initial consonant clusters in English: There is a rule that says the initial consonant must be /s/ if it is followed by any consonant other than /l/ or /r/. It rules out such syllable-opening sequences as /pt/, /mg/, /dn/, or /rt/, but not /pl/ or /fr/. There is also a rule that says that once voicing terminates in the post-nuclear consonants, it cannot begin again until the next syllable. It rules out such syllable-closing sequences as /pz/ or /tm/. *Spree* has a complex onset but a simple rime.

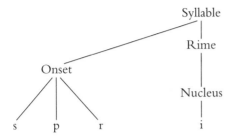

Sixths illustrates how strings of consonants can pile up as various rules of word formation do their work. Starting with *six,* which has two terminal consonants, /sɪks/, we first add a voiceless *-th* to change it to *sixth,* which has three terminal consonants, /sɪksθ/, and then add *-s* to get the plural *sixths* with four terminal consonants, /sɪksθs/. This syllable has a simple onset but a complex rime.

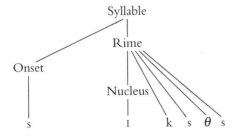

These additions illustrate two kinds of morphological rules of English. This *-th* suffix is added by a derivational rule: Its field of application is limited to numbers, it derives a new word, *sixth,* from the root *six,* and it changes the meaning. The *-s* is added by an inflectional rule: Its field of application is any noun and it changes the meaning from singular to plural—whether or not it results in a new word, *sixths,* different from *sixth,* depends on what you count as a word.

The rule for plurals is worth closer attention, because the same rule for the *-s* suffix is used, not only to create plural nouns, but also for the possessive form and for the third person singular form of verbs. Compare the plurals of *nose, lip,* and *chin.* To form the plural of *nose,* another syllable is added, /ɨz/; to form the plural of *lip,* an /s/ is added; to form the plural of *chin,* a /z/ is added. Speakers of English can do this correctly, not because they have memorized the plural of every word separately, but because they have learned a general rule that enables them to form the plural of any word, even words that they have just encountered for the first time. People who speak English know, for example, that the suffix is added to *flitch* just as it is added to *nose;* that *plast* is treated like *lip;* and that *thole* is treated like *chin.*

What is this rule that everyone obeys but few can state? In order to formulate it, words must be categorized according to their terminal sounds: Words with this kind of ending take one addition, words with that kind of ending take a different addition. So, what are the three categories of word endings? One way to characterize them is by listing all of the terminal phonemes in each category, but this solution offers no insight into what is going on. It turns out that the simplest way to state the rule—to describe categories of words that take different inflections—is not by listing the terminal phonemes that take each inflection, but by formulating the rule in terms of distinctive features.

> **P1.**   If a word ends in a phoneme that is dental-alveolar and fricative (formed by raising the tongue blade and directing the airstream at the upper teeth), add /ɨz/; if the preceding stipulation does not apply and the word ends in a phoneme that is unvoiced, add /s/; otherwise, add /z/.

Why is this formulation preferable to simply listing the terminal phonemes? Morris Halle offers the following answer. Try this test: Listen to yourself as you read aloud this sentence, *I like Johann Sebastian Bach's music.* How did you pronounce *Bach's*? If you relied on a list of terminal English phonemes, you would not know how to pronounce it, because the terminal sound is not an English phoneme. But if you relied on the rule just stated, you would have recognized that the German *ch* is unvoiced and so takes the terminal /s/.

Yet even this rule seems complicated. Is there not some better way to understand what is going on? Suppose that the underlying idea here is to form plurals by adding the dental-alveolar (sometimes termed coronal), fricative (sometimes termed strident), voiced consonant /z/ at the ends of words. This convention works reasonably well for most words that end in a voiced phoneme, but it cannot work for words that end in unvoiced phonemes: It conflicts with the general rule that says voicing cannot start again in a syllable once it has stopped. So, there are two possibilities: Let the unvoiced antecedent assimilate the /z/, turning it into an /s/; or start a new syllable and let it end with /z/. In general, assimilation is the rule for English where it can apply; a new syllable is the solution whenever two strident, coronal phonemes would occur successively in the same syllable.

Feature assimilation is a common phonological process: A given value of a feature spreads from one phoneme to adjacent phonemes. In the case of the -s suffix, consider this representation of the plural of *lip*.

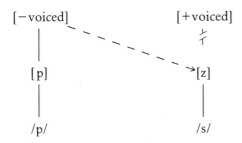

The dotted arrow indicates the spreading of the unvoiced feature from [p] to [z], and ⫫ indicates that the [+voiced] feature is disconnected from the terminal phoneme.

In this example, a single distinctive feature spreads to an adjacent phoneme. It is sometimes the case that more than one feature will be assimilated, but when this occurs it is always one of a small number of feature subsets that go together. The assimilable subsets have been studied and found to coincide with the sets of features associated with the various major articulators illustrated earlier in this chapter. That is to say, a feature subset controlled by a switch in that figure can be shared with an adjacent phoneme, but a subset that is not dominated by a single switch (Nasal and Labial, for example) cannot be shared.

The details are complex but the moral is simple. Speech sounds are not discrete segments. They overlap. Speaking flows like dancing; as good dancers take one step, they are already preparing for the next.

■ ■ ■

Analysis of speech forces attention to the many respects in which the speech signal differs from alphabetic writing. The spoken word has a biological basis that the written word lacks. And that biological basis, shared equally by all human beings, is a major source of what is most general about language in general.

▲ *"Grammar" is portrayed as a prudent gardener by Laurent de la Hire in this painting of 1650.*

▶ *Every schoolchild memorizes the eight "parts of speech" (in the old-fashioned terms of traditional grammar): word families that, since they play similar roles as constituents of sentences, form syntactic categories. Context determines the syntactic family to which an individual word belongs in a given phrase or sentence. Here, square is successively (clockwise from top) a verb, an adjective, an adverb, and a noun.*

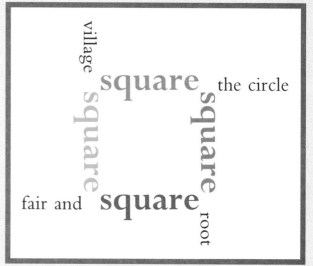

Word Families

"Divide and conquer" is a basic scientific strategy. In fact, analysis is a good strategy for attacking any hard problem. Take a large problem and divide it into smaller problems, then conquer the smaller problems one by one. The trick, as William James once said, is to "carve the bird at its joints"—to find smaller problems whose solutions do not depend on each other. To apply this analytic strategy to the problem of understanding the vocabulary, which is certainly a large problem, the vocabulary must be divided into classes of similar words that can be studied separately. The trick is to find the right classes of words.

What classes of words are there? Properties and relations define classes of words: All the words that have the property or that satisfy the relation are said to belong to the same class. However, the variety of possible classes of words is so great that it would be impossible to consider them all, even if anyone wanted to. The building blocks of language have by definition—and acquire by use—an indefinite variety of connections, associations, similarities, and affinities: A word is a bundle of connections with a label on it. Take any two words at random and a moment's reflection will reveal some property they share or some relation they satisfy: *Goodness* and *gracious* are spelled with eight letters; *river* and *shiver* rhyme; *taped* and *adept* are anagrams; *afternoon* and *foot* are nouns; *sad* and *happy* are opposites; *lame* and *sugar* associate with *cane; oxygen* and *generous* derive from the same root *gen;* and so on and on. But which of these many properties and relations carve the lexical bird at its joints? For example, the class of words spelled with a *q* (or, for that matter, the class spelled without a *q*), or the class of words that satisfies the relation longer-than-five-letters, and indefinitely many other arbitrary classes, are of no intrinsic interest.

What classes of words do linguists find interesting? A synchronic answer to that question is not the same as a diachronic answer. From a synchronic point of view, the interesting classes are those that reflect linguistic knowledge. If word families are defined as classes of words that depend on knowledge that a person must have to use a language acceptably, then the apparently endless variety of conceivable classes of words can be narrowed considerably. When discussion is limited to those word families, there is hope for efforts to classify and bring order into this intimidating heterogeneity.

A diachronic approach is also concerned with those word families, but an additional kind of family emerges from the historical record, one that can be called a family of cognates—a family of words assumed to be descended from the same root in some ancestral language. A special pleasure seems to derive from knowledge of obscure cognates. Did you know, for example, that the words *tow* and *educational* are related? Both are descended from an Indo-European root *deuk-,* meaning *to lead.* In one line of descent the inflected form *duk-a-* became the Germanic *tugon,* which led to Old English *togian* and eventually to modern *tow.* In another line of descent *duk-a-* became the Latin verb *educare* (with the prefix *ex-*), whose past participle entered Middle English as *educaten.* Such facts enrich one's appreciation of English, but they are not scientific facts about language in general. They are not, indeed, even facts that you need to know to speak English fluently.

The discussion here will focus on synchronic families. Three kinds have been studied in considerable detail: syntactic, morphological, and semantic. Words that can play the same syntactic roles in sentences are syntactically related. Words that share a common stem or root are morphologically related. And words that share components of meaning are semantically related. All three kinds are discussed in this book; this chapter looks at syntactic families.

Syntactic Categories

A syntactic category—or part of speech, to use an older terminology—is a family of words that can all be used as the same constituent of a sentence. In the sentence *Wealthy people instinctively fear revolution,* a variety of words can be used in place of *wealthy: poor, fat, little, foreign,* and so forth. The words that are acceptable in that position all belong to the same syntactic category—adjectives, in this case. Substitutions change the meaning of the sentence, of course, but the sentence remains grammatical; its syntactic structure remains unchanged. Similarly, all the words that can be used in place of *people—women, insomniacs, turkeys,* whatever—belong to another syntactic category, nouns. And so on through the sentence—and all other sentences. Linguists call this the distributional approach: Words that have the same distribution (that are usable in the same grammatical slots) belong to the same syntactic category. The advantage of having syntactic categories is that rules for forming grammatical sentences can then be stated in terms of these categories, rather than in terms of specific words. There is no syntactic rule, for example, that makes explicit mention of the word *wealthy* or the word *people;* rather, the classes adjective and noun are invoked. Syntactic categories, not individual words, provide the atoms for building grammatical molecules.

Traditional grammars typically recognize eight parts of speech: noun, verb, adjective, adverb, pronoun, preposition, conjunction, and interjection. These are the parts of speech that children still study in the early grades, where they still memorize the definitions: "A noun is the name of a person, place, or thing," "A verb is the name of an action," and so on. (Of course, *explosion* is a noun that names an action and *remain* is a verb that does not, but such facts have never dented teachers' devotion to the familiar notional definitions.) The eight traditional categories grew out of ancient and medieval attempts to integrate grammar, logic, and metaphysics. The distinction between nouns on the one hand and verbs and adjectives on the other was drawn in ancient Greece on logical grounds: Nouns serve as subjects of a proposition, verbs and adjectives as predicates. During the Middle Ages, when Scholastic philosophers tried to use language instead of observation to analyze the structure of reality, the parts of speech were metaphysical conceptions, and grammar was assumed to be the same in every language. The history of the parts of speech is long and complex—and unrewarding. Its principal value is to show (if a demonstration is needed) that the Big Eight are not as self-evident or obligatory as they are made to appear to schoolchildren.

In most languages, nouns form by far the largest family, and verbs—the most important family (see Chapter 11) because they make sentences possible—are less numerous than nouns; the number of adjectives and adverbs is highly variable from one language to another. Those four are generally considered the major families. They are open families, in the sense that you can borrow words in those categories from other languages, or even invent new ones, and

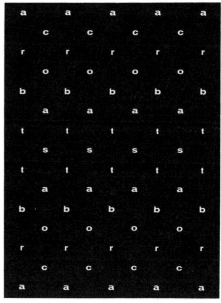

This concrete poem, conceived in 1966 for a playground, uses a noun to convey verbal dynamics. The artist, Ian Hamilton Finlay, comments: "Isolated, single letters are pattern but letters joined in words (as these are) are direction. Those in the 'Acrobats' poem are both, behaving like the real circus acrobats who are now individual units, now—springing together—diagonals and towers."

René Magritte, in his painting La Clef des Songes *(The Key of Dreams), plays with the naming function traditionally assigned to nouns.*

have them accepted by other speakers. Words belonging to the major families are called open-class words or, sometimes, content words. Minor families—pronouns, prepositions, conjunctions, interjections—are closed; new words in those categories are rare indeed. Words belonging to the minor families are called closed-class words or, sometimes, function words, because they are used to indicate the grammatical functions of other words.

These eight families, inherited from medieval grammars of Greek and Latin, work reasonably well for Indo-European languages, but elsewhere the picture is not so simple. In their fieldwork, linguistic anthropologists often run into languages that call for rather different descriptions. Closed-class distinctions are especially variable. It has been claimed that some of the so-called synthetic languages, like Eskimo, with exceedingly long and complex words, have no closed classes at all; much of the work done by closed-class words in analytic languages, like Vietnamese, is done by affixes in synthetic languages. In the earliest studies of non-Indo-European languages, an amateurish attempt was made to force the lexicon of every language into the eight traditional families, even when these families were clearly unsuitable. The shortcomings of those attempts stirred an interest in the criteria for defining syntactic categories. The old formulas were found to be misleading even for modern Indo-European languages and totally unworkable for non-Indo-European languages.

Consequently, defining syntactic categories is a basic problem that every serious grammarian must struggle with. If this were a treatise on syntax, such matters would have to be carefully resolved, since the syntactic structure of acceptable sentences has to be described in terms of patterns of such elements. Here, however, the concern is only with those places where theories of sentence structure and theories of word structure seem to interact, and most of what needs to be said requires only four large syntactic categories: nouns, verbs, modifiers, and particles.

Within these large families, of course, there are subfamilies. Nouns are either proper nouns (*Mary, Australia, Madison Square Garden*) or common nouns (*woman, continent, arena*); common nouns are either count nouns (*book, table*) having both a singular and a plural form or mass nouns (*bacon, furniture, oats*). Verbs are either auxiliary verbs (*be, have, can, must*) or full verbs (*say, see, make*). Full verbs differ in the number of arguments (noun phrases) they take: Intransitive verbs (*fall, die*) take a subject but no object, transitive verbs (*lose, kill*) take one object, doubly transitive verbs (*give, throw*) take two. Modifiers differ in what they modify: Adjectives (*bright, formal*) modify nouns, adverbs (*brightly, formally*) modify anything else, and sentential adverbs (*probably, seldom*) modify whole clauses or sentences. Particles include all the function words: pronouns (*I, you, she*), prepositions (*in, on, of*), conjunctions (*and, or, when*), determiners (*a, the, some*), and perhaps a few others. Such a list of subfamilies may seem compulsively detailed, but a careful grammarian would need to distinguish still further sub-subfamilies.

How do speakers of English learn to recognize these distinctions? Recognition would be easier if, as in certain other languages, some formal stigmata indicated membership—if words in each syntactic family began or ended in a different phoneme, say—but that is not the case. The closed-class or function words grouped together here as particles are hopeless; nothing will do but to memorize them and their uses. Fortunately, there are only a few hundred. A psychological justification for grouping these words together as a single syntactic family can be based on the fact that they all disappear together, along with grammatical inflections, in cases of the type of disorder called agrammatism. Since this family is closed, and since the members of this family work in conjunction with open-class words, particles will be neglected in this discussion.

The major families are also learned: Each new content word that is added to a person's vocabulary must be added to one of these families. This learning is complicated by the fact that the major families are not mutually exclusive—a word can belong to more than one. In English there are words (*back, paper, surface*) that belong to all three major families, and many more that belong to two. In such cases, the only way to tell the syntactic category of a particular token is by analyzing the sentence in which it occurs.

Should a word in two syntactic categories be considered one word or two? Those who favor a one-word–many-uses analysis point out that any word can be forced to play any syntactic role if the context is right. For example, *lamp* is ordinarily used as a noun, but it could be used as a verb (*He lamped the closet*) if the context supported the idea that *to lamp* something is to install a lamp in it. Since the connection between a word and the syntactic role it plays is so loose in English, it would not be unreasonable to assume that, say, in some deep sense, *back* really is a noun, but that this noun is sometimes used in sentences as a verb or modifier.

Those who favor the alternative one-word–one-use analysis respond that syntactic categories cannot be so freely negotiable in context. Nonce words (for example, using *lamp* as a verb) require a carefully prepared context, and their special interpretation is temporary. When one word is normally used in two or three different syntactic roles, the common solution is to assume that it is more than one word. For example, *back* as a noun is $back_a$, as a verb is $back_b$, and as a modifier is $back_c$. In some cases, no other solution is feasible. If, say, *bear* really is a noun, is it a noun that can appear as a verb? $Bear_a$ the noun and $bear_b$ the verb are accidental homonyms; it would be absurd to assume they are the same word.

These syntactic families of words are defined for the convenience of describing sentence structure. It is time now to move on to morphological families, which are generated by rules of word structure. However, one class of morphological rules is so closely related to the syntactic component of language that it is hard to tell where syntax stops and morphology begins.

Inflectional Morphology

Nowhere is the relation between syntax and morphology closer than it is for inflectional morphology. An inflection is an affix that is added to the stem of a word to indicate the syntactic role that the word plays in a particular grammatical context. How an inflection should be added is describable by morphological rules, rules that are assumed to be invoked automatically by the syntax of the sentence in which the word is to occur. A rule for adding an inflection (like morphological rules in general) has three parts:

    1. The rule must specify its domain of application—it must characterize the family of stems to which the affix can be added.

    2. The pronunciation of the inflected word must be given.

    3. Any change that the inflection makes in the meaning of the stem must be described.

In English, for example, the plural of a noun is formed by adding /z/ at the end of a noun. In this case, part 1, the domain of application, is the syntactic family of count nouns; part 2, the rules of pronunciation for plural forms, has been described in Chapter 4; and part 3, the semantic change, is from *one N* to *more than one N.*

    Note that the domain of application of an inflectional rule is described in terms of stems, rather than words. In English, this distinction is irrelevant: The stem to which affixes are added is always a word. Many other languages, however, have stems that are not words. In Latin, for example, the noun *populus* (people) is formed from the stem *popul-* plus the nominative singular suffix *-us;* there is no word in Latin corresponding to the naked stem *popul.* Or in German, to take a more modern example, the verb *sagen* (to say) is formed from the stem *sag-* plus the infinitive suffix *-en;* there is no word in German corresponding to the naked stem *sag.*

    The domains of application for different inflectional rules are normally specified by syntactic categories. Indeed, it is sometimes proposed that the syntactic categories be defined in terms of the inflections they take. In English, for example, the major syntactic categories take the following inflections:

        Noun: *book, books, book's, books'*
        Verb: *lock, locks, locked, locking*
        Modifier: *nice, nicer, nicest, nicely*

Someone who wanted to program a computer to cope with written English would undoubtedly use these inflections (along with any other available information) to decide which syntactic category each word belonged to. Inflections do more, however. They also give information about the syntactic role that the word is playing.

Paul Broca and Agrammatism

Paul Broca.

phasia is a loss of the ability to produce or comprehend words, usually resulting from a brain lesion. Although references to speech loss attributable to head injuries can be found as far back as 400 B.C., it was the French surgeon Pierre Paul Broca (1824–1880) who first proved that aphasia is caused by specific lesions to the brain and showed that those lesions are predominantly in the anterior part of the left half of the brain. In 1861 Broca reported on two patients with almost total loss of speech (which he termed "aphemia") whose brains he had been able to examine in post-mortem examinations. In 1863 he published comments on eight more autopsied cases. The area of damage that was common to all these patients was in the third frontal convolution of the left cerebral cortex, an area that is still known today as Broca's area. A lesion confined to Broca's area of

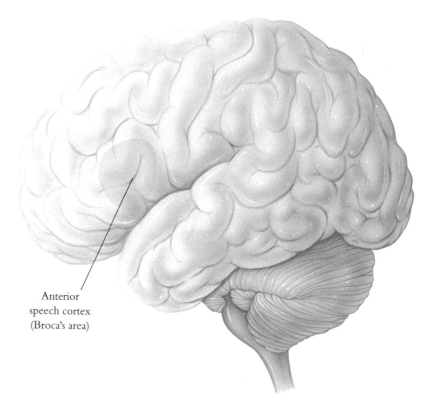

Anterior
speech cortex
(Broca's area)

The left hemisphere of the human brain, showing the position of Broca's area relative to other important cortical areas.

the cortex does not, however, result in the full range of language difficulties that he described; destruction of a larger area is required. Some neurologists believe that connections between Broca's area and the rest of the brain must be damaged to produce a permanent aphasia of Broca's type.

A characteristic symptom of this type of aphasia is called agrammatism. Agrammatic speech is nonfluent and oddly inflected—slow, emitted in bursts and only with great effort, never initiated with an unstressed word—with frequent omission of the inflectional endings and closed-class words (pronouns, prepositions, articles, conjunctions) that play important grammatical roles. For example, part of the Boston Diagnostic Aphasia Examination developed by Harold Goodglass and Edith Kaplan requires a patient to describe what is happening in a picture of three people in a kitchen. The following transcript is the response of a nonfluent aphasic, B.L.; note the absence of function words and of tense inflections.

B.L.:	Wife is dry dishes. Water down! Oh boy! Okay. Awright. Okay. . . . Cookie is down . . . fall, and girl, okay, girl . . . boy . . . um . . .
Examiner:	What is the boy doing?
B.L.:	Cookie is . . . um . . . catch
Examiner:	Who is getting the cookies?
B.L.:	Girl, girl
Examiner:	Who is about to fall down?
B.L.:	Boy . . . fall down!

In mild cases, agrammatism may involve only an occasional dropped inflection and a preference for certain simple verb forms; in severe cases, only single words are possible.

This drawing of three people in a kitchen is part of a standardized psychological test used to determine the nature and severity of aphasic symptoms. The patients' speech is recorded while they try to describe the picture.

The inflectional variants of a word form an inflectional family; each of the three lines of examples in the previous paragraph lists the members of such a family. One would like to say that all the members of such a family are inflectional variants of a single word, but the terminology gets a little tangled. Consider an example. From a purely formal point of view, *book, books, book's,* and *books'* are four distinct words, but from a morphological point of view, they are four different forms of the single word *book.* Which is it, four words or one? Clearly, two different senses of "word" are involved. When ambiguity between these two senses might arise, linguists use "lexeme" (or sometimes "entry," in the sense of a dictionary entry) to refer to the inflectional family: The lexeme *book* includes four different words.

Inflectional families in Modern English are small. That is to say, on the scale of languages that runs from synthetic to analytic, Modern English stands nearer the analytic end. It is not a good language in which to illustrate inflectional morphology. The history of English is characterized by the gradual but progressive disappearance of inflections (there is no evidence that it happened suddenly, as it might have following the Norman Conquest). And it is still going on: Distinctions expressed by *thou, thee, thine, thy,* and *ye,* for example, have now vanished in America from all but Biblical texts and Quaker discourse. Pronouns seem to be the slowest to change; traces of gender and case distinctions are still found. *He/she/it* provide a faint echo of the masculine, feminine, and neuter genders of Germanic languages, although it is natural gender, not linguistic gender, that they express. *I/me/my, he/him/his,* and *who/whom/whose* illustrate case distinctions (see tables on next page), which seem to be growing weaker in American English.

Other Indo-European languages typically have much more complex inflectional systems. The inflectional morphologies of Sanskrit, ancient Greek, Latin, and Balto-Slavonic have led linguists to assume that Proto-Indo-European must have been a richly inflected language. Much of that richness is assumed to have been preserved in Latin, which provides a representative picture of the kinds of inflections found in most Indo-European languages. In Latin, every noun is marked for number and gender: as singular or plural and as masculine, feminine, or neuter. Moreover, Latin nouns are marked for case: nominative (to mark the subject of the sentence), vocative (the case of address), accusative (to mark the object of a transitive verb), genitive (the case of possession), dative (to mark the indirect object of a doubly transitive verb), and ablative (which has a variety of uses that usually confuse schoolchildren). Taken together, these inflections generate word families that are ordinarily summarized in tabular form. Three such tables for the masculine *lupus* (wolf), the feminine *puella* (girl), and the neuter *bellum* (war) illustrate the complexity of this system.

There are, of course, exceptions to these tables. Certain classes of verbs take objects in cases other than the accusative, different prepositions select their own cases, and so on. In addition to these elaborate noun declensions, Latin conjugations inflect verbs for tense (present, past, future), person (first,

Three Latin Declensions

	Masculine	Feminine	Neuter
Singular:			
Nominative	lupus	puella	bellum
Vocative	lupe	puella	bellum
Accusative	lupum	puellam	bellum
Genitive	lupī	puellae	bellī
Dative	lupō	puellae	bellō
Ablative	lupō	puellā	bellō
Plural:			
Nominative	lupī	puellae	bella
Vocative	lupī	puellae	bella
Accusative	lupōs	puellās	bella
Genitive	lupōrum	puellārum	bellōrum
Dative	lupīs	puellīs	bellīs
Ablative	lupīs	puellīs	bellīs

second, third), number (singular, plural), and so on. And modifiers must agree with the words they modify.

The details are not important here; the point is simply that inflectional families in English are abnormally small. On the other hand, a dozen inflected forms is not an abnormally large family. In languages that make extensive use of inflections, an inflectional family can be much larger. For example, in Passamaquoddy, an Algonquian language spoken by native Americans in New Brunswick and northeastern Maine, every verb has more than ten thousand forms. In such a language, the use of word forms never heard before could be a regular occurrence.

English pays a price for its lack of inflections. The advantage of inflections is that they can signal directly the grammatical role that the word is playing. In Modern English, such information must be given by word order. For example,

> *The boy sees the girl*
> and
> *The girl sees the boy*

say something different because the word order is different, but the Latin equivalents can have the words arranged in any order. In both

> *Puer puellam videt*
> and
> *Puellam puer videt*

Adpositions

Closed-class words are typically adjoined to—that is, occur in specific combinations with—open-class words, subject to syntactic rules that vary considerably from one language to another. Adpositions, which are adjoined to nouns, illustrate some of the complexities that can arise.

In English, for example, adpositions occur in front of nouns and so are known as prepositions: *with a gun at the corner of the house.* Other languages have closed classes of words that serve a comparable purpose, but follow nouns; they are known as postpositions. It has been observed that languages like Japanese and Turkish, where the preferred sentence structure is Subject-Object-Verb, nearly always have postpositions, whereas languages like Hebrew or Welsh with a Verb-Subject-Object structure nearly always have prepositions. Languages like English or Swahili that have a Subject-Verb-Object structure can have either prepositions or postpositions (but not both).

Adpositions can indicate grammatical case. In English, for example, the dative case can be indicated by *to,* as in *She gave the candy to the boy;* the instrumental case can be indicated by *with,* as in *He opened the door with his key;* the genitive case can be indicated by *of,* as in *the door of the car.* Many English prepositions can indicate location; some linguists speak of this as the locative case. Thus, *at, in, on, under,* and many others can serve as locatives.

Prepositions have many different senses and are notoriously hard to translate—consider the difference between *the boat on the lake* and *the house on the lake.* Or explain the difference between being *at the hospital* and being *in the hospital;* or say what is wrong with *the pencil near Italy.* Moreover, prepositional phrases can attach to sentences at different points: *She saw the man with the binoculars* leaves it uncertain whether *with the binoculars* goes with *she saw* or with *the man.*

The house on the lake.

for example, the accusative -*am* inflection on *puella* indicates that the girl is seen by the boy, whereas in both

Puerum puella videt

and

Puella puerum videt

the accusative -*um* inflection on *puer* signals that the boy is seen by the girl. As inflections disappeared from English, the work that they did, and still do in other Indo-European languages, had to be taken over by word order and by prepositions. That is to say, what is treated by inflectional rules in other Indo-European languages must be handled by syntactic rules in English.

■   ■   ■

Different senses of "word" are now accumulating. A phonological word is a string of phonemes that conforms to certain rules of syllable formation. A syntactic word is an atom in terms of which grammatical sentences can be described. The two are not necessarily the same: *I've* and *can't,* for example, are each one phonological word and, at the same time, two syntactic words. But this is just the beginning. Morphology has still another definition of "word."

LLANFAIRPWLLGWYNGYLLGOGERYCHWYRNDROBWLLLLANTYSILIOGOGOGOCH

ST MARYS CHURCH IN THE HOLLOW OF THE WHITE HAZEL NEAR TO THE RAPID WHIRLPOOL OF LLANTYSILIO OF THE RED CAVE

▲ *Living languages constantly shape new words from old. Sometimes they proceed by accretion, as in this Welsh place name.*

▶ *Lewis Carroll's poem, "Jabberwocky," which Alice encounters in mirror writing, synthesizes words to describe the denizens of the Looking-Glass world.*

JABBERWOCKY

'Twas brillig, and the slithy toves
Did gyre and gimble in the wabe:
All mimsy were the borogoves,
And the mome raths outgrabe.

Word Formation

dward Sapir once said that using language the way people ordinarily do is like using a dynamo to power a doorbell. There is a richness in language that only orators and poets dare to exploit, and even they cannot explain their art. But surely one important source of linguistic power derives from the connectingness of words: Every word is a generalization over life's specificities, every sentence a realization of new associations. The connectingness of words weaves a cloak of coherence to cover the endless heterogeneity of experience.

JABBERWOCKY

'Twas brillig, and the slithy toves
  Did gyre and gimble in the wabe;
All mimsy were the borogoves,
  And the mome raths outgrabe.

'Beware the Jabberwock, my son!
  The jaws that bite, the claws that catch!
Beware the Jubjub bird, and shun
  The frumious Bandersnatch!'

He took his vorpal sword in hand:
  Long time the manxome foe he sought—
So rested he by the Tumtum tree,
  And stood awhile in thought.

And as in uffish thought he stood,
  The Jabberwock, with eyes of flame,
Came whiffling through the tulgey wood,
  And burbled as it came!

One, two! One, two! And through
  and through
  The vorpal blade went snicker-snack!
He left it dead, and with its head
  He went galumphing back.

'And hast thou slain the Jabberwock?
  Come to my arms, my beamish boy!
O frabjous day! Callooh! Callay!'
  He chortled in his joy.

'Twas brillig, and the slithy toves
  Did gyre and gimble in the wabe;
All mimsy were the borogoves,
  And the mome raths outgrabe.

From *Through the Looking-Glass,*
Lewis Carroll, 1871.

The integrative resources of language are tuned and amplified by the machinery of word formation. When a simple word fails to capture a complex thought, rules of morphology can often nudge it in the right direction. Consider, for example, the variety of shades of meaning expressed by different members of the derivational family of English words built on the Latin root *liber-*: *liberty, liberality, liberalization, liberation, liberticide, liberationism, liberalness, liberalism, libertinism, liberationist, liberator, libertarian, libertine, liberticidal, liberal, liberally, liberalist, liberalistic, to liberate, to liberalize.* Somewhere in that pile you should find the word you need to paint the picture you have in mind. The study of how such modulations are introduced is called derivational morphology.

Some of the most interesting morphological questions, however, are concerned with what is NOT derivable. Why, for example, does *liber-* not also yield such words as *libertary* or *liberarchy* or *liberment* or *libertocracy*? (And how do you know that it does not?) Questions about nonwords are endless. If, for example, the verb *to orchestrate* derives from the noun *orchestra*, why is there no verb *to symphony orchestrate* bearing a similar relation to the compound noun *symphony orchestra*? Again, if *street wise* is an acceptable adjective, why is *street wiser* unacceptable as its comparative form? Such puzzles are the stock-in-trade of professional morphologists.

This chapter asks where words come from. That is to say, it looks at rules of word formation. The examples will be taken largely from English, although similar morphologic processes are known in other languages. But first, before you lose your morphological innocence, you should pause to answer some questions. Right now you can answer them without being confused by the claims and counterclaims of different theorists.

If you encountered the following letter-strings used as words in a printed text,

ject   cran   vert   fer   sist   mit   boysen

would you know:

1. How to pronounce them?

2. What syntactic category they belong to?

3. What they mean?

The reason for asking will become clear shortly.

Derivational Rules

Where do new words come from? Nearly always, new words are fashioned out of old words. Speakers of English have always been willing to borrow ("steal" might be more descriptive), so the old words are often taken from another language. But usually the old words are already familiar, and the new words come to form families of related words clustering about their common roots. When the new words are formed by adding affixes, they are said to be *derived*; the study of derivative forms is said to be the study of derivational morphology.

The derivational morphology of English is rich and interesting. Superficially, derived words look much like inflected words. For example, *moved* is *move* plus *-ed,* and *movable* is *move* plus *-able.* But linguists say that the addition of the derivational suffix *-able* is different from the addition of the inflectional suffix *-ed.* Nearly all linguists are convinced that this is an important difference, although not always for the same reason—many descriptions of the difference have been offered. The larger theoretical picture is complicated by the fact that something that is inflectional in English may be derivational in another language, and something inflectional in another language may be derivational in English. The simplest account is the one already proposed here: Inflections are under the control of syntax, and derivations are not.

Nevertheless, the similarities are striking. Derivational rules look very much like inflectional rules. Derivational rules have four parts:

1. Domain of application: There is, first, a characterization of the base for the affix; that is, the stems to which the affix can be added.

2. Pronunciation: The pronunciation of the derived word is specified. Often the derived pronunciation is simply the combination of the pronunciations of its parts, but sometimes there are changes of a complex but regular kind.

3. Meaning change: Each affix has a more or less consistent effect on the meaning of the stem, so a description of that change must be given.

4. Syntactic category: The syntactic category of the derived word is specified.

The only thing new here—that is not required for inflectional rules—is a need to state the syntactic category of the derived word. Derivations frequently change the syntactic category of the stem; inflections do not.

One difference between the two kinds of morphology is that regular inflectional affixes always appear outside derivational affixes. The youth of two boys, for example, cannot be referred to as their *boyshood.* In English, another difference is that words can have several derivational affixes, but only one inflectional affix. In other languages, however, multiple inflections are possible. The Latin word *amabatur,* for example, has two inflectional suffixes added to *ama-,* the indicative stem: *-ba* to indicate the imperfect and *-tur* to indicate the third person singular passive.

Words that have more than one derivational affix raise questions about the order in which the affixes are added. Sometimes the answer is obvious. In a word like *governmental,* for example, the suffix *-ment* must be added to the verb *govern* before there is a noun to add the *-al* to. But other cases can be ambigu-

Lewis Carroll (1832–1898).

ous. Take *unbelievable,* for example. The root is *believe,* to which a prefix and a suffix have been added, *un-* and *-able.* How should those additions be described? One way would be to have a morphological rule that adds both affixes at the same time, but that answer is not promising—the domains of application for compound rules would become too restricted. Morphologists assume that two separate rules are involved, one for adding *un-* and another for adding *-able,* so that *unbelievable* would be formed from *believe* in two steps. But in what order are the steps taken? Is *un-* first prefixed to *believe,* giving *unbelieve?* Or is *-able* first suffixed to *believe,* giving *believable?* The standard answer is that *-able* is added first, because the result, *believable,* is an actual word. If it were derived in the other order, an intermediate nonword would be created, *unbelieve.* In contrast, *unfoldable* or *undressable* should be ambiguous, because either order of affixing yields an actual word—and, indeed, they are ambiguous.

This line of argument leads to the conjecture that the domains of derivational rules are always actual words:

M1.   Derivational rules operate on words to yield other words.

M1 is a strong claim, with some surprising implications.

An example of derivational rules at work is the word *antidisestablishmentarianism,* which has been said (erroneously) to be the longest word in the English language. Someone who knew the rules of derivational morphology for English and who encountered this word for the first time might build its meaning out of its constituent morphemes, perhaps along the following lines:

—Start with the root, the verb *to establish,* meaning to set up on
 a permanent basis.
—Add the prefix *dis-* to obtain the new verb *to disestablish,*
 meaning to deprive of its permanent status.
—Add the suffix *-ment* to turn the verb into a noun,
 disestablishment, meaning the act or state of being
 disestablished.
—Add the suffix *-arian* to obtain the noun *disestablishmentarian,*
 meaning a believer in or advocate of disestablishment.
—Prefix it with *anti-* to produce the noun
 antidisestablishmentarian, meaning someone opposed
 to disestablishmentarians.
—Add the suffix *-ism* to obtain, finally, the noun
 antidisestablishmentarianism, meaning the doctrine
 of antidisestablishmentarians.

There is nothing wrong with this derivation. It does add the necessary affixes to obtain the desired word. Yet it starts with the wrong sense of *establish* and never recovers. Anyone familiar with the history of this notorious word knows that the sense of *to establish* that is appropriate here is to make something a national institution—in this case, to enact a law making a church the official church of the nation, called the established church. Then *to disestablish* refers to the political act of cutting this relationship between the state and the national institution—in this case, to abolish the established church. In fact, terminating a national institution is the ONLY meaning of *disestablish;* the word is not used in any other context. That is to say, the verb *to disestablish* does not have the more general meaning derived above, and so, according to M1, this nonword should not serve as a basis for subsequent derivational steps leading to the more general sense of *antidisestablishmentarianism.* According to M1, derivational rules apply only to actual words, but sometimes it is not entirely clear whether intermediate steps have produced words or not.

Domains of Application

Not all linguists accept the idea that the domain of application for a derivational rule must always be a word. One objection to this word–based approach is that it excludes certain Latinate derivations that begin with roots that are not words. *Liber,* for example, is not an English word, yet a large family of words derives from it. Or again, the verb *to invert* derives from the root *-vert* by the addition of the prefix *in-.* Both parts seem to combine freely; *infer, invent, insist, induct,* and *inject* all have the same *in-* prefix; *divert, revert, subvert,* and *convert* all have the same *-vert* root. But *vert* is not an English word.

How should morphological theory deal with such examples? One possibility is to revise the requirement that the domains of derivational rules must always be words. Suppose that morphological rules were to apply to morphemes:

M2.   Derivational rules operate on morphemes to yield words.

M2 seems an attractive alternative to M1; it defines morphology as the theory of how words are constructed out of morphemes. The roots *liber-, -ject, -vert,* and so forth, are bound morphemes; the affixes are also bound morphemes; they combine to yield words, which are free morphemes. This morpheme-based approach would also accommodate inflectional morphology in those languages in which the stem to which inflections attach is not itself a word.

This discussion has now wandered onto a battlefield. Many linguists resist a morpheme-based theory of morphology. The basic objection is that many of the morphemes involved are meaningless outside of the words in which they occur. Morphemes are defined as the smallest individually meaningful elements of language (see Chapter 2), so a morphology based on morphemes should have individually meaningful elements as its atoms. But is that the case?

For example, consider the verb *to subject*. What does *ject* mean? (What did you decide at the beginning of this chapter?) If *ject* does not have a meaning, how can it be a morpheme? And what about *sub-?* People who insist that *ject* is a meaningful unit claim to detect some trace of the Latin verb *jacere,* to throw, although admittedly the sense of throwing has become rather abstract. And *sub-* has a variety of interpretations in different words, but generally means below or downward or under. Can some hint of a sense of this verb be gleaned from this combination? Can all the senses of this verb be predicted from this combination? Is the sense assigned to *-ject* in *subject* the same as the sense assigned to it in *inject, deject,* or *project?* Those who prefer word-based morphology would direct such questions to an etymologist.

On the other hand, the main objection to word-based morphology is that, since the basic atoms are words, somewhere there must be a list of all the words. This list, the lexicon, must be consulted to determine whether the result of applying a derivational rule to a particular word is or is not a permissible word. Critics of word-based morphology argue that morphology is generative, that it is unnecessary to list thousands of words that could be generated from a list of morphemes by the rules of derivation. An advantage of morpheme-based morphology is that its list of all the morphemes would be much shorter than a list of all the words. Brevity is not a trivial advantage here, because it is not obvious that anyone COULD construct a list of all words. New words are being coined every day, but that is not the worst problem. Consider: What would a list of all the English words contain? Would it contain *anti-missile* and *anti-anti-missile missile* and *anti-anti-anti-missile missile missile* and so on ad infinitum? Would it contain *Boston-to-Chicago trip* with all possible place names substituting for *Boston* and *Chicago?* How many integers would it contain names for? How many names of biochemical compounds? The idea of constructing a list of all the words runs into trouble because it assumes that (1) "word" is a well-defined concept, and (2) there is a finite number of them. Neither assumption is plausible. Moreover, advocates of morpheme-based morphology argue that even if a finite list of all words could be drawn up, it would be a hodgepodge containing morphemes, words, and phrases—units at different levels of analysis having no clear linguistic status at any level.

Part of the problem here is how to distinguish between possible words and actual words. At the beginning of this chapter words were said to have the property of connectingness because they facilitate the connecting of ideas. Attentive readers surely hesitated over *connectingness*. It is a possible word, but is it an actual word? In fact, *connectingness* is NOT an actual word. It was coined for this chapter—no other use of it is known to the author—to illustrate the productivity of derivational morphology. The first thing to note is that the coinage, though unfamiliar, is interpretable, which indicates that it was put together according to familiar rules; it is a possible word. In English, *-ness* is a suffix that can be freely appended to adjectival modifiers or to past participles to form nouns that express a state or condition: *Hardness* is the state or condition of being hard; *connectedness* is the state or condition of being connected, and so on. The novel derivative *connectingness* pushes the limits of this derivational rule. Although purists will surely dislike it, *connectingness* can be defended: *Connecting* can be used to modify nouns (*connecting rod, connecting link*), so the *-ness* suffix, which has great freedom of application, is not totally alien to it (compare *willingness, lovingness, clingingness, thrillingness*). According to the derivational rule for *-ness*, if *connectingness* were an actual word, it should refer to the state or condition of being connecting.

The fact that *connectingness* is interpretable is congenial to morpheme-based theories, which are geared to explain how words built up from simpler morphemes can be understood without consulting a lexicon. On the other hand, the fact that readers notice something odd about *connectingness* suggests that they did try to look it up in their mental lexicon, but did not find it. Perhaps both kinds of information processing are available. When word-based morphology fails, morpheme-based morphology tries to come to the rescue. Adopting two theories to do the work of one is not parsimonious, but it does explain how people are able to guess the meanings of many unfamiliar words.

A major problem for any theory of morphology is to explain why so many possible derivations are missing, leaving holes in the delicate structure of the lexicon. For example, compare the similar verbs *amend* and *emend*. Why does *amend* nominalize as *amendment* and *emend* as *emendation?* Why not the other way round, or both the same? Again, compare the derivational families that can be built with three verbs that, on the surface, look very similar: *permit, commit,* and *transmit.* Parentheses mark the derivatives that were NOT found in *Webster's Second New International Dictionary,* a dictionary that is notoriously permissive about what it will accept as a word of English.

permit	*commit*	*transmit*
permission	*commission*	*transmission*
permissive	*commissive*	*transmissive*
permissiveness	*(commissiveness)*	*transmissiveness*
permissible	*(commissible)*	*transmissible*
impermissible	*(incommissible)*	*intransmissible*
permissibility	*(commissibility)*	*transmissibility*
permissibly	*(commissibly)*	*(transmissibly)*
(permissioner)	*commissioner*	*(transmissioner)*
(permitment)	*commitment*	*(transmitment)*
permittee	*committee*	*(transmittee)*
(permittal)	*committal*	*transmittal*
(permittance)	*(committance)*	*transmittance*
permitter	*committor*	*transmitter*
permittable	*committable*	*transmittable*

Which derivatives have been useful and which have not been needed is apparently a matter of historical accident. Or, to put it otherwise, if someone were to introduce a new verb, *demit,* it would not be possible to know in advance which of these derivative forms it would eventually take.

Explaining why so many derivations that seem to follow the rules do not succeed in generating acceptable words poses a difficult question for those who favor a morpheme-based theory of derivational morphology. One possibility is to assume that the morphological component of language actually does generate them, but the lexicon then filters out those products that no one has ever used. This approach could explain why a user of English might hesitate in deciding whether or not *permittable* or *commissible* or *transmitment* are actual words of English: The morphological component generates them, but the lexical filter cannot decide whether they are in general use or not. Morpheme-based morphology with a lexical filter does succeed in drawing a sharp distinction between the morphological and the lexical components of language. But it does not avoid the requirement that somewhere there must be a lexicon that lists all the actual words. Indeed, it creates a new problem, for now there are two lexicons: first, an implicit list of all the possible words that could be generated by the morphemes and rules of derivation; second, an explicit list, a subset of the first lexicon, that contains only the actual words of the language. But even if this double lexicon were acceptable, the second list would not be complete, because (history and social conventions being what they are) derived words do not always mean what derivational rules say they should. Derived words that have picked up idiosyncratic uses (using *transmission* to refer to a part of an automobile, for example) would still have to be added to the lexicon of actual words.

Specifying the domain of application is not the only problem to be resolved in stating derivational rules. The rules also specify changes that occur in sound and meaning. How meaning changes are to be described has been illustrated in passing, but so far little has been said about phonological changes.

Rules for Pronunciation

Two kinds of derivational affixes must be distinguished when discussing the pronunciation of derived words: those like *-ness* that are simply tagged onto words and those like *-ion* or *-al* that change the pronunciation of the words they are tagged onto. For example, when the noun *deduction* is derived from the verb *deduct,* the final /t/ of *deduct* is softened to /š/ (the initial phoneme of *shun*). A slightly larger change occurs when the noun *revision* is derived from the verb *revise:* Not only is the final /z/ of *revise* softened to /ž/, but the pronunciation of the stressed vowel changes. And sometimes, as when *radiation* is derived from *radiate,* not only is there a sound change, but there is a stress change as well—from the first to the third syllable, in this example.

Derivational changes in pronunciation follow complex rules that are hotly debated by the experts. To follow their arguments in any detail would necessitate a long detour, but one point is worth noting. When an affix and a word are adjoined, a boundary is created between the two segments. Not all boundaries behave the same way. There are two kinds of boundaries in English: word boundaries and morpheme boundaries. The -*ness* suffix, for example, takes a word boundary, and so can be written #*ness;* for example, *happy* → *happi#ness,* with no change in the pronunciation of the stem. The -*ion* suffix, on the other hand, takes a morpheme boundary, written +*ion;* for example, *investigate* → *investigat+ion,* where the terminal phoneme changes and the main stress is shifted to the syllable immediately preceding the suffix. The difference can be illustrated by comparing the verb *refuse,* meaning to decline or reject something, with the verb *re#fuse,* meaning to fuse again, where *re#* is prefixed to the verb *fuse.*

Derivational rules tend to lengthen words, and rules for assigning stress to the syllables of long words in English are complicated. Consider, for example, that in *telegraph* the main stress is on the first syllable, in *telegraphy* it is on the second, and in *telegraphic* it is on the third. To assign the correct pitch contour to such words, a speaker must know far more than how to form the individual phonetic segments. In some cases, he or she must know whether the word is a noun or a verb: In the sentence *Will they convict the convict?* the verb receives stress on the second syllable but the noun on the first. Thus, syntax as well as morphology enters in.

Considerations governing the correct pronunciation of derived forms are complex; it is difficult to imagine that they are computed as needed in the act of speaking. Probably pronunciations are stored in the lexicon of actual words and can simply be retrieved when needed. It is possible to compute them when necessary, however. An English-speaking person who encounters a new word in a written text can usually make a plausible guess about how to pronounce it. For example, the written word *histaminase* may be unfamiliar, but you would probably guess that it has four syllables and that the accent falls on the second one. The first few times you saw the word you might hesitate slightly while repeating the calculation. Soon learning would take over, however, and *histaminase* would be added to the ever-growing collection of word tokens that flow gracefully from the tongue. But there is more to mastering a new word than just learning what it means.

Affix Ordering

Affixes must be added to words in a certain order. From the root word *talk* you can form *talks* and *talker* and even *talkers,* but not *talkser.* The #*s* affix cannot apply before the #*er* affix applies. From the root word *red* you can form *reddish* and *redness* and even *reddishness,* but not *rednessish.* The #*ness* affix cannot apply before the +*ish* affix applies. From the root word *human* you can form *antihuman* and *inhuman* and even *antiinhuman*, but not *inantihuman*. The *in*+ affix must be applied before the *anti#* affix. Dozens of such examples could be displayed and the result might seem chaotic and confusing, but the morphological rules controlling the ordering of affixes are simple and quite general.

Three kinds of English affixes can be distinguished: inflections and two kinds of derivational affixes. Derivational affixes apply before inflectional affixes, and derivational affixes at morpheme boundaries apply before derivational affixes at word boundaries. This ordering creates three levels of affixation.

Order	Examples	Description
First	+*ion*, +*ish*, +*al*, +*ous*, *in*+	Derivational affixes at morpheme boundaries
Second	#*ness*, #*hood*, #*ist*, #*ism*, *anti*#	Derivational affixes at word boundaries
Third	#*s*, #*ing*, #*ed*	Inflectional affixes at word boundaries

This scheme can be extended. Irregular forms act like derivational affixes at the first level: Whereas *legsless* and *gumsless* are clearly ill-formed, *feetless* and *teethless* are unusual but not illegal. That is to say, an irregular plural can apply before the #*less* affix applies, but the regular plural, #*s,* cannot. Moreover, compounds act like derivational affixes: *House cats* is fine, but *houses cat* is not a compound word—the plural inflection cannot apply before the compound is formed.

To test whether children know these rules, the psycholinguist Peter Gordon first told three-, four-, and five-year-old children about *X-eater* compounds (*meat-eater, candy-eater,* and so forth). He then asked, "What would you call something that eats rats?"

"A rat-eater," they replied.

"And what would you call something that eats mice?"

"A mice-eater."

Even the youngest children clearly rejected *rats-eater,* but accepted *mice-eater,* thus showing they knew that regular inflectional rules apply after compounding, but that irregular inflectional rules can apply before compounding.

How could such young children have learned this obscure fact about the morphology of English words? Compounds like *people-mover* or *lice-infested,* containing irregular plurals, are possible in English, but they are rare; it is unlikely that the children would have heard them. How children could recognize that such compounds are acceptable poses the kind of puzzle that tempts students of language development to believe in innate knowledge.

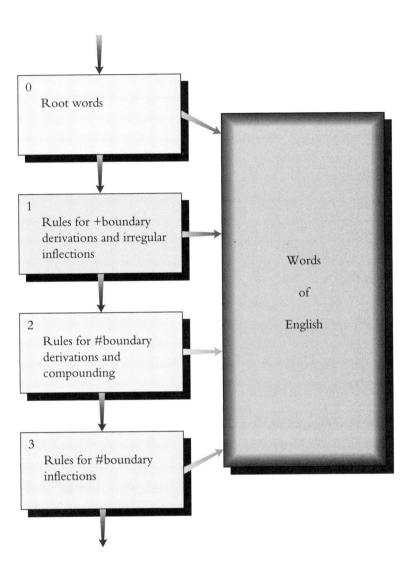

A flowchart indicating how the morphology of English words is organized into three levels. Derivations apply before regular inflections; irregular inflections and derivations at morpheme boundaries apply before derivations at word boundaries.

Compound Words

The simplest way to make new words is to put old words together; the result is called a compound. When, for example, conveyances are invented that fly through the air, it is a simple thing to combine *air* and *craft,* thus producing a compound noun *aircraft* to distinguish these new vehicles from land or water craft. This trick is so simple, in fact, that it can be overworked. It is a test of one's definition of "word" to tell which compounds are words and which are not.

German is notorious for its freedom of compounding. For example, the following compound was printed on the passenger ticket for a steamship excursion up the Danube:

Donaudampfschiffahrtsgesellschaft

which breaks down more or less as follows:

Donau (Danube)
Dampf (steam)
Schiff (ship)
Fahrt (excursion)
Gesellschaft (company)

But when the process is continued, say, to refer to the widow of the captain of this company's steamship:

Donaudampfschiffahrtsgesellschaftskapitänswitwe

then even the Germans think it is funny.

The German convention of writing compounds without spaces makes the result more intimidating, but the same kind of compounding occurs in English. For example, the following sentence is taken from a Sunbeam Corporation advertisement for its Oster division Osterizer: "Occasionally we hold friendly and informal Osterizer blender and Kitchen Center brand food preparation appliance Creative Cookery Classes in many cities around the country." This twelve-word nominal compound,

Osterizer blender and Kitchen Center brand food preparation
appliance Creative Cookery Classes

is susceptible of more than one interpretation, but everyone would agree that it refers to some kind of classes. Similarly, when the *Congressional Record* included the thirteen-word nominal compound,

liquid oxygen liquid hydrogen rocket powered single stage to orbit
reversible boost system

it obviously referred to some kind of system. The last word in such constructions has a preferred status as the head of the compound, and the other words are modifiers of some kind. But the point is that it is a construction. No one would expect to find these compounds—German or English—in a dictionary.

Unpacking Meanings

"You seem very clever at explaining words, Sir," said Alice. "Would you kindly tell me the meaning of the poem called 'Jabberwocky'?"

"Let's hear it," said Humpty Dumpty. "I can explain all the poems that ever were invented—and a good many that haven't been invented just yet."

This sounded very hopeful, so Alice repeated the first verse:

"'Twas brillig, and the slithy toves
Did gyre and gimble in the wabe;
All mimsy were the borogoves,
And the mome raths outgrabe."

"That's enough to begin with," Humpty Dumpty interrupted; "there are plenty of hard words there. *'Brillig'* means four o'clock in the afternoon—the time when you begin *broiling* things for dinner."

"That'll do very well," said Alice; "and *'slithy'*?"

"Well, *'slithy'* means 'lithe and slimy.' 'Lithe' is the same as 'active.' You see it's like a portmanteau—there are two meanings packed up into one word."

"I see it now," Alice remarked thoughtfully; "and what are *'toves'*?"

"Well, *'toves'* are something like badgers, they're something like lizards, and they're something like corkscrews."

"They must be very curious-looking creatures."

"They are that," said Humpty Dumpty; "also they make their nests under sun-dials; also they live on cheese."

"And what's to *'gyre'* and to *'gimble'*?"

"To *'gyre'* is to go round and round like a gyroscope. To *'gimble'* is to make holes like a gimlet."

"And *'the wabe'* is the grass-plot round a sun-dial, I suppose?" said Alice, surprised at her own ingenuity.

"Of course it is. It's called *'wabe,'* you know, because it goes a long way before it and a long way behind it—"

"And a long way beyond it on each side," Alice added.

"Exactly so. Well, then, *'mimsy'* is 'flimsy and miserable' (there's another portmanteau for you). And a *'borogove'* is a thin, shabby-looking bird with its feathers sticking out all round—something like a live mop."

"And then *'mome raths'*?" said Alice. "I'm afraid I'm giving you a great deal of trouble."

"Well, a *'rath'* is a sort of green pig; but *'mome'* I'm not certain about. I think it's short for 'from home'—meaning that they'd lost their way, you know."

"And what does *'outgrabe'* mean?"

"Well, *'outgribing'* is something between bellowing and whistling, with a kind of sneeze in the middle; however, you'll hear it done, maybe, down in the wood yonder, and when you've once heard it you'll be *quite* content. Who's been repeating all that hard stuff to you?"

"I read it in a book," said Alice.

From *Through the Looking-Glass,* Lewis Carroll, 1871.

The German word Strasse *means* street, *but* Einbahnstrasse *does not mean* Einbahn Street. *Since the correct English translation is* one-way street, *this pair of signs poses something of a riddle.*

Some compounds, however, are actual words. Something like *cornflower blue* strings three words together, but the result is frozen in the dictionary as a compound word. The English lexicon includes hundreds of such words. For example, a *cloth* spread over a *table* before food is served is a *tablecloth; water* that has fallen as *rain* is *rainwater;* a *prize* passed out at the *door* for a winning ticket is a *door prize;* a *knob* on a *door* is a *doorknob;* a *wiper* for a *doorknob* is a *doorknob wiper;* the list could go on at great length. These examples combine two old nouns to make a new noun, but adjective-noun compounds are also common (*gentleman, safe-conduct, dry goods*), as are verb-noun compounds (*pushcart, crybaby, dragnet*). All these are examples of compounds that a linguist would call endocentric. The compound is a species of the general class of things named by the final word of the pair: A *shade tree* is a kind of *tree,* and a *highroad* is a kind of *road*. (Exocentric compounds refer to something other than what their parts refer to: A *turnkey* is not a *key*, a *pickpocket* is not a *pocket*.)

Endocentric compounding is the easiest way to create a new word, and newspapers add them to the language every day. The question is: How do actual compound nouns differ from nonlexicalized expressions created freely? The nature of the difference may be clarified by a specific example: How does *a gentleman* differ from *a gentle man?* For one thing, the stress is different—on the first syllable of *gentleman,* but on the final word of *gentle man.* For another thing, *very* can be introduced into the noun phrase to modify the adjective, *a very gentle man,* whereas the adverb *very* cannot modify *gentleman.* Similarly, in French, the noun phrase *une sage femme* (a wise woman) differs from the compound *une sage-femme* (a midwife) because only the adjective *sage* can be modified: *une très sage femme* (a very wise woman). When standard syntactic moves that can be made with normal noun phrases are not applicable, the chances are that you are dealing with a compound word.

The clearest examples of the difference between compound nouns and noun phrases are those in which one member of the compound is not a word, so that the combination cannot occur as a noun phrase. Among the potential words listed at the beginning of this chapter were *cran* and *boysen*. These occur in English only in the words *cranberry* and *boysenberry*. It is conceivable that *blackberry* and *strawberry* could be viewed as noun phrases, *black berry* and *straw berry,* but *cranberry* and *boysenberry* cannot.

These "cranberry morphs" provide a standard argument in favor of word-based theories of morphology. A morpheme-based morphology would probably assume that these words are formed by combining the morphemes *cran* and *boysen* with the morpheme *berry*. But if morphemes have to be meaningful outside of the words in which they occur, then *cran* and *boysen* do not qualify. That looks bad enough for a morpheme-based morphology, but the berry situation gets even worse. Consider *blackberry,* which does compound two meaningful morphemes, *black* and *berry*. But not all blackberries are black berries, and not all black berries are blackberries, so *black* must have some special meaning in *blackberry* that it does not have elsewhere. Otherwise said, the meaning of the word *blackberry* cannot be inferred from the meanings of the morphemes that make it up.

To create a new lexical unit, any syntactic group can be given some meaning that is not composed from the meanings of its elements in the normal manner. *Man in the street, stock-in-trade,* or *dog in the manger* are well-formed syntactic groups, but they have been frozen as compound words with special meanings.

Most compound words in English are nouns, many are adjectives (*care-free, man-made, airborne, homesick*), and a few, mostly of recent origin, are used as verbs (*to handcuff, to rubber-stamp, to sight-read*—most of the verb compounds seem to be derivatives from compound nouns). The great variety of compounds that occur in English has inspired attempts at classification, but with little success. Would-be classifiers generally paraphrase the compounds by fully grammatical constructions—for example, *coffee cream* is cream for coffee—then classify the paraphrases, rather than the compounds themselves. For example, the critical term that must be supplied to formulate a paraphrase can be listed:

Relation	Compound
CAUSE	*tear gas, sleeping pill*
HAVE	*picture book, writer's cramp*
MAKE	*rainwater, daisy chain*
USE	*waterwheel, steam iron*
BE	*whitecap, target site, machine tool*
IN	*hillbilly, house cat, country club*
FOR	*ashtray, carbarn, fish pond*
FROM	*fingerprint, whalebone, sea breeze, knife wound*
ABOUT	*tax law, book review*

Different workers favor different paraphrases, however, and no proposal has created an exhaustive and mutually exclusive set of relations, so the results are generally considered to be inconclusive. English compounds remain a difficult obstacle for anyone learning English as a second language.

Etymology

It should now be obvious that derivational and compound morphology can be highly irregular and unpredictable in English. When you ask why one form is a word and a closely analogous form is not, or why some roots take affixes and others do not, the only answer seems to be historical accident. That is simply how the vocabulary developed. It might have happened differently, but it did not. Great efforts have been made to reconstruct the history and publish it in such monumental works as the twelve-volume *Oxford English Dictionary*. The historical study of word origins—historical morphology—is called etymology.

As comparative linguistics developed during the nineteenth century, it was recognized that words change gradually over the centuries, in both sound and meaning. The critical part of the task of establishing correct relations between languages consisted of following those changes in detail. For many words, the historical origins are incomplete or totally unknown. But it is possible to trace some of them all the way back to their hypothetical origins in Proto-Indo-European. As the physician and sometime philologist Lewis

Thomas remarked in *The Medusa and the Snail: More Notes of a Biology Watcher* (New York: Viking Press, 1979):

> When you do run across a primary, original word, the experience is both disturbing and vaguely pleasurable, like coming across a friend's picture in an old high-school annual. They are all very old, and the most meaningful ones date all the way back to Indo-European roots which become the parents of cognate words in Sanskrit, Persian, Greek, Latin, and much later, most of the English language. *Sen* meant old, *spreg* meant speak, *swem* was swim, *nomen* was name, a *porko* was a young pig, *dent* was a tooth. . . . Using basic Indo-European and waving your hands, you could get around the world almost as well as with New York English.

But most of today's vocabulary is the outcome of a series of small inadvertent blunders that have accumulated over thousands of years.

Many people who know English are aware of certain etymological facts about its vocabulary, the most obvious being that some words derive from Anglo-Saxon and others from Latin. Sometimes it is possible to recognize a root that is common to a family of words and to enjoy discovering relations between words that otherwise go unnoticed. But most of the etymological details have no significance for how people learn and use the language today. For example, compare *ear* and *palm:* The two senses of *ear,* "organ of hearing" or "fruiting spike of a cereal," are derived from two different Anglo-Saxon words, whereas the two senses *palm,* "part of the hand" and "a kind of tree," are derived from the same word (because the leaf was thought to resemble an outstretched hand). Such information is not part of what a person needs to know to use a language in social interactions, and this book forgoes the diachronic pleasures of etymology in favor of a synchronic look at what is in the mental lexicons of present-day language users.

■ ■ ■

Two kinds of word families have now been visited: syntactic families and morphological families. Syntactic families include nouns, verbs, modifiers, and particles. Morphological families include inflectional families, derivational families, and compound families: From the root *bake* comes the inflectional family *bakes, baked, baking;* the derivational family *baker, bakery;* and the compound family *clambake, bakeshop, half-baked.* How all this is known to someone who speaks the language is the next topic to be considered.

◀ *Familiar written words are perceived as units, not as strings of letters. Jasper Johns plays on this automatic and immediate recognition in his 1959 painting,* False Start.

▼ *A quarter-century earlier, experiments had found this reflex word recognition to be so powerful that people asked to name the colors in which a series of words were printed faltered when, say, the word in green ink was R-E-D.*

RED	**RED**	**RED**
BLUE	**BLUE**	**BLUE**
GREEN	**GREEN**	**GREEN**
BLACK	**BLACK**	**BLACK**
YELLOW	**YELLOW**	**YELLOW**
BLUE	**BLUE**	**BLUE**

The Mental Lexicon

Villiam James (1842–1910), the father of scientific psychology in America, told a story about a practical joker who, "seeing a discharged veteran carrying home his dinner, suddenly called out 'Attention!' whereupon the man instantly brought his hands down, and lost his mutton and potatoes in the gutter." People who know a word are like well-drilled veterans. They may not lose their dinner in the gutter when they hear it, but they cannot help but respond.

The reflex recognition of words is a topic of much importance to scientists who study the mental lexicon, but a caveat is needed before that story is told. In general, it is easier to explore people's knowledge of words using written rather than spoken materials, simply because inscriptions are easier than sounds for an investigator to control. This is one reason that so much experimental information about the mental lexicon is available only for the written word—and for alphabetically written English words, at that. This limitation is ethnocentric and generally deplorable, but until cross-cultural replications are available there is little that can be done but to report results for this special case. A thoughtful reader will be cautious in drawing generalizations.

The Word-Superiority Effect

More than a hundred years ago James McKeen Cattell (1860–1944), another pioneer American psychologist, reported an unexpected finding: Letters are easier to read when they form a word than when they do not. Cattell compared haphazard strings of letters with short words by measuring the shortest exposure time that was needed for correct recognition. He found that at short exposure durations, where only four or five random letters can be recognized, it is possible to read two or three short words that together contain more than five letters. For example, the nine letters,

FONHGTAEW

are much harder to read when shown in that arrangement than when presented as:

FOG HAT NEW

Words are seen as individual units, not as strings of letters.

This phenomenon waited more than fifty years for a plausible explanation. It came in the form of probability theory. Students of the statistical properties of written messages observed that written words are highly redundant (see Chapter 2). That is to say, a string of nine letters conveys more selective information when any letter can occur in any position than when the same nine letters are constrained to spell familiar words. If one assumes that selective visual information is received at the same rate for both displays, words should be recognizable faster (after less information has been assimilated) than should nonredundant strings of letters. In other words, Cattell's subjects had a much better chance of guessing the letters correctly when they saw them in words than when they were random strings. Someone who saw only

FO★ H★T ★★W

had a much better chance of filling in the missing letters when they spelled words than when they did not.

That explanation was accepted for another twenty years until the experimental psychologist Gerald M. Reicher figured out how to test it. The trick is to eliminate the effects of guessing. People try to read a short string of letters that is flashed briefly, then answer a question about the final letter in the string. For example, they might see

HEAR

very briefly and then be asked whether the final letter was a D or an R. This question cannot be answered by guessing the final letter that forms a word, because both alternatives form a word. For the purpose of comparison, other people see

AEHR

and are asked the same question: Was the final letter D or R? Obviously, this question cannot be answered by guessing the final letter that forms a word, because neither letter forms a word. If Cattell's phenomenon were simply a matter of guessing from the context, then under these conditions—where context provides no help for either condition—the difference should disappear.

In fact, however, the phenomenon does not disappear. Accuracy in reporting the final letter is significantly better in words than in nonwords. In fact, the final letter is reported more accurately in a word than when it is presented in isolation. This finding, known to psycholinguists as "the word-superiority effect," put a sharp point on Cattell's observation.

A string of letters is flashed on the screen for a tenth of a second and viewers are asked whether the final letter was a D or a K. Their responses are significantly more accurate when the letters spell a familiar word than when they do not.

After much experience with printed words, people come to see them as unitary wholes—not as strings of letters, but as integrated chunks of information whose constituent parts are not identified separately. The precise nature of these learned patterns is not yet established, but the important implication of this explanation is that literate adults have acquired, one way or another, a large store of complex visual units that are immediately available in reading.

Evidence that these unitary percepts are involuntary, as well as immediate, comes from another observation, called the Stroop effect after its discoverer, J. Ridley Stroop. For his doctoral dissertation in 1935, Stroop printed color names in different colored inks: The word *red* might be printed in blue, the word *yellow* in green, *brown* in red, and so on through a long list of colored color words. Then he asked people either to read aloud the list of words or to name the sequence of colors. He found that people could read words printed in colored inks almost as rapidly as they could read them in black ink, but they had great difficulty naming the colors of the inks. When they looked at the letters R-E-D printed in green ink, they could not avoid reading *red*, which interfered with saying "green." Reading the words was so automatic that they were unable to suppress this reaction and concentrate on the task at hand.

Familiar words are coherent perceptual units, so immediately and automatically available that a literate person is no longer able to control their recognition. The totality of these acquired perceptual units has been likened to a dictionary that people carry around in their heads.

The Familiarity Effect

The ability to recognize words as coherent units is acquired through learning, and like most learned abilities, it improves with practice. The more times a word is encountered, the more familiar it becomes and the faster it can be recognized.

This relation holds even for meaningless words. To demonstrate the familiarity effect, try the following experiment. Take ten 7-letter words in, say, Turkish and make up a deck of 86 cards in such a way that two words are printed on 25 cards each, two more on 10 cards each, two on 5 cards each, two on 2 cards each, and the final two on only 1 card. Then shuffle the deck, hand it to a friend who knows nothing about Turkish, and ask him or her to go through it one card at a time, spelling each word aloud and then pronouncing it. After the entire deck has been read in that manner, announce a surprise test: Measure the shortest exposure duration required to recognize each of the ten words. If you do the experiment correctly, you will find that the more frequently a word was seen the more rapidly it could be recognized. It will take about three or four times as long to recognize words seen only once as to recognize words seen twenty-five times.

It is well known that everyday language provides optimal conditions for the development of large differences in the familiarity of different words. One

BLUE	BLUE	BLUE
GREEN	GREEN	GREEN
BLACK	BLACK	BLACK
YELLOW	YELLOW	YELLOW
BLUE	BLUE	BLUE
BLACK	BLACK	BLACK
RED	RED	RED
GREEN	GREEN	GREEN
A. Control	B. Matched	C. Mismatched

The Stroop effect. People are first shown column A and asked to read the words aloud as fast as they can; that calibrates their reading speed. Then they are shown column B and asked to name aloud the colors of the words as fast as they can; their speed for naming the colors in B is the same as their reading speed for A. Finally, they are shown column C and again asked to name the colors of the words as fast as they can. At this task, people go much more slowly and make many mistakes, frequently reading the word instead of naming its color.

of the most firmly established statistical facts about words is that some of them are used far more than others. For example, Hartvig Dahl has counted the frequency of different words (word types) in a transcript of 1,058,888 running words (word tokens) of spoken conversation. Of course, his definition of "word" was crude (any string of letters between successive spaces; see definition D1 in Chapter 2), because that is the easiest unit for a computer to count. Thus, for example, the *uh* that fills pauses was counted as a word, and *be, am, are, is, was,* and *were* all were counted as different words, not as different forms of the same word, *be.* The results were so massive, however, that no refinements in the definition of "word" would have changed them significantly. Dahl found that the most frequently spoken word was the first person singular pronoun; on the average, every sixteenth word was *I.* The top twenty words are listed in the table on the next page—taken together, those twenty made up more than 37 percent of all the words uttered. Note, incidentally, that only one of the frequent words, *know,* is an open-class, or content, word; all the others are closed-class words, little words that give grammatical shape to phrases and sentences. As the list continues beyond the twentieth word, more content words begin to appear, but slowly at first. Just 42 different word types made up 50 percent of the word tokens counted; 848 different word types made up 90 percent of the corpus.

The Twenty English Words Occurring Most Frequently in Personal Discourse

Rank	Word type	Frequency	Cumulative frequency	Percentage
1	*I*	65,213	65,213	6.2
2	*and*	38,020	103,233	9.7
3	*the*	29,753	132,986	12.6
4	*to*	29,653	162,639	15.4
5	*that*	27,558	190,197	18.0
6	*you*	26,598	216,795	20.5
7	*it*	20,542	237,337	22.4
8	*of*	20,290	257,627	24.3
9	*a*	19,385	277,012	26.2
10	*know*	15,285	292,297	27.6
11	*was*	15,091	307,388	29.0
12	*uh*	14,017	321,405	30.4
13	*in*	12,964	334,369	31.6
14	*but*	9,799	344,168	32.5
15	*is*	8,875	353,043	33.3
16	*this*	8,815	361,858	34.2
17	*me*	8,506	370,364	35.0
18	*about*	8,377	378,741	35.8
19	*just*	8,318	387,059	36.6
20	*don't*	8,307	395,366	37.3

From H. Dahl, *Word Frequencies of Spoken American English.* Essex, Conn.: Verbatim, 1979.

Similar data for written texts show greater variety in the choice of words. For example, whereas Dahl found only 17,871 different word types in his transcript of 1,058,888 spoken words, Henry Kučera and W. Nelson Francis at Brown University counted 50,406 different word types in their sample of 1,014,232 written words. But the general picture is the same. A few words are overworked, most are neglected. From such statistics it is inevitable that some words will become much more familiar than others.

It is a general observation that the more familiar a word is, the less time people require to read it. Faster recognition is a consequence of highly familiar words being seen as perceptual wholes, not as strings of letters. For example, if people are handed a printed text and asked to scan it for all occurrences of the letter *t*, they are more likely to overlook a *t* in *the* than in other less frequently used words. That is to say, people see the highly familiar *the* as a complete unit, not as a string of three letters. Moreover, it is not the meaning of the text that makes people overlook *t* in *the*, because the same thing happens when they are asked to scan a haphazard list of words. The familiarity effect is strong and

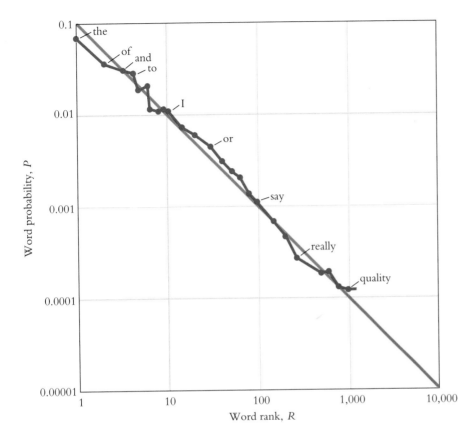

The standard curve for English words in written texts. The probability P of a word occurring is plotted as a function of the word's rank R when ordered with respect to frequency of occurrence. The product PR is approximately constant, which yields the straight line with a slope of −1 when plotted on doubly logarithmic coordinates.

pervasive; psycholinguists systematically design their experiments in such a way that the familiarity effect does not swamp other variables in which they are interested.

An obvious implication of the familiarity effect is that the dictionary in your head must be very different from the dictionaries that are sold in bookstores. How long it takes you to find something on a printed list depends on the length of the list, but how long it takes you to recognize a word does not seem to depend on how many different words you know. If you look up such infrequently used words as *tun* or *ire* in a hand-held dictionary, it does not take any longer than it takes to look up the frequently used words *the* or *but*. But when you look up these words in your mental lexicon, the less used words take much longer to find.

The comparison is questionable, of course, because it takes so long to find anything in a hand-held dictionary, but it does pose a question about how a mental lexicon might be organized. Are familiar words somehow imprinted on the brain in larger letters? Perhaps as words are used they are returned to the top of a pile, so that frequently used words are always near the top. Perhaps frequently used words are easy to find quickly because they are stored in many different places in the brain.

It is no great trick to demonstrate that the mental lexicon is not organized the way a hand-held dictionary is. What is not so easy to figure out is how the mental lexicon IS organized. It is not even obvious how many mental lexicons there are.

Multiple Vocabularies

The word *lexicon* has two senses. One is synonymous with dictionary: a printed book containing an alphabetized list of words and their meanings. The other is more abstract: the words of a language, whether or not they have been written down. An unabridged, printed dictionary can be regarded as a rather tedious theory—or a very detailed description—of the abstract lexicon. That, at least, is what a good dictionary aspires to be. But it is not a satisfactory description of a mental lexicon.

The term *mental lexicon* introduces still a third, more personal, sense. What you know, your personal word knowledge, is but a subset of the abstract lexicon, the lexical component of the language. The abstract lexicon can be thought of as the sum total of all the different words in all the mental lexicons of all the people who know and use the language. Nobody knows every word, but somebody knows each one.

What does it mean to say that someone knows a word? Does it mean that they use it in speaking? In writing? Does it mean that they can define it? Or does it mean merely that they are sure they have seen it before? There are many words that a person can recognize in reading and might even use in writing, but would never utter or expect to hear in ordinary conversation. In a printed dictionary, a word is either on the list or it is not; in a mental lexicon, the edges are fuzzy.

One way to describe these differences in how words are known is in terms of multiple vocabularies. A literate person has at least two vocabularies, a phonetic vocabulary for talking and listening and an orthographic vocabulary for reading and writing; an illiterate person, in contrast, has only the phonetic vocabulary.

Once this notion of multiple vocabularies is introduced, it is natural to ask how many there are. In addition to the distinction between spoken and written, is there not also a difference between input and output? Combining the two distinctions gives four vocabularies: a phonetic input vocabulary for listening, a phonetic output vocabulary for speaking, an orthographic input vocabulary for reading, and an orthographic output vocabulary for writing.

These are not trivial or unimportant distinctions. Neuropsychologists, who study patients with brain injuries that interfere with speech or language in various ways, claim that they need at least those four vocabularies to describe

Presumed signs of dyslexia such as mirror writing are often seen in the early stages of learning to write. Here Amanda, in preschool, mirror-writes her name and about "my blanket I love the best."

the clinical symptoms that they see. A type of disorder known as *dyslexia* can serve to illustrate how independent the different vocabularies are. Dyslexia denotes a reading difficulty; when it results from brain injury it is called acquired dyslexia to distinguish it from the apparently innate reading difficulties of certain children. Loss of the ability to read is known as *alexia*. Moreover, since many patients with acquired dyslexia also show *agraphia* (inability to spell or write), the more interesting cases for the present discussion are those designated as having alexia without agraphia. These patients can hold a conversation and they can write, but they read only with great difficulty.

Each clinical case has its own unique features that make generalization difficult, but studies of alexic patients have shown that their reading of letters is usually better than their reading of words. When asked to read a word, they may try to build it up from its letters in a slow and labored way. Shown the printed word *ball*, they might say aloud "B, A, L, L, . . . ball." How successful they are depends on how good they are at spelling. When shown handwritten words they have even more difficulty, because individual letters are harder to isolate and identify in cursive script than in printed form. Finally, when groups of letters are presented briefly, alexic patients have no greater success in reading words than in reading haphazard strings of letters or digits—no word-superiority effect is obtained. It might be possible to explain these symptoms as consequences of difficulty in recognizing letters, but a more plausible theory is that there is a particular area in the brain where visual word forms are stored and recognized. When that area is damaged, the patient tries to compensate for the loss with letter-by-letter spelling.

The converse of patients showing dyslexia without agraphia are those showing agraphia without dyslexia—patients showing impairments of the writing process without serious difficulties in speaking, listening, or reading. Lexical agraphia is probably the simplest form. In a language whose written form is regular, these patients may not be seriously handicapped, but in English, where a variety of spellings sometimes correspond to the same spoken

The Berlin Wall in its last days (December 1989) suggests the polyglot multiples that contemporary history can impose on the mental lexicon.

utterance, their difficulties are very noticeable. Patients afflicted in this way are not simply poor spellers; they can spell regular words and even nonwords perfectly well by relying on a nonlexical phonological route. It is only irregular spellings that give them trouble. Similar evidence argues for a distinction between input and output processes for spoken language; clinical neurology seems to provide evidence for at least four different vocabularies.

Four vocabularies may seem like a lot, but why stop there? Why not go on? Why not include tactile input and output vocabularies for those who read and write braille? Or telegraphic input and output vocabularies for those who send and receive Morse code? And that is only for one language. Someone who knows two languages could double the number, and someone who knows three could triple it. There is almost no limit to the number of vocabularies a determined polyglot might accumulate.

At this point a thoughtful reader will become uncomfortable with this way of describing the situation. A vocabulary is a large store of information: It contains tens of thousands of words, most of them with multiple meanings. Building just one vocabulary is a major learning task. Is it credible that some people would acquire dozens of these elaborate knowledge structures? And, if so, is there a separate vocabulary matrix for each one? How would polyglots make room in their heads for anything else?

Obviously, all these different vocabularies cannot be totally independent. Consider an analogy. Everyone knows that different signals can carry the same message. An acoustic signal corresponding to the spoken word *hello* is picked up by a microphone and transduced into an electronic signal; the signals are different, but the message remains invariant. A handwritten note is typed into a computer and transmitted to a remote computer screen; several different signals convey the same message. Are the different vocabularies that have been distinguished by neuropsychologists like that? Can they be regarded as little more than different collections of signals for transmitting the same messages?

A test of this analogy would be whether messages remain invariant under transformation from one kind of signal to another. In some cases, such invariance must obtain. A word as spoken and as heard cannot be associated with different meanings, if only because speakers hear their own speech: It would be totally confusing if, when you uttered *table*, you heard yourself saying something else. Or if, when you wrote *table*, you saw something different on the page. Input and output vocabularies must be closely related. Moreover, in languages that are written alphabetically, the spoken/heard "table" is related to the written/read *table* by well-learned rules of spelling. Literacy would be even harder to acquire than it is if *table* could be spelled by some arbitrary string of letters. Even people who know a second language do not have totally independent vocabularies: For someone who knows both English and Italian, *tàvola* and *table* will not be drastically different in meaning. And for a familiar English word like *table*, it seems safe to assume that the same set of meanings is associated with the spoken, heard, written, and read representations. The real ques-

Lexical Access and Positron Emission Tomography

Computerized tomography is the construction of a three-dimensional image of a bodily structure from a series of X-ray pictures. Positron emission tomography (PET) adds a measure of blood flow to this imaging technique. If a subject—patient, volunteer, animal—is given an intravenous injection containing a radioactive isotope, the resulting radiation can be recorded tomographically. As metabolism at a site increases, blood flow increases; as more blood flows to it, radiation from that site increases; as the radiation increases, it is registered on the tomographic image.

This technology has been used to study blood flow in the brain during simple verbal tasks. Volunteers received intravenous injec-tions of water that contained oxygen-15 (half-life 122 seconds). Then PET scans were taken for 40 seconds while the subjects stared at a fixation point (the control condi-tion) or while they passively listened to or looked at a series of familiar English nouns (the experi-mental condition). The effect of this passive perceptual processing on blood flow was estimated by subtracting the scans for the con-trol condition from the scans for the experimental condition.

Listening to words increased the blood flow in the primary au-ditory projection areas in both hemispheres and in the nearby temporoparietal areas in the left hemisphere. Looking at words increased activity in the primary visual projection area (the striate cortex) and in the nearby extrastriate cortex in both hemi-spheres, although more intensely in the left hemisphere. When sub-jects were asked to look at pairs of words and press a key if they rhymed, increased activity was observed in both the extrastriate and temporoparietal areas. These observations were consistent with the belief that the left temporopari-etal area is where auditory word-images are formed and the extrastriate area is where visual word-images are formed.

1
2
3
4
5
6
7

Primary auditory projection area

Temporoparietal area

Extrastriate cortex

Primary visual projection area (Striate cortex)

The left hemisphere of the human brain, locating the slices made by the PET scans pictured.

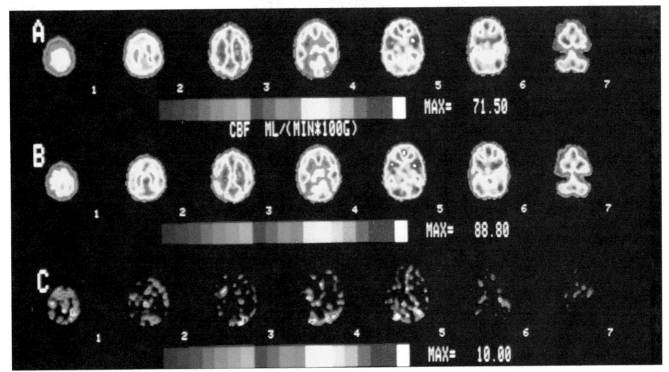

A subtraction procedure makes it possible, using PET scans, to identify brain areas related to lexical processing. Here, for example, the top row (A) shows the brain blood flow measured while the person viewed a fixation point (the control state). Each image is a slice through the brain, going from the top of the brain (slice 1) to the bottom (slice 7). The top of each slice is the anterior part of the brain and the bottom is the posterior. The middle row (B) shows the blood flow while the person looked at words that were presented at a rate of one per second (the experimental state). The bottom row (C) is obtained by subtracting the control images from the experimental images; the difference shows the change in blood flow induced by visual word presentation. It can be seen from slices 4 and 5 in row C that the peak response occurred in the posterior part of the brain, the visual input center.

tion is not how many vocabularies there are, but how so many different signals can all gain access to the same message.

In short, to speak loosely of multiple vocabularies can be misleading. Dyslexics do not lose the words they are unable to read; agraphics still know the words they cannot spell. Such patients are simply unable to gain access to what they know via the usual associations. What psycholinguists have in mind is a single lexical matrix with multiple ways of getting in and out of it.

Vocabulary Size

A lexical matrix is too large to imagine building totally new ones for each use. It is a sobering thought to realize how much lexical knowledge you have acquired. Some of it you know firmly, but a lot is known only at the level of recognition—and often held so tentatively that it might better be called lexical belief, rather than lexical knowledge. But it is obvious that you know a great deal. It is a challenging problem to estimate how much.

The standard procedure for estimating an individual's vocabulary size is to administer a multiple-choice test. Words are presented and the test-taker is asked to choose correct definitions from lists of four or five alternatives. Since the person being tested merely has to recognize the right defining phrase, the results of the test might be called the size of the person's reading vocabulary. The problem is to develop a test in such a way that the test score can be translated into an estimate of vocabulary size. Dictionary sampling is the popular method for achieving that result. The basic assumption (and the source of most of the disagreements among estimators) is that the number of words in the language is given by the number of words in a dictionary. For this basic assumption to be even marginally plausible, it is necessary to use the largest dictionary available.

Consider the following arithmetic. Suppose you start with a dictionary that contains 500,000 words. If you sample 500 of them at random to estimate the size of your friend's mental lexicon, then your sampling factor is 1,000. That is to say, for every word that your friend recognizes, you give credit for knowing 1,000 words that you might have sampled but did not. If your friend recognizes 100 of the 500 words, the estimated vocabulary size is 100 × 1,000, or 100,000 words. But note, however, that if you had started with a dictionary containing only 100,000 words, your friend would have to recognize every test word to achieve the same estimated size. The general rule is: The larger the dictionary on which your test is based, the larger the estimates that you are likely to obtain.

Since the size of the dictionary that you sample is so important, you might ask what the largest English dictionary is. The answer depends on when you ask—over the past four hundred years there has been a steady increase in the number of words that dictionaries contain.

Author/editor	Brief title	Date	Approximate number of words
Robert Cawdrey	*Table Alphabeticall*	1604	2,500
John Kersey	*New English Dictionary*	1702	28,000
Nathan Bailey	*Dictionarium Britannicum*	1730	48,000
Samuel Johnson	*Dictionary*	1755	40,000
Noah Webster	*American Dictionary*	1828	70,000
Noah Porter	*Dictionary of English, unabridged*	1864	114,000
William D. Whitney	*Century Dictionary*	1891	200,000
Isaac K. Funk	*New Standard Dictionary*	1913	450,000
James A. H. Murray	*Oxford English Dictionary*	1928	400,000
William A. Neilson	*Webster's New International*	1934	600,000
Philip B. Gove	*Webster's Third New International*	1961	450,000

If you extrapolate this growth, it rapidly approaches infinity, taking the sampling factor with it. Fortunately, the number seems to have leveled off in the twentieth century at around half a million words. But your friend may still know some perfectly acceptable words that are not on a list of 500,000.

Another hazard for such estimates is that, even after you have chosen the largest dictionary you can find, you still have to estimate how many words it contains. You might think that you could rely on the publisher's claims. For example, the dust jacket of one best-selling collegiate dictionary says that it has "almost 160,000 entries and 200,000 definitions." But remember, this is advertising, and most customers think that more is better. So take a look inside. This particular dictionary has 1,373 pages, which should work out to 160,000/1,373 = 115 entries per page. If you sample a few pages at random, however, you will find only 50 to 60 headwords per page. (A headword, sometimes called the main entry, is the uninflected form, or citation form, that identifies the entry and is used to place it in alphabetical order with other entries.) Where are the rest of the entries? They are there, but you have to read the headword entries to find them because the "160,000 entries" are not all headwords. In this case, there are about 71,000 headwords. To get the count up to 160,000 you have to count as a word everything that is printed in boldface. For example, inside the entry alphabetized under the headword **obfuscate** are the inflected forms **obfuscating** and **obfuscated** and also the run-on (appended) derivatives **obfuscation** and **obfuscatory**.

This format may be a good way to publish and advertise a dictionary, but think what it does to the person who wants to sample its entries in order to

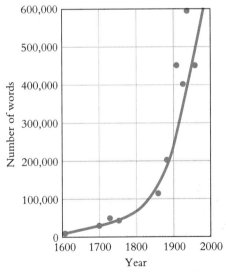

The size of large English dictionaries has grown exponentially over the past four hundred years, indicating how questionable it is to assume that the number of words in the English language is given by the number of words in any particular English dictionary.

construct a vocabulary test. If the dictionary is assumed to contain 160,000 words, then the test will be counting all five forms of *obfuscate* as separate words. Most test makers have recognized that the dictionary's operational definition of "word" was not what they had in mind when they set out to estimate how many words people know.

In short, what seem on the surface to be straightforward questions—How many words are there? How many words does the average person know?—turn out, on closer inspection, to be rather complicated. And the ultimate complication—that some words have many different meanings—has not yet been mentioned. It is a curious fact that the most familiar words tend to have the most meanings; people perversely persist in using most frequently those polysemous words most likely to be ambiguous. Should polysemy be taken into account in estimating vocabulary size? The word *press*, for example, has dozens of meanings, both as a noun and as a verb. Does it count no more than, say, *press agent*, which has only one meaning?

Faced by such problems, vocabulary estimators have been forced to make some arbitrary decisions. Suppose the question is slightly rephrased: not "How many words does the average person know?" but rather, "How many words has the average person learned?" That is to say, some expert looks at every root word and asks, "If you learned this word, what other related words would you probably understand?" The answer would define as "one word" an entire family of words that, according to the judge's lexical intuition, people come to understand when they master the central word of the family. For example, *obfuscate* would count as one word, not five.

What kinds of decisions would such a judge need to make? Some of them are easy. A person who speaks English should not have to learn inflected forms as if they were totally new words; if you know *book*, for example, you should also know *books* and *book's*. But what about derivatives and compounds? Most derivatives formed with such regular affixes as #*ness* or #*ly* can be understood in context if the stem is understood, but derivatives formed with morpheme boundaries should be considered one by one. For example, consider some of the problems with the #*er* suffix. A person who has learned *run* will understand *runner*, but a person who has learned *walk* could easily miss one sense of *walker*, and a person who has learned *tell* will not understand *teller* at all. So knowing *run* and *runner* would count as knowing one word, knowing *walk* and *walker* could count as either one or two, and knowing *tell* and *teller* should count as two. By such a criterion, most compounds count as new words—it is a characteristic feature of compound words that their compound meaning is not given by the meanings of their parts, although sometimes it is possible to guess what the coiner had in mind.

At the University of Illinois, William Nagy and Richard Anderson went through a list of 227,553 different words using this learning criterion. According to their count, the list contained 45,453 headwords. They judged that 139,020 of the remaining 182,100 derivative and compound forms could be understood in context by someone who knew their root forms, but that 42,080

Notable Lexicographers of English: Samuel Johnson

It is sometimes assumed that a good dictionary of a language should contain all the words in that language. No English dictionary meets that requirement—it is not even obvious that the number of English words is finite. And it was certainly not the intention of the great lexicographers of English to create an archive for every word that has been or could be uttered. Their goals were ambitious, but not THAT ambitious.

The most famous English lexicographer was Dr. Samuel Johnson (1709–1784), the poet, essayist, literary critic, and conversationalist. In 1746 Johnson, always in need of money, signed a contract for the *Dictionary of the English Language*. The following year he published his *Plan of a Dictionary of the English Language*, which was addressed to Lord Chesterfield in hope of enlisting support for the project. It was a well-reasoned plan, showing familiarity with the best lexicographic practices of the day. He discussed criteria for including words and set his policies for dealing with spelling, pronunciation (by the use of rhyming words), morphology, contexts, and idiomatic expressions. And he planned to hire experts to include encyclopedic material in some entries.

Samuel Johnson.

Johnson hoped that his dictionary would serve to "fix" the English language in a pure state—a project that he knew Chesterfield favored. But to no avail. Chesterfield soon lost interest. Lacking financial support, many of Johnson's plans proved too ambitious for one man to implement.

The *Dictionary* was published in 1755, after nine years of prodigious effort. The work is so important in the history of English lexicography that it is often cited as the first to have had this or that feature. But Johnson was not an innovator. There is no ingredient of his *Dictionary* that had not been introduced already by other lexicographers. Johnson simply did the standard things better than they had ever been done before. His spellings were traditional, his treatment of pronunciation was as sketchy as that of other dictionaries, and his etymologies were uncertain, but his definitions were lucid gems, illustrated by a choice of literary quotations drawn from his own vast scholarship. By illustrating every sense with quotations from great authors, he hoped to preserve "the wells of English undefiled" to serve as a permanent standard of good writing.

Today, Johnson's *Dictionary* is remembered mostly for a few highly quotable definitions. His famous definition of *lexicographer* as a harmless drudge was certainly modest. And his definition of *oats* as a grain that in England is generally given to horses, but in Scotland supports the people, was, he later confessed, meant to vex the Scots. At the time Johnson's *Dictionary* appeared, however, it was unequaled, and for more than a century it remained the most authoritative dictionary in English. But even Dr. Johnson's great prestige was not enough to halt the irresistible process of linguistic change.

were semantically opaque. To master the complete list of 227,553 different words, then, a student would have to learn 45,453 + 42,080 = 88,533 word families. The Illinois team went on to ask how many of these 88,533 lexical elements most people know. They estimated that the average high school graduate knows about 45,000 of them.

The Illinois estimate is conservative. It excludes proper names, numbers, foreign words, acronyms, and many undecomposable compound words that occur regularly in newspapers. If these were included, the average high school graduate would probably be found to have learned some 60,000 different "words." Superior students, because they do more reading, would probably know twice that many.

It is not worth arguing over these numbers, however, because so many subjective and intangible factors contributed to the estimates. Shouldn't there be some more objective way to decide which words are learned together and can be regarded as a family?

Retrieval from the Mental Lexicon

If you are a good reader, as your eyes skim along the lines of print, you set in motion a sequence of complex interpretive processes whose outcome is the conscious appreciation of meaning. Fortunately for you, but unfortunately for linguistic scientists, the information processing required to produce that awareness does not clutter your mind or obscure the meaning. The process is simply unavailable to introspection. To build a picture of what is going on behind the scenes, it is necessary to make inferences on the basis of the performance itself or to conduct psychological experiments designed to choose among different hypotheses.

Anyone who considers such matters in detail, however, quickly realizes that recognizing the words is a critical component of the reading process. It is easy to see how that part of the process could be studied experimentally: Simply flash the words and see how long an exposure is required to read them. When Cattell tried it he found that words can be read much faster than nonwords, and his discovery was generalized to the principle that the more familiar a word is, the less time people need to recognize it.

A variety of techniques have been used to demonstrate that familiarity breeds speed, but perhaps the most popular is the lexical decision task. People are asked to indicate as rapidly as possible whether or not a string of letters spells an English word. Subjects do not have to say what word it is or what it means—just "Yes, it is a word," or "No, it is not a word." The reaction time is the time between the instant that the word appears and the instant that people answer yes or no. (Reaction times for mistaken responses are discarded.)

Notable Lexicographers of English: Webster and Worcester

*W*hereas Samuel Johnson hoped to "fix" the language, the goal for Noah Webster (1758–1843) was to replace Johnson's *Dictionary* as the American standard. Webster first became famous for his blue-backed speller, *The American Spelling Book* (1783), which sold more copies than any other schoolbook that had ever been published.

Webster had no respect for Johnson. He criticized Johnson's choice of words, simplified his spellings, decided that literary citations are unnecessary (he made up his own examples), and vigorously pressed his claim that American English needed its own dictionary. Webster's attempt to fill that need, his two-volume *American Dictionary of the English Language*, was published in 1828. Historians have judged it a minor contribution to lexicography that would have disappeared had it not been actively promoted and heavily revised by its publishers.

Two years later, when the more conservative lexicographer Joseph Emerson Worcester (1784–1865) published his *Comprehensive Pronouncing and Explanatory Dictionary of the English Language*, a battle began. Webster and Worcester were natural antagonists. The brash Webster, contemptuous of tradition and proudly American,

Noah Webster.

was associated with Yale; the scholarly Worcester, who admired British lexicography, was associated with Harvard. But the real "war of the dictionaries" was the commercial rivalry between their publishers. Webster's publishers eventually won by commissioning a German philologist to rewrite Webster's etymologies in light of the recent growth of linguistic knowledge in Europe. In 1864 their new dictionary appeared and rapidly gained international fame—ironically beating Worcester at his own conservative game.

The lexical decision task consistently shows faster response times for high-frequency, high-familiarity words—as expected. An early finding that was not expected, however, was that people respond faster to homographs than to nonhomographs. That is to say, words like *crane* or *chest* that have more than one sense were recognized as words slightly faster than equally familiar words like *neighbor* or *cliff* that have only one sense. Indeed, the more meanings a word has, the faster it is recognized as a word. Even though subjects are not asked to identify the word or think of its meaning(s), they obviously cannot prevent themselves from doing so, since the variety of meanings influences the test results. The natural inference is that a homograph is really two or more entries in the mental lexicon and that the response time is the time it takes to find any one of them.

To illustrate how this task can be used to probe into the workings of the mental lexicon, consider an experiment in which native speakers and readers of Serbo-Croatian (the principal language of Yugoslavia) made rapid lexical decisions about inflected singular nouns in three cases: nominative, dative/locative, and instrumental. Serbo-Croatian has a complex case system, in that there is no simple relation between the form of the affix and the case that it marks. Some cases, moreover, are used more frequently than others. For example, the feminine noun *frula* (flute) occurs 31 percent of the time in the nominative case (written *frula*), 10 percent of the time in the dative/locative case (both are written *fruli*), and less than 1 percent of the time in the instrumental case (written *frulom*). So it is possible to ask the following question: Does the familiarity effect for Serbo-Croatian nouns depend on the stem frequency or on the frequency of the inflected form? It was found that the nominative form could be recognized as a word slightly (but significantly) faster than could the dative/locative or the instrumental forms, but there was no difference in response times between the dative/locative and the instrumental.

What could this mean? Consider one possible hypothesis, derived from the morpheme-based theory of morphology described in Chapter 6. Suppose that the mental lexicon contains only a list of morphemes and that words containing two or more morphemes cannot be looked up, but must be synthesized on the fly, so to speak. Then the nominative singular noun *frula* must be synthesized out of the root *frul* and the suffix *-a*. Since *frul* is shared by all cases, the activation threshold for *frul* cannot explain why the nominative singular is recognized faster than are the other forms. So the difference must be attributable to the suffix *-a*. But that is improbable, because *-a* has that effect only when it is used to mark the nominative case. So the morpheme-based hypothesis can be dismissed. The mental lexicon must contain more than a list of morphemes.

A subtler method for exploring the role of morphology in lexical organization involves a variation of the lexical decision task known as repetition priming. If a word or nonword is presented twice (with an intervening lag), the second lexical decision time will be faster than the first. It is assumed that the first presentation (the prime) facilitates the decision on the second presenta-

Notable Lexicographers of English: James Murray

James Murray's goal was to establish the histories of English words by arranging literary quotations in chronological order. In 1857 Richard Trent presented a proposal for such a dictionary to the Philological Society, which decided to sponsor *A New English Dictionary on Historical Principles.* Temporary editors began the task, and a network of volunteer readers was assembled to contribute quotations. But the real work did not begin until 1879, when Murray (1837–1915) was persuaded to become the editor.

He worked diligently, and by 1884 the first volume had been published. To speed the work, three more editors were eventually added, but the final volume did not appear until 1928. By that time what had come to be called the *Oxford English Dictionary* contained 240,000 headwords and 400,000 entries, filled 15,487 large pages, and was based on a file of more than 5,000,000 quotations. Not only were sense divisions precise and detailed, with clear definitions, but the history of every sense was documented with quotations. The etymologies were the best that existed up to that time. The wonder is not that it took fifty years to complete, but that it was ever completed at all.

James A. H. Murray.

Although he edited the largest English dictionary, it is clear that Murray had no ambition to include all the words of English. Vulgar words were excluded, and the growing vocabularies of science, technology, commerce, and indus-

try were largely omitted—all in keeping with the nineteenth century's conception of good taste. But the goal that Murray and his companions set for themselves— the creation of a valid historical record—was achieved in a manner that evoked such adjectives as "monumental," "massive," "indispensable," and "without parallel." Perhaps the magnitude of the task was best described by Murray himself in his presidential address to the Philological Society:

Only those who have made the experiment know the bewilderment with which editor or subeditor, after he has apportioned the quotations for such a word as *above* . . . among 20, 30 or 40 groups, and furnished each of these with a provisional definition, spreads them out on a table or on the floor where he can obtain a general survey of the whole, and spends hour after hour in shifting them about like pieces on a chess-board, striving to find in the fragmentary evidence of an incomplete historical record, such a sequence of meanings as may form a logical chain of development. . . . Those who think that such work can be hurried, or that anything can accelerate it, except more brain power brought to bear on it, had better try.

tion (the target), and the size of the difference is taken as the priming effect. For example, when the singular dative/locative form of the feminine Serbo-Croatian noun *rupi* (hole) was repeated, the second lexical decision time was 90 milliseconds shorter than the first. When the prime was changed to the nominative form *rupa*, the priming effect on *rupi* was 79 milliseconds. And when the instrumental *rupom* was used as a prime, the priming effect was 69 milliseconds. Regular inflected forms of the same word do prime each other, indicating that there is a close association among them.

The results in English are even stronger: Inflected words prime their uninflected forms just as well as the uninflected forms prime themselves. This result provides objective support for the intuitive impression that someone who has learned, say, *pour* or *burn* does not have to learn *pours* or *burned* as separate words. The vocabulary estimators are right in counting all the inflected forms as a single entry in the mental lexicon.

But what about derivative words? The vocabulary estimators seem to have been on the right track there, too. For example, the inflected form *manages* and the derivative forms *manager* and *management* all facilitate a subsequent recognition of *manage* as much as *manage* facilitates itself. By contrast, repetition priming does not occur between morphologically unrelated words whose initial letters coincide; for example, *cancel* does not prime *can*.

In general, therefore, the results of experiments using repetition priming with a lexical decision task support the general idea that morphologically related words are stored together in the mental lexicon. Activate any member of a morphological family and all the others are ready to spring into action. Moreover, these effects are not limited to reading printed words—the same kinds of results have been obtained with auditory priming, although the temporal duration of the priming effect seems to be shorter. Experts still argue over details, but the general conclusion has been that the organization of the mental lexicon reflects the way different morphological forms are learned together.

Those who want to estimate vocabulary size in terms of the number of root words that must be learned in order to understand all the different but morphologically related words can take comfort from this picture. But they should not overlook the fact that lumping all morphologically related forms together as a single word in a single lexical entry leaves the psycholinguist with a very unappealing characterization of the entries in the mental lexicon. What use is a lexical entry that fails to differentiate inflected and derived forms? It cannot be assigned to any single syntactic category. It cannot be used in the statement of morphological or syntactic rules. It cannot be associated with any single definition. And how differences in the familiarity of the different forms are to be registered is left a mystery.

In the end, therefore, a theorist is driven back to the conception of the mental lexicon as a lengthy list of individual words, not a collection of undifferentiated word families. But on top of this lengthy list there must be an elaborate network of morphological associations among words. When a word is used—activated—the activation spreads over this network of morphological associations. Words are not only associated with meanings. They are associated with one another.

■   ■   ■

It is a general observation that the human brain seems to have more storage capacity than computing power, so the idea of storing separately every form of every word may not be too outrageous. But it is a puzzle to understand why the brain stops where it does. When people encounter a new word they list it in their mental lexicons and associate it with its morphological relatives, but when a new, regular syntactic phrase is heard, it is not listed in memory. Presumably there comes a point when even the vast storage capacity of the human brain can no longer cope with the exponential principle.

▲ In James Murray's Scriptorium, built in his back garden, the first edition of the Oxford English Dictionary (OED) took shape. More than half of the 44-year project, which drew on a file documenting word usage in over five million quotations, was his own work.

▶ This entry (for abaptistan, an obsolete instrument for cranial surgery) in Murray's hand was for the first installment (A-ANT) of the OED, published in 1884.

Word Meanings

*L*isten to someone speaking a language you do not know. You hear an unsung song, ever changing, rising and falling, occasionally illuminated by flashes of feeling. The sounds themselves are little more than vocal noises. If there are words, you cannot disentangle them; if there is a message, you cannot understand it. Interest evaporates. You might as well stare at a brick wall.

Now listen to a good friend. It is the same kind of vocalization, but you cannot hear it in the same way. The noises are there, but they are totally transparent. Your mind passes right through the sounds, through the words, through the sentences, and into the mind of your friend. Your experience is totally different.

The difference, of course, is meaning. Phoneticians and telephone engineers may be able to ignore it, but to an average person meaning is crucial. It is meaning that makes language useful. Without meaning, assertions are noise, promises are empty, threats are ignored, warnings go unheeded, questions cannot be answered. And meaning is not something subtle. To appreciate meaning differs from hearing noise as waking differs from sleeping. The difference between meaning and nonsense is—must be—a major dimension in any serious account of human experience.

Many psychological processes work together in the comprehension of language. Understanding the words is only a part of an enormously complex and important phenomenon. But it is a necessary part, one that lays the foundation for understanding larger linguistic units. In the preceding pages the word forms themselves, the physical utterances and inscriptions, have held center stage. But utterances and inscriptions are like labels on file folders; you need them to organize your filing system and to retrieve information from it, but in and of themselves they tell you very little. When you pull the file, however, the meaning of its label opens up.

Semantics

The academic name for the study of meaning is semantics. It is not an easy subject, and beginning students can be misled because two different intellectual enterprises go by that name. One is philosophical semantics, dignified and inscrutable; its goal is to formulate a general theory of meaning. The second is lexical semantics, grungy and laborious; its goal is to record meanings that have been lexicalized in particular languages. The concern here is with lexical semantics, but something must be said about philosophical semantics, if only to explain why the high road has not been taken.

A philosophical theory of meaning is an attempt to give an adequate characterization of the word *mean* and related terms—as they are used, for example, in such expressions as "*Circumvent* means to get around something," or "*Zebra* refers to (denotes, signifies) a kind of horse with stripes." That is to say, an adequate theory should provide an explicit and logically coherent account of what you are saying about a linguistic expression when you specify its meaning. Many different philosophical theories of meaning have been proposed, but for every theory there is a list of problems that it either fails to solve or fails to treat.

A theory of meaning that once enjoyed considerable popularity holds that there are two kinds of meanings, extensional and intensional. The extensional meaning of a word is whatever it can be used to refer to: The extension of the word *chair*, for example, is all the chairs there are; the extension of the word *gold* is all the gold there is. The intensional meaning of a word is whatever determines its extension: The intensions of *chair* and *gold* are the sets of conditions something must satisfy to be included in their extensions. Thus, to know the meaning of a word is to know its intension: To know the meaning of *chair* is to be able to recognize chairs; or, more technically, to know the meaning of *gold* is to know the conditions under which the sentence *This object is gold* would make a true statement. Knowing the meaning of an expression is thus a matter of knowing the truth conditions for its use.

This way of talking about meaning seems plausible until you realize that many words—indeed, the very words that are most used—*the, of, and,* and so forth—must be meaningless because they have no extensions. One response to this objection is suggested by the fact that these overworked particles come to life only when they are used in sentences. Perhaps the domain of linguistic meaning should be limited to sentences, and any claims that isolated words can have meanings should be dropped. This tactic would make it possible to say something like this: The meaning of sentence S is the set of conditions—the individually necessary and jointly sufficient conditions—under which the statement that S makes would be true. Since isolated words are neither true nor false, they acquire meaning only insofar as they participate in meaningful sentences. Although unattractive to anyone who thinks that isolated words can be interesting, this approach does confer certain advantages, and its theoretical consequences have been explored in detail. Of course, it poses a puzzle about questions and commands, which do not make statements and so cannot be either true or false, but that oddity can be shrugged off as a problem of sentence use, not sentence meaning.

Unfortunately, however, the theory does not escape a second objection: that truth and meaning are not so closely related. To return to the example of *gold,* many people who use this word successfully in discussions of finance, dentistry, or jewelry are totally unable to determine, in any particular instance, whether or not the statement made by the sentence *This object is gold* is true or false. That determination is work for a metallurgist. In short, it is possible to understand the meaning of a sentence without knowing its truth conditions.

Philosophical semantics is a serious business. Some of the best minds of Western civilization have struggled with it, and their failure to come up with a satisfactory definition of meaning stands as a worrisome warning to scientists trying to understand human understanding. So worrisome, in fact, that some behavioral psychologists have abandoned the notion of meaning entirely. A less radical possibility is to retain the notion of meaning, but to abandon the philosophical approach to it—to turn instead to less ambitious brands of semantics.

Relational Semantics

Sentences are not the only contexts that can endow individual words with meaning. A different way to think about such matters was suggested by the German psychologist Karl Bühler, who proposed a "field-theoretical" approach to language. In 1934, before Hitler's invasion dislodged him from his professorship at the University of Vienna and sent him to the United States,

Some Philosophical Semanticists

hilosophical interest in meaning has ancient roots, but the modern history of philosophical semantics begins with the English philosopher John Locke (1632–1704). In 1690 Locke, in his *Essay Concerning Human Understanding*, argued that words are the "sensible" (tangible) marks of ideas—the meaning of a word is the idea that speakers have when they use it and that listeners have when they hear it. For Locke, ideas arose from perception, so perception provided the necessary and sufficient conditions for determining a word's meaning. The theory seemed to work for words that refer to concrete things, but not for abstract or imageless words. How Locke's approach should be qualified or extended became a recurrent question for the next two hundred years of British empiricism.

In the twentieth century, philosophical semantics became increasingly logical. In 1892 the German mathematician and philosopher Gottlob Frege (1848–1925) published a seminal article distinguishing between a word's reference (denotation or extension) and its sense (meaning or intension). Two expressions can refer to the same thing, yet have different meanings: *George Washington* and

John Locke.

the first American president, for example. Or an expression can have a sense without referring to anything: *unicorn,* or *the present king of France.* Frege emphasized that the idea aroused by a word should not be confused with its reference or its sense—no one can know what ideas another person has, but denotations and meanings are determinable.

In 1905 the English philosopher Bertrand Russell (1872–1970) put forward a theory of denotation

in which he argued that a denoting phrase by itself—*a man,* for example—means nothing, although when it is used in a statement—*She met a man*—it acquires a definite meaning. This approach, now known as Russell's theory of definite descriptions, moved questions of meaning from words to statements, with the advantage that formal logic can be applied to statements. But the way Russell applied it—especially to such examples as *The present king of France is bald*—stirred heated debate. Russell claimed that *The present king of France is bald* must be false; many of his critics claimed that it is neither true nor false because it fails to make a statement at all.

Logic introduces questions of truth, and truth is no easier to define than meaning is. In 1931 the Polish logician Alfred Tarski (1902–1983) read a paper on the concept of truth before the Warsaw Scientific Society. Tarski claimed that a formally correct definition of "true sentence" depends in an essential way on the particular language under consideration. He proposed a definition for such formalized languages as logic or mathematics, but concluded that natural language, by its very nature, does not permit a consistent

Bertrand Russell.

with the meaning of ordinary language and the many perplexities it creates for philosophers. In his posthumous *Philosophical Investigations*, Wittgenstein argued that to know the meaning of a word is to be able to use it in the conventional way. The word *game*, for example, denotes a variety of activities that are classed together, not because of any feature common to them all, but because they share a family resemblance. He likened meaning to a thread spun from many fibers: "The strength of the thread does not reside in the fact that some one fiber runs through its whole length, but in the overlapping of many fibers."

Some ordinary-language philosophers attempted to pursue Wittgenstein's claim that major philosophical questions can be dissolved by avoiding traps inherent in their own habits of speech. It was in this spirit that John Austin in 1955 visited Harvard University from Oxford to lecture about performative verbs and speech acts, and H. P. Grice followed in 1967 to argue that the alleged divergences of formal logic from ordinary language can be dispelled if adequate attention is given to social conventions governing the conversational use of language.

Ludwig Wittgenstein.

use of the expression "true sentence." Tarski phrased the traditional correspondence theory of truth in the general form: "*It is snowing*" *is a true sentence if and only if it is snowing*, then showed how it leads to the Liar's Paradox: "*This is a false sentence*" *is a true sentence if and only if it is a false sentence.*

The ordinary-language philosophers took a different tack. As a young man, the Austrian-born philosopher Ludwig Wittgenstein (1889–1951) made important contributions to the logical analysis of meaning, but in his later years he became increasingly concerned

Bühler wrote *Sprachtheorie: Die Darstellungsfunktion der Sprache (Language Theory: The Representational Function of Language),* an uneven but fascinating book that is full of original insights. Bühler saw language as having two components: the words and the structures, or fields, in which words are arranged. A word achieves its full meaning, its field value, by its location in a field.

Bühler supported his theory by examples, rather than experiments, which results in some oversimplification of his ideas. He compared words, for instance, to the printed signs of musical notes; in isolation they signify nothing, but when those same signs are placed relative to five horizontal lines, they achieve their meanings. Similarly, isolated names of cities, rivers, or mountains say very little until they are placed on a geographical map. The coordinates of the map provide a field within which the words are related to one another. In that field, therefore, the words take on meaning.

Bühler distinguished two kinds of fields that serve to relate words, a pointing field and a symbolic-syntactic field. The pointing field is helpful in understanding the meaning of such words as *you, here,* or *now,* which refer to different things when used by different people in different places at different times. All natural languages are studded with such words—Bühler called them deictic or pointing words—which are clearly meaningful, yet have no constant denotation, no fixed extension. Deictic words achieve their full meaning and significance in terms of the concrete situation, or deictic field, in which they are used.

But there is also a symbolic-syntactic field. To Bühler, the basic field structure of language is the sentence; individual words do not achieve their full meanings until they are located in such structures. The word *line,* for example, takes different meanings in the different sentences *He drew her a line* and *He threw her a line.* And the sentence *He threw her a line* takes different meanings in the different fields of boating and courtship. Bühler recognized that grasping the syntactic relations among words is a necessary part of understanding the meaning of a sentence. The meaning of *They are flying planes,* for example, is different depending on whether *flying* is taken as a modifier or as a verb. Bühler emphasized structural relations. Even his truth is a relational truth, determined by the correspondence between relations in the sentence and relations in the situation or event being referred to.

Bühler's approach can be called a relational theory of semantics, but there is one glaring omission. He fails to discuss lexical fields. In their 1963 book, *Symbol Formation,* the developmental psychologists Heinz Werner and Bernard Kaplan noted this gap and proposed to add a third field, which they called a lexical-conceptual field, to Bühler's deictic field of pointing and his symbolic-syntactic field. In isolation, most nondeictic, open-class words—which is to say, most words—are not as empty of meaning as are deictic words, nor are they as fully meaningful as when they are used in grammatical sentences. The word *line* can take different meanings in different sentences, but there are limits to its versatility; setting aside nonce usages, even a noun as polysemous as *line* cannot refer to as many different things as can the demonstrative pronoun *that.* There are lexical-conceptual constraints on the meaning of *line,* and a semantic theory must take them into acccount.

All three fields contribute to meaning by providing structures within which words can be located. The major difference is that deictic and syntactic fields are observable in a way that lexical-conceptual fields are not. A speaker can provide deictic and syntactic cues for a listener, but the lexical-conceptual structure—the knowledge of words and their meanings that is sometimes called the mental lexicon—must already be in place in the long-term memory of the listener. And because they are internalized, a scientist must analyze the structures of lexical-conceptual fields indirectly, by inferences based on observations of the contribution that words make to the meanings of larger expressions. Insofar as they are known, those lexical memory structures are the subject of this and the next three chapters.

In this book, the lexical-conceptual field is represented as a matrix, a hypothetical array in which each word form heads a separate column and each word meaning heads a separate row. An entry in a cell of the matrix means that the word form in that column can, in an appropriate context, express the word meaning in that row (see Chapter 2). Thus far, the lexical matrix has been regarded as a phonological-morphological system of word forms whose meanings have been of interest only insofar as a change of meaning signaled a distinctive feature of the word forms. Now it is necessary to shift perspective and look at the matrix as a semantic system of lexicalized concepts whose phonetic or orthographic forms are of interest only insofar as they serve as pointers to the meanings under discussion. In box-and-arrow terms, the shift is from the Word Forms box to the Word Meanings box. This new perspective reveals another complex network of relations—the semantic relations, which are every bit as intricate as the relations among word forms.

How can this complex network of meanings be analyzed? One way, a way most people are familiar with, is exemplified by dictionary definitions. A dictionary definition is a prime example of giving meaning to a word by locating it relative to the meanings of other words. The rationale behind this lexicographic strategy is worth examining.

Definitions

To think seriously about a lexical matrix, it is necessary to have some definite idea of what a row of the matrix stands for. So, the first problem that must be solved is how to talk about meanings. Word forms as column heads pose no great problem; everyone speaks, hears, writes, or reads word forms constantly. But word meanings as row heads are intangible and difficult to characterize.

Begin with the relatively innocuous assumption that a word meaning is a concept of some kind. Not just any concept can serve to head a row of the lexical matrix, of course. Only a tiny fraction of the limitless variety of con-

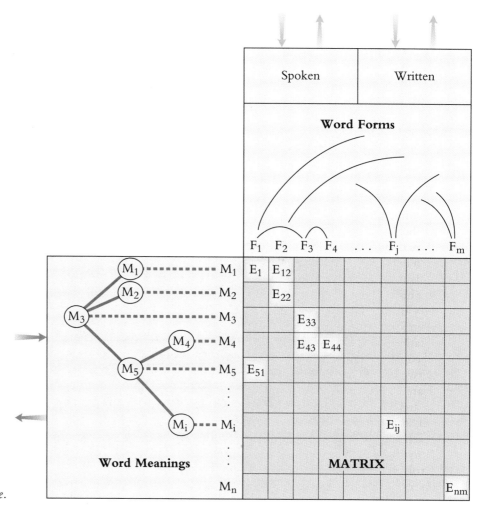

The lexical matrix maps between word forms and word meanings, both of which have their own complex internal structure.

cepts that the human mind can entertain have been deemed of sufficient generality, permanency, and social value to merit lexicalization. These selected concepts are mental elements that stand in various semantic relations to nonlinguistic referents and to one another. But to define word meanings as lexicalized concepts merely shifts the question from "What is a meaning?" to "What is a concept?" No easy answer commands universal agreement, for much about the fundamental nature of concepts is not yet understood. But a few things can be said.

If the lexical-conceptual field is thought of as a kind of mental structure—a mental coordinate system within which lexical concepts are located—then the place to begin an exploration of it is with the relations among lexical concepts. These semantic relations are relatively accessible, in the sense that people can understand questions about them and agree about the answers. By patiently collecting these relations, therefore, it is possible to sketch the general outlines of this structure, much as a cartographer constructs a map by patiently collecting distances and angles between landmarks.

Two kinds of semantic relations are usually distinguished, denotative relations and sense relations. Consider first the denotative (or referential) semantic relations. Concepts do not simply float about freely; a concept must be a concept OF something. In the simplest case, it will be a concept of something familiar: a shoe, for example. The relation between a shoe and the concept of a shoe is usually said to be one of representation; the concept is a mental representation of the physical thing. (This notion of mental representation has worried some philosophical semanticists, but their misgivings need not be reviewed here.)

Where do words come in? For English-speaking people, the word *shoe* can be used to express the mental concept of a shoe. As a consequence, the word *shoe* stands in a denotative semantic relation to a certain class of physical objects. The only connection between physical shoes and the word *shoe* is the one created by this relation by means of a mental representation. In these simple cases, therefore, a word's meaning can be said to be the concept, the mental representation, of the word's extension.

A second kind of semantic relation, a sense (or purely linguistic) relation, holds between lexicalized concepts. For example, the meanings of *shoe* and *footwear* are related; a shoe is one kind of footwear. The most familiar sense relations are synonymy and antonymy, which play important roles in definitions and so are often noted explicitly in dictionaries. Linguistic semanticists call the semantic relation between *footwear* and *shoe* hyponymy (from *hypo* under + *nym* name); *shoe* is a hyponym of *footwear*. Hyponymy plays an important role in the definitions of nouns.

This raises another question. What is a definition? Definitions play an important role in any theory of meaning, but a definition is not a meaning; meanings are concepts in the minds of people, whereas definitions are written by lexicographers. You might say that definitions play the same role in a theory of lexical knowledge that meanings play in the mind of a knower. Just as the meaning of *shoe* is a mental representation of shoes, so a definition of *shoe* is a lexicographer's theory of that mental representation. An ostensive definition of *shoe* can be given by simply pointing to some instances, but a lexicographic definition must be a verbal description, given in terms of semantic relations. For example, the definition *a kind of footwear, usually made of leather with a stiff sole and heel* states a lexicographer's theory of the lexicalized concept *shoe* by locating it relative to a string of other lexicalized concepts.

It is usually assumed that, if the lexicographer got it right, a dictionary definition will communicate a new concept to someone who has never encountered it before. But that assumption sets the lexicographer a difficult task. Fortunately, definitions can play an important role even when they are not

lexical
concept

representation   meaning

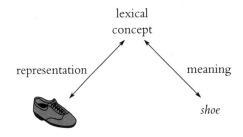

shoe

a kind of footwear, usually made of leather, with a stiff sole and heel

description   definition

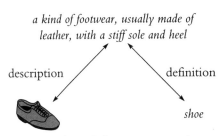

shoe

A lexicographer's definition is assumed to play the same role in a theory of lexical knowledge that a word meaning plays in the mind of a person.

adequate for teaching new meanings. Definitions can help someone learn a new term for a familiar concept, or refine a concept they already have, or discover a relation between concepts. But as long as theorists remain uncertain about the nature of concepts, the lexicographer will remain uncertain about the best way to help people construct new ones.

A distinction can be helpful here: A theory of lexical knowledge can be constructive, or it can be merely differential. In a constructive theory, the theoretical representation contains (or should contain) sufficient information to support an accurate construction of the concept. In a differential theory, on the other hand, meanings can be represented by any symbols that enable a theorist to distinguish among them—in principle, numbers could serve, for example. The requirements of a differential theory are much more easily satisfied.

In the differential case, a definition is merely a label that enables a theorist to designate the particular lexicalized concept under discussion. It can be assumed that a person reading the definition has already acquired the concept and will use the gloss merely to identify it. A single word is often sufficient. Someone who knows, say, that *fast* can mean either to go for an extended period of time without food or accomplishment in an unusually short period of time will be able to pick out the intended meaning with no more help than *abstain* or *rapid*. That is to say, the synonym sets { *fast, abstain*} and { *fast, rapid*} are adequately unambiguous designators of the meanings that these words can express. The synonyms serve to locate lexical concepts relative to other lexical concepts. (The curly brackets, { and }, will be used to surround sets of synonyms that serve to identify lexicalized concepts.)

Of course, dictionaries are sometimes used by learners who have not already mastered the concept in question, but who hope to construct it from information in the definition. In this age of communication, even young children know that unfamiliar words should be looked up in a dictionary. To accommodate such users, lexicographers must add more than a disambiguating synonym. They must include a phrasal definition (and sometimes excerpts illustrating usage) from which they hope a reader can induce the intended concept.

Expanded glosses can be very helpful, but they can also be baffling or misleading. Lexicographers who try to write them tread a narrow path. On the one hand, precision may require terminology more difficult to understand than the word being defined. Anyone so innocent as to need to look up the meaning of *fox,* for example, can hardly be expected to understand *carnivorous mammal* in its definition. On the other hand, if a definition is phrased in terms that innocent users are sure to know, there is a risk of misunderstanding: The most familiar words are also the most polysemous, and words with multiple meanings always run the risk of misinterpretation. As a cautionary tale when you next go to a dictionary to learn the meaning of some unfamiliar word, remember the little girl who looked up *erode,* found a definition that looked familiar—*to eat out, eat away*—and wrote "Our family erodes a lot." A lexicographer tries, not always successfully, to steer a course between incomprehension and miscomprehension.

It is not obvious that words alone can provide all the information required to construct novel concepts. Children learn many names for concrete objects, not from verbal definitions, but from watching someone point to an instance (or a picture of an instance) while uttering the name. But ostensive definitions can go only so far. They can work for perceptible nouns and adjectives, but try explaining *traffic* or *custom* or *unusual* by pointing at something. And even the commonest verbs are hard to explain by pointing.

If there were a satisfactory theory of concepts, it might provide a principled way to determine when it is possible to write definitions from which novel concepts can be acquired. As matters stand, writing definitions is a difficult and little-appreciated art. Because words are daily pressed into countless uses that no lexicographer could foresee, it is always necessary to leave room for negotiation—to provide enough pliancy to fit the word into oddly shaped slots. Most words in natural languages have a hard core of meaning that cannot be tampered with, but there is also a part that can be interpreted according to the symbolic-syntactic field in which it is used. A verb like *bring,* for example, should be so defined that *Bring me the cup* can be satisfied in a variety of ways: in the right hand, in the left hand, on a tray, filled, or empty. Or again, a word like *container* must be defined to accommodate both *container of lemonade,* where it has the sense of *bottle* or *glass,* and also *container of apples,* where it has the sense of *bag* or *basket;* bottles of apples or baskets of lemonade would be quite surprising. To allow an appropriate degree of modifiability without drowning in the sea of infinite polysemy, a lexicographer must have sensitive intuitions about words and their nuances.

The difficult question of how new concepts are formed will be set aside here in favor of the easier question of how familiar concepts are related, since those are the relations from which the semantic structure of the field of lexical concepts can be inferred. Definitions can guide those inferences by making many semantic relations explicit, but before that lead is followed up, a more direct way of surveying the contents of the mental lexicon should be considered.

Word Associations

Direct evidence for the variety and complexity of semantic relations comes from the word association test, one of the oldest methods psychologists have for studying lexical fields. The test was invented by the English scientist Sir Francis Galton (1822–1911), a cousin of Charles Darwin. Galton wrote some words on separate cards and put them away for several days, then looked at the cards one at a time. With a stopwatch he measured the time it took for each word to suggest two different ideas. He recorded the ideas, but refused to reveal them. "They lay bare the foundations of a man's thoughts with a curi-

Francis Galton.

Carl G. Jung (1875–1961), as a young man, used word associations to reveal emotionally significant groups of ideas—which he called "complexes"—in the unconscious regions of the mind. A serious difficulty, however, soon arose. There was no means of differentiating with statistical precision the associations of the abnormal from the normal. To remedy this, Jung and his colleagues collected thousands of associations from normal subjects. Because the most frequent and rapid responses are usually uninteresting from a diagnostic point of view, Jung tried various kinds of distractions, but with little success. The best indicator of an emotional complex was obtained by going through the list a second time, asking the patient to reproduce the original response. When the reproduction differed from the original, Jung suspected that an emotional distraction had disrupted recall. In his interpretations of unusual, delayed, or unreproduced word associations, Jung borrowed from Freud, which provided the initial impetus for their closer acquaintance.

ous distinctness," he wrote, "and exhibit his mental anatomy with more vividness and truth than he would probably care to publish to the world."

Psychologists quickly adopted Galton's idea and standardized its administration. For example, the Swiss psychiatrist Carl Jung used it to explore repressed emotions. He reasoned that slow or unusual responses should indicate that the stimulus word had probed some guilty knowledge or emotional complex. To recognize that a response is slow or unusual, it is necessary to know how long it takes an average person to give a popular response—only departures from that norm would be of clinical interest. So the test was given to large numbers of people, and their pooled results were used to define the norm. The first large-scale study for English was reported in 1910 by two American psychiatrists, G. H. Kent and A. J. Rosanoff, who read aloud a list of 100 probe words, one at a time, to a person who was instructed to give "the first word that occurs to you other than the stimulus word." They repeated this procedure with 1,000 men and women of different occupations and levels of education, then published their tabulated results.

Although the data were collected out of an interest in odd or unusual responses, the results offer striking evidence for uniformity in the organization of people's lexical fields. The same word associations are given over and over by different people—the result that would be expected if people share stable networks of connections among words.

Word associations show the familiarity effect: Responses are faster to familiar words. And when a stimulus word is familiar, adults tend to give responses that are in the same syntactic category. In one carefully controlled study, it was found that a noun stimulus elicited a noun response 79 percent of the time, adjectives elicited adjectives 65 percent of the time, and verbs elicited verbs 43 percent of the time. Since grammatical speech requires a person to know (at least implicitly) the syntactic privileges of different words, it is not surprising that such information would be readily available. It is as if people developed three separate lexical matrices, one for each major syntactic category.

The kinds of associations that the test reveals can best be appreciated by considering an example. Take the responses that Kent and Rosanoff obtained to the probe word *chair.* The data reveal a variety of associative relations. A few responses are clearly idiosyncratic—*beauty, careful, myself, rubber,* for instance—but nearly all responses given by two or more people bear some recognizable semantic relation to *chair.* The most frequent response to *chair* is *table,* which is a coordinate word: *Table* and *chair* are both hyponyms of *furniture.* Another response is *furniture,* the superordinate term; still another is *rocker,* a hyponym of *chair.* Responses like *comfortable, wooden, hard,* or *soft* designate attributes of chairs. Responses like *seat, cushion, legs, arm,* or *rung* are parts of chairs. And the many responses like *sit, sitting, rest, comfort, rocking, ease,* or *seated* designate things that chairs do or that can be done with them.

The word association test demonstrates that a single word can make available, or activate, a wide range of lexical knowledge. But wait—each person makes just one response. Can the pooled data for a large group of people be taken as representative of the mental lexicon for any single individual? The answer is yes. The psychological validity of these associations can be tested with the priming technique; the priming observed for words that are morphologically related (see Chapter 7) is also obtained for words that are related in other ways. If any common response to *chair (table, seat, sit, furniture)* is used in a lexical decision task, the time required to recognize it as a word will be shorter if *chair* is presented shortly before. The statistical distribution of responses to a word association test, therefore, reflects the distribution of response strengths within each individual.

Frequency of Word Associations for 1,000 Men and Women
Probe Word: CHAIR

191	table
127	seat
107	sit
83	furniture
56	sitting
49	wood
45	rest
38	stool
21	comfort
17	rocker
15	rocking
13	bench
12	cushion
11	legs
10	floor
9	desk, room
8	comfortable
7	ease, leg
6	easy, sofa, wooden
5	couch, hard, Morris, seated, soft
4	arm, article, brown, high
3	cane, convenience, house, large, lounge, low, mahogany, person, resting, rung, settee, useful
2	broken, hickory, home, necessity, oak, rounds, seating, use
1	back, beauty, bed, book, boy, bureau, caning, careful, carpet, cart, color, crooked, cushions, feet, foot, footstool, form, Governor Winthrop, hair, idleness, implement, joiner, lunch, massive, mission, myself, object, occupy, office, people, place, placed, plant, platform, pleasant, pleasure, posture, reading, rubber, size, spooning, stand, stoop, study, support, tables, talk, teacher, timber, tool, upholstered, upholstery, white

From Kent and Rosanoff, 1910.

Setting aside idiosyncratic associations, most of the associative responses that adults give to noun probes can be classified as instances of just four kinds of connotative semantic relation:

1. Superordinate, coordinate, and subordinate terms: terms that arrange things in a taxonomic tree

2. Attributive terms: modifying terms that state the values of attributes of things

3. Part-whole relations: terms that name a part of something, or that name the whole of which something is a part

4. Functional terms: terms that designate the ends that things serve— what things normally do or what is normally done with them

Problems encountered in trying to apply this classification scheme are mostly uncertainties about which category the subject had in mind. For example, did people who said *arm* in response to *chair* have in mind *armchair,* which is a subordinate name, or *chair arm,* the name of a part? Whatever the answer, such uncertainties do not contradict the claim that these four kinds of semantic relations are salient in the lexical organization of most speakers of English.

To appreciate how these four kinds of associations are related to one another, it is necessary to develop a picture of how noun meanings are organized in the semantic memory of the normal adult speaker of English.

Reference, Nouns, and Hyponymy

In the everyday use of language it is frequently important to designate clearly what is being talked about, but it is seldom necessary to make absolute identifications. Relative distinctions usually suffice; an expression can refer successfully if it is informative enough to distinguish an intended referent from other things that are also relevant to the purposes of the communication. The important thing for successful communication about concrete objects is not an ability to identify referents correctly by name in any conceivable situation, but rather an ability to distinguish one object from any others with which it is likely to be confused at the time.

To enable its speakers to draw such distinctions, a language must provide not only names for objects, but also names for features by which objects can be distinguished. In one situation, for example, it might suffice to ask for *the book,* but in another it might be necessary to specify *the little book with the tan binding at the end of the second shelf,* where a description including size, color, and location supplements the head noun.

These distinguishing features are essential not only for referring expressions, but also in definitions. The prototypical definition of a noun relates it first to a superordinate term, then adds a relative clause that differentiates this instance from all others. Distinguishing features are needed to provide that differentiation. An example (using slightly simplified definitions to avoid obscuring the point) can illustrate how distinguishing features are incorporated:

> **canary:** a finch that is characteristically (but not necessarily) green to yellow and is bred for song.

Note the form of the defining phrase. The superordinate noun phrase "a finch" identifies a category of objects; the relative clause, "that is characteristically green to yellow and is bred for song," is intended to distinguish canaries from other members of that category. A canary is a kind of finch, and that biological relation is reflected in the lexicon by a semantic relation: *Canary* is a hyponym of *finch*.

A finch, in turn, is a kind of songbird, so the same pattern can be traced out again:

> **finch:** a songbird that is small and has a short bill.

And a songbird is a kind of bird:

> **songbird:** a bird that utters a characteristic musical song.

And a bird is a kind of animal:

> **bird:** an animal that is warm-blooded, has feathers, wings, and a bill, and characteristically (but not necessarily) can fly.

Canary is a hyponym of *finch*, which is a hyponym of *songbird*, which is a hyponym of *bird*, which is a hyponym of *animal*. These semantic relations follow directly from the familiar animal taxonomy, of which canaries, birds, and animals form a tiny fragment.

The familiar taxonomic principle for organizing lexical data is based on set inclusion. The set of canaries is included in the set of finches, and the set of finches is included in the set of songbirds, and so on. The semantic relation between the words that are used to denote these nested sets has been called superordination, or hyponymy (subordination), or simply the ISA relation (from "an x IS A y"); the resulting semantic structure has been called a taxonomy, a hierarchy, or simply a tree. Much experience has shown that tree structures are extremely useful in organizing certain parts of the lexicon—nouns, in particular, lend themselves to this kind of semantic organization. *Roget's Thesaurus,* for example, attempts to arrange all the words of English in a hierarchical structure.

But trees, valuable as they are, do not provide a complete solution to all the problems of representing semantic relations. Some account of the features

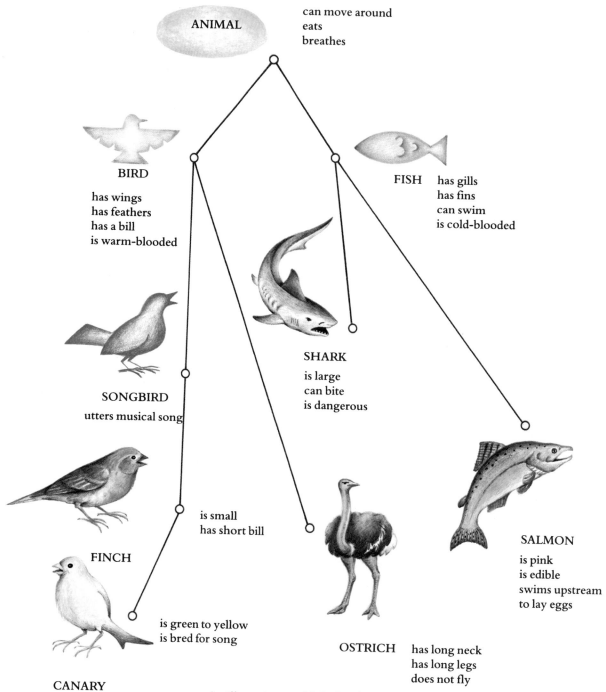

An illustration, modeled after the work of Alan Collins and Ross Quillian, of how the meanings of animal names are hierarchically related in the mental lexicon. The lexical hierarchy reflects the biological taxonomy.

that are used to differentiate hyponyms is also necessary. The *canary* example can make the point. Canaries, being finches, have all the features that define finches plus the additional features that distinguish canaries from other finches. Moreover, finches are songbirds, so canaries also have all the features that define songbirds. And so on. When all the features of canaries, finches, songbirds, and birds are collected together, it becomes apparent that they fall into three important types:

1. Attributes: "is small," "is green to yellow," "is warm-blooded"

2. Parts: "has feathers," "has wings," "has a short bill"

3. Functions: "sings," "is bred for song," "can fly"

Taken together, these features should enable a person to distinguish canaries from other animals. The validity of that particular claim is not at issue here. Here the interest is in the kinds of features that can be used to state such distinctions.

Note that these three types of distinguishing features are the same ones used before to categorize word associations. And note also that these three classes of distinguishing features lead beyond nouns and into other syntactic categories. Attributes, parts, and functions could not enter into definitions at all if they were not expressible in words. Attributes are most conveniently expressed by adjectives and adjectival phrases, parts by nouns and nominal phrases, functions by verbs and verb phrases.

Attributes and Antonymy

Whereas words that refer to objects are organized hierarchically, words that denote values of attributes are not. The basic relation organizing adjectives has generally been assumed to be antonymy.

Perhaps one reason nouns have been studied more than adjectives is that antonymy is hard to define. Although some antonyms are mutually exclusive and exhaustive (*male/female* or *alive/dead,* for example), antonyms like *hot/cold* are not; they cannot both be true, but both can be false: *Not hot* does not mean *cold.* Because many antonyms have this property, antonymy cannot be defined logically in terms of simple negation.

The important generalizations are that adjectives presuppose attributes, and attributes tend to be bipolar. When the semantics of antonymy are phrased in terms of attributes rather than negation, the distinction between exclusive and nonexclusive antonyms can be seen to follow from the fact that attributes can be gradable or ungradable. Exclusive antonyms express values of those attributes, like gender, that are ungradable. In other words, the semantics of adjectives, and the fact that lexical fields of adjectives are organized in terms of antonymy, follow directly from commonsense assumptions about the bipolar attributes whose values such adjectives are used to express.

Dr. Roget's Classification of Ideas

At the age of sixty-one, the English physician Peter Mark Roget (1779–1869) retired from professional practice and from his duties as Secretary of the Royal Society to devote his full energies to various scholarly projects that had aroused his curiosity over the years. One of those projects was the publication of the thesaurus for which he is still remembered. For many years he had made a hobby of grouping words according to their meanings, which was a novel idea at that time. Retirement gave him an opportunity to pursue this interest and to prepare his catalog for publication. The first edition appeared in 1852 under the title *Thesaurus of English Words and Phrases, Classified and Arranged so as to Facilitate the Expression of Ideas and Assist in Literary Composition*. Its immediate popularity created a family enterprise; revised and expanded versions were subsequently edited by his son, John Roget, and by John's son, Samuel, until it became known simply as *Roget's Thesaurus*.

Dr. Roget hoped that his thesaurus not only would help authors who were "struggling with the difficulties of composition," but also would interest scholars "engaged in the more profound investigation of the Philosophy of Language." For writers who want their memories jogged, the book contains two sections, one an alphabetical index of all words in the

Peter Mark Roget.

thesaurus, the other a sequence of several hundred categories of related words. Users who seek a particular word first consult the index for some related word; there they are directed to appropriate categories of semantically similar words. That way of using Roget's thesaurus is so standard that most people, even avid users, are unaware of a third section of the book. Yet for Roget, that third section, the Synopsis of Categories, represented a major contribution to "the more profound investigation" of language. Roget expected that users of his book would master his system of categories and would begin their word searches with it—conceptually—rather than with the alphabetical index.

The Synopsis of Categories is a hierarchical arrangement of all the ideas that can be expressed by English words or common phrases. Roget established six primary classes of categories: (1) Abstract Relations, such as existence, resemblance, quantity, order, number, time, power; (2) Space, including motion; (3) Material World, including properties of matter such as solidity, fluidity, heat, sound, and light, the phenomena they represent, and the simple perceptions to which they give rise; (4) Intellect and its operations, such as the acquisition, retention, and communication of ideas; (5) Volition, including such voluntary and active powers as choice, intention, utility, action, antagonism, authority, compact, property; and finally (6) Sentiment and Moral Powers, such as feelings, emotions, passions, and moral and religious sentiments. The classification has expanded and evolved over the years, but about seven levels of subcategories are usually provided. For example, in the 1977 edition, revised by Robert L. Chapman, the word *thesaurus* is found in three places, as shown in the diagram below.

This hierarchical arrangement was constructed for nouns and noun phrases; morphologically related words in other syntactic categories—verbs, adjectives, a few adverbs—were simply assimilated into the noun taxonomy.

Roget's comprehensive classification system exemplifies the best thinking of his day, but seems oddly antiquated to a modern eye. It is remarkable that the system of categories he took such pains to construct and name has proved to be so peripheral to the practical usefulness of his thesaurus. The hierarchical system of categories was a tool that Roget needed in order to build the thesaurus; once it was built, the tool was no longer needed.

A word of warning, however. Defining adjectives by values of perceptual attributes may be necessary, but it is not sufficient. In particular, this account ignores the influence of the head noun on the interpretation of adjectives that modify it. A canary is a small bird and a pony is a small horse, but the size conveyed by *small* is different in the two cases.

Shape and Meronymy

Although shape is frequently regarded as an attribute, on a par with such bipolar attributes as *big/little, good/bad, common/uncommon, animate/inanimate,* or *familiar/unfamiliar,* shape is clearly not bipolar. A relatively simple vocabulary of antonymous adjectives suffices for communication about bipolar attributes, but communication about the shapes of objects requires a more elaborate lexicon for the description of part-whole relations.

Although the importance of parts for the perception of shape has long been recognized, psycholinguists have paid less attention to the role of part names than to the role of hyponymy in the organization of lexical fields. Sometimes the "part of" relation (meronymy) is compared to the "kind of" relation (hyponymy). Both are asymmetric and transitive, and both can relate terms hierarchically, since parts can have parts: A finger is a part of a hand, a hand is a part of an arm, an arm is a part of a body. Linguists call the part-whole relation meronymy (from *meros* part + *nym* name): *Finger* is a meronym of *hand, hand* is a meronym of *arm, arm* is a meronym of *body*. But the "part of" construction is not always a reliable test of meronymy.

In many instances transitivity seems to be limited. For example, *handle* is a meronym of *door* and *door* is a meronym of *house*, yet it sounds odd to say "The house has a handle" or "The handle is a part of the house." Such failures of transitivity may indicate that different part-whole relations are involved in the two cases. For example, "The branch is a part of the tree" and "The tree is a part of a forest" do not imply that "The branch is a part of the forest" because the *branch-tree* relation is not the same as the *tree-forest* relation. The *handle-house* example fails because "part of" is used where "attached to" would be more appropriate: The "part of" relation should be transitive, whereas the "attached to" relation clearly is not—your toe is attached to your foot and your foot is attached to your leg, but no one would say that your toe is attached to your leg. "The house has a door handle" is acceptable because it negates the implicit inference in "The house has a handle" that the handle is attached to the house.

Such observations raise questions about how many different "part of" relations there are. At least seven types of meronyms can be differentiated:

1. Component-object (*branch-tree*)

2. Member-collection (*tree-forest*)

Some examples, borrowed from J. D. Bransford and N. S. McCarrell, of the importance of function. Lacking information about the uses to which these implements are put, it is difficult to know what they should be called. (The functional information is provided on page 166.)

3. Portion-mass (*slice-cake*)

4. Stuff-object (*aluminum-airplane*)

5. Feature-activity (*paying-shopping*)

6. Place-area (*New Haven-Connecticut*)

7. Phase-process (*adolescence-growing up*)

Meronymy is obviously a complex semantic relation—or set of relations.

Some components can serve as parts of many different things: Think of all the different objects that have gears. It is sometimes the case that an object can be two kinds of thing at the same time—a cairn is both a pile of rocks and a marker, for example—but that situation is rare in the hyponymic hierarchy. In the meronymic hierarchy, on the other hand, it is common, and it is remarkable that this situation causes so little confusion.

Visual imagery is important in part-whole judgments, so important that some theorists have used it in a general argument that meanings cannot be defined by specifying categories of objects that are characterized by lists of individually necessary and jointly sufficient conditions. A more conservative formulation might be that lists of features are useful, perhaps even necessary, for characterizing contrasts between categories of objects, but the importance of configurational or topological features in the understanding of meronymic relations indicates that mere lists of features are not sufficient.

Functions and Predication

Whereas perceptual attributes have been studied extensively by psychologists for many years and part-whole relations are a familiar psychological problem, the third type of distinguishing feature, the ends that things serve, has received far less attention. Attributes and parts can usually be recognized perceptually, but recognizing the function of an object—what it does or what can be done with it—depends far more on general knowledge. For example, the objects depicted in the margins are probably unfamiliar and so have little meaning. The attributes and part-whole relations of these objects are clear enough, but by themselves these relations provide little information about the objects. It helps a bit to know that each object is a tool designed to perform a special function; when the functions are explained (see next page), the objects become meaningful.

If it is granted that part-whole relations are important, it is difficult to exclude functional judgments. Parts frequently enjoy a duality that is not apparent in simple attributes. Part names refer both to a perceptual entity and to a functional role: The *leg* of a table or the *handle* of a door not only have particular shapes, but also have particular functions. Knowledge of a part's function can influence where its boundaries are perceived.

Once their functions are known, it is easy to agree on appropriate names for the implements.

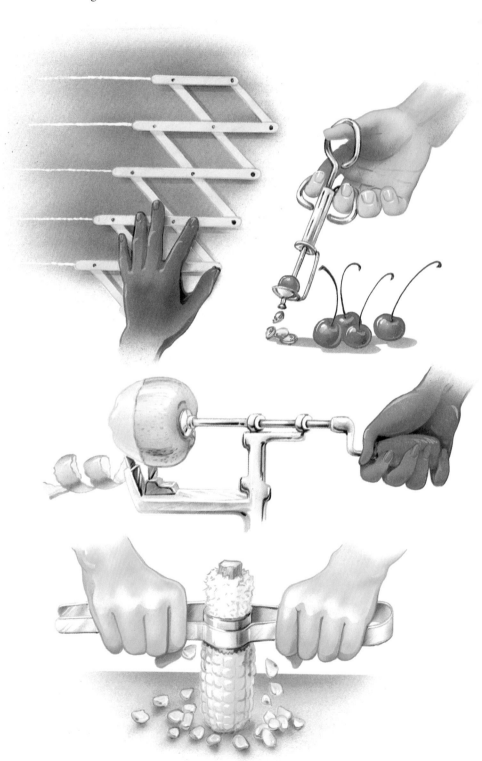

Unfortunately, however, although good design dictates that function should determine form, the correlation between shape and function, even for artifacts, is not always close. Even table legs and door handles come in a variety of shapes and are recognizable as much by their place in the total configuration of a table or a door as by their shapes in isolation. The shape of a concrete object is ordinarily a static feature of an object; its function is revealed over time. If a concrete object has any function, the function can usually be determined by watching the thing long enough to determine what it does or what is done with it.

The slippage between structure and function is best illustrated by cases in which an object serves a familiar function but does not have a familiar shape. Consider the case of two people using a tree stump for a picnic. One of them says, "This stump is a good table." A stump, of course, is not a table; calling a stump a table doesn't make it one. But calling it a good table seems perfectly acceptable. How can something that is not a table be a good table? A plausible answer has been suggested by the philosopher Jerold J. Katz, who proposes that functional information is stored with most head nouns.

Katz's proposal resembles an assumption already noted. From the fact that a small horse is larger than a small bird, it was assumed that part of the meaning of *horse* and *bird* must be the expected sizes of horses and birds. Katz's proposal for *good* is similar: From the fact that a good table need not be a table at all, he concludes that part of the meaning of *table* is the expected function of tables. The functional information determines the interpretation of the adjectives *good* and *bad*; these adjectives select the functional component of the noun's meaning and assign it a positive or negative value. Something is a good table, for example, if it serves well the function that tables are supposed to serve; a poor table serves that function poorly. Thus, a good knife is a knife that cuts well, a good violinist is a violinist who plays well, a good chair is a chair that supports well, and so on. If Katz is right—if *good* selects functional information—then the function that an object is expected to serve is a separable component of the meaning of the noun used to refer to that object. (Indeed, for words like *ornament*, the functional component seems to be all there is to the meaning.)

Usually it is an advantage to know the function of an object, but sometimes it can be a handicap. Psychologists who study the behavior of people who are trying to solve simple, set problems have observed a phenomenon called functional fixedness, in which the name given to an object blocks people's ability to see how it could be used for some different function. For example, a box is normally used as a container; to call some object a box is to invoke the container function, thus making it more difficult to see that the object could be emptied and used for some other purpose. Or again, asked to get a Ping-Pong ball out of a fixed vertical tube, people found it easier to think of floating it out when a pitcher of water was available than when a bottle of champagne was available: Water has many uses, but champagne is for drinking.

Benjamin Lee Whorf

Benjamin Lee Whorf.

Benjamin Lee Whorf (1897–1941) was an amateur linguist who studied chemical engineering at the Massachusetts Institute of Technology and became a highly skilled fire inspector for the Hartford Insurance Company. Whorf's interest in the Hebrew language led him to read linguistics, and he soon discovered that Hartford had an excellent collection in American Indian languages and folklore. He began to study the Aztec language and visited Mexico. When Edward Sapir went to Yale as Professor of Anthropology in 1931, Whorf enrolled in his courses.

Whorf is best remembered for his articles arguing that the language a person speaks controls the ideas the person can have, an idea borrowed from Sapir that is known as the Whorfian Hypothesis or the Sapir–Whorf Hypothesis. Whorf extended Sapir's idea and illustrated it with examples drawn both from his knowledge of American Indian languages and from his experience as a fire-prevention engineer. Critics have argued that his linguistic examples are little more than poor translations. But Whorf's accounts of fires that had, in effect, been caused by the names assigned to conditions still provide dramatic instances of functional fixedness—

of the way an object's function is mentally fixed by the name it is given. He wrote:

A tannery discharged waste water containing animal matter into an outdoor settling basin partly roofed with wood and partly open. This situation is one that ordinarily would be verbalized as "pool of water." A workman had occasion to light a blowtorch nearby, and threw his match into the water. But the decompos-

ing waste matter was evolving gas under the wood cover, so that the setup was the reverse of "watery." An instant flare of flame ignited the woodwork, and the fire quickly spread into the adjoining building.

Whorf had many such examples. "We always assume," he commented, "that the linguistic analysis made by our group reflects reality better than it does."

From such observations it seems plausible to conclude that the meanings of many words have a functional component. There is an unfortunate vagueness to the concept of function, however. It is true that for many human-made artifacts known directly through manipulation—spoon, ball, comb, hammer, food—the function is an intrinsic part of the relevant action system. But for other artifacts—wall, bridge, mine, building—the function is obvious although a distinctive action system is not. Similarly for natural objects: Some have been assigned familiar functions—apples are eaten, horses are ridden, trees provide shade—but others—atoms, clouds, mountains—have not. These distinctions must be learned for each individual object.

From a lexical point of view, to characterize the function of some category of objects is to indicate the class of verbs (or verb phrases) that can be predicated of that object. For example, since foods are eaten, *eat* can be predicated of *food* and all of its hyponyms; since blades are for cutting, *cut* can be predicated of every noun having *blade* as a meronym; and so on.

Much of this functional information appears in dictionary definitions. Conceivably, more complete lists of the predication relations between verbs and nouns could be added to the lists of attributes and parts already discussed. Even more than for attributes and parts, however, the interpretation of lists of predicates would depend on perceptual and general knowledge that could not be made explicit by merely listing the predicates.

■   ■   ■

The meaning of a sentence depends on the local situation in which it is used (the deictic field), on the grammatical relations among words in the sentence (the syntactic field), and on the concepts that those words conventionally express (the lexical-conceptual field). Of these three, the lexical-conceptual field is probably the most difficult to investigate scientifically, for it must be inferred from the patient analysis of semantic relations among particular lexical concepts. Definitions must play a central role in any serious exploration of the lexical-conceptual field, and definitions rely on a relatively limited set of distinguishing features. The analysis of words denoting these features—attributes, parts, functions—leads beyond lexical fields and deep into the organization of general knowledge. The acquisition of the lexical-conceptual field goes hand in hand with the acquisition of a general conceptual structure in terms of which people try to understand the world in which they live.

▲ *Although they differ in many details, these three structures are all quickly generalized under the label* flower.

▶ *Three semantic relations among lexical concepts in the noun network are illustrated here. Maroon arrows denote semantic opposition (antonymy). Purple arrows indicate part-whole relations (meronymy);* corolla *is a part of* flower, *while* petal *is a part of* corolla. *The hierarchical relation that orders nouns from the generic to the specific (hyponymy) is marked by yellow arrows. Daisy, rose, lily, and so forth are thus recognized as a class of lexical equals: hyponyms of* flower.

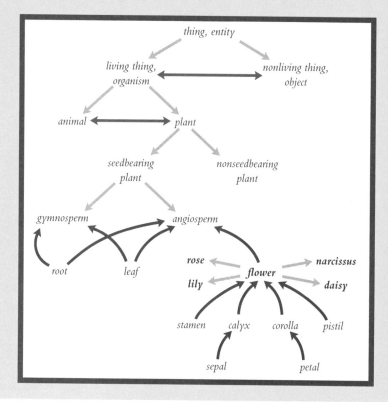

Categorizing Experience

Human beings consider themselves to be the most intelligent creatures in the animal kingdom. Intelligence can be defined in many ways, but the definition that best justifies this human pride is the ability to profit from experience. People can usually learn to avoid making the same mistake over and over, and when something works well it is usually remembered. People are clever at solving problems, very clever in remembering solutions and adapting them to new problems, and uniquely clever in passing on solutions to successive generations.

Language plays an important role in this human cleverness, not merely in spreading knowledge, but also in acquiring it. To recognize that a familiar and practiced response is appropriate in a new situation, it is necessary to have some way to classify situations—to recognize that the old situation and the new situation are situations of the same kind, meriting the same response. All higher animals possess this ability to some extent, but the human aptitude for categorizing experience is enormously extended by the ability to use words to denote recurring situations.

Nouns serve, in the mental lexicon, to reflect the categories into which people sort their experience.

The words that best serve as names of recurring individuals and events are the words known as nouns. The structure of this part of the mental lexicon is determined by the structure of categories that people develop for dealing with their experiences. Of course, categorization is not the only way that people manage their experience and put it to use, but it is a major way and one with enormous consequences for the languages they speak. The thousands of nouns that people know and use are all different, one from another, yet are all the same in the way they are known. Nouns are bound together by semantic relations that hold only for nouns. Indeed, nouns are so cohesive in their diversity that an injury to the brain can effectively eliminate them from a person's linguistic competence while leaving everything else relatively intact.

Sometimes the categories into which nouns divide the world are so important that they spill over into the morphology of a language. When a language has different classes of noun forms, linguists speak of differences in gender. In Indo-European languages, gender is associated with sex: The masculine and feminine genders of French or the masculine, feminine, and neuter genders of German are familiar examples. It is often noted that these genders, considered as semantic categories, contain mistakes—surely Germans know that a girl is really feminine, not neuter. Typically, gender is based in part on meaning, but in part is arbitrary. Nevertheless, the fact remains that a categorization into masculine and feminine goes far back into the ancient origins of Indo-European languages.

Because gender is sex-related for most speakers of Indo-European languages, the news that there are languages with a dozen or more genders is usually received with amazed misunderstanding. For example, the Bantu languages spoken in the southern half of the African continent have many genders, which are marked by prefixes; attempts to reconstruct Proto-Bantu have listed nineteen classes of nouns. For example, the first class contains nouns that take the prefix *m-* and refer to (singular) human beings: *mtu* (*person*), *mtoto* (*child*), *mgeni* (*stranger*). Class three contains nouns that also take the prefix *m-*, but have a different plural and refer to thin or extended things: *mti* (*tree*). Other genders refer to instruments, animals, qualities, body parts, locations.

Some languages indicate semantic classes by noun adjuncts; that is, by words that are typically used with nouns to form noun phrases. Thus Thai, the Siamese language, uses classifier + noun constructions, where the meaning of the head noun determines the choice of classifier. As in the case of gender marking, Thai classifiers are partly semantic and partly arbitrary. For example, the classifier for nouns denoting human beings is *khon;* for animals, furniture, and clothing it is *tua;* for cigars and cigarettes it is *muan;* for books, carts, and sharp instruments it is *lêm;* and so on. There are more than sixty such classifiers, which are obligatory when certain numerals are also used.

In English, a handful of nouns have classifiers—*a grain of sand* or *salt* or *sugar,* for example—but most semantic classes of nouns are not overtly marked. Even gender is marked only for pronouns. But nouns themselves are classifiers. Every noun denotes a class of referents, and classes can be combined into superclasses or divided into subclasses. The result is a classificatory hierarchy or taxonomy. Tracing out these hierarchies reveals the semantic classes of English nouns.

Lexical Hierarchies

Things that have names usually have many names. A steed is a horse, an equid, a perissodactyl, a herbivore, a mammal, a vertebrate, an animal, an organism, an object. Moreover, the words can be ordered. All steeds are horses, all horses are equids, all equids are perissodactyls, and so on to larger and more

The Man Without a Noun

*P*atients who experience difficulty naming things are said to suffer from anomia. Anomia comes in many forms, and some degree of naming difficulty is observed in almost every case of aphasia. Sometimes the difficulty is restricted to particular semantic domains: Proper nouns pose special problems; rare words are usually harder to recall than common words; color naming is often particularly sensitive; names of body parts may be spared while other names are lost; actions may be named correctly but not objects, or vice versa. Some forms of anomia are modality-specific: Patients can name objects by touch, but not by sight; others by sight, but not by touch. Rare cases of fluent aphasia have been reported in which a patient's difficulty is predominantly in recalling verbs, but the vast majority of anomic patients have trouble only with nouns.

The standard method for investigating these difficulties is confrontation naming; the patient is shown an object and asked to name it. When H.W. was shown an apple, for example, he could not say "apple," although he understood the word—if it was supplied for him, he would recognize that it was the word he could not produce. When asked to point

Carl Wernicke (1848–1905), who first described fluent aphasias.

out the apple in a pile of fruit, he could do so. He could draw a picture of an apple, but could not name what he had just drawn. And he could say that an apple is "something to eat." But he could not produce "apple" on demand.

Unlike patients with lesions in and around Broca's area, H.W. spoke fluently and had few problems of comprehension. But he did have considerable difficulty in finding the words he wanted, a problem that was most severe with respect to nouns. For example, when Dr. Kathleen Baynes of the Dartmouth Medical School asked H.W. to describe the "cookie theft" picture (see page 97), he began as follows (nouns are printed in **bold**):

H. W.: First of all this is falling down, just about, and is gonna fall down and they're both getting something to eat . . . but the **trouble** is this is gonna let go and they're both gonna fall down . . . but already then . . . . I can't see well enough but I believe that either she or will have some **food** that's not good for you and she's to get some for her, too . . . and that you get it and you shouldn't get it there because they shouldn't go up there and get it unless you tell them that they could have it. And so this is falling down and for sure there's one they're going to have for **food** and, and didn't come out right, the uh, the **stuff** that's uh, good for, it's not good for you but it, but you love it, um mum mum (*smacks lips*) . . . and that so they've . . . see that, I can't see whether it's in there or not.

Examiner: Yes, that's not real clear. What do you think she's doing?

H. W.: But, oh, I know. She's waiting for this!

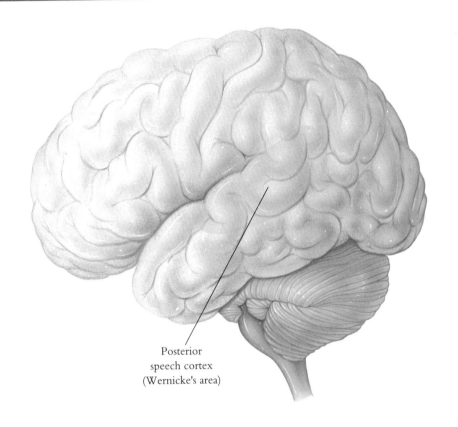

Posterior
speech cortex
(Wernicke's area)

The left hemisphere of the human brain, showing the location of Wernicke's area relative to other important cortical areas.

Examiner: No, I meant right here with her hand, right where you can't figure out what she's doing with that hand.

H. W.: Oh, I think she's saying I want two or three, I want one, I think, I think so, and so, so she's gonna get this one for sure it's gonna fall down there or whatever, she's gonna get that one and, and there, he's gonna get one himself or more, it all depends with this when they fall down . . . and when it falls down there's no **problem**, all they got to do is fix it and go right back up and get some more.

H.W. continued at length, but this is representative. Note that his grammar is reasonably intact and his speech contains many pronouns and noun phrases, but few nouns. There are only four nouns in this sample; all are highly generic. Two of them, *trouble* and *problem,* were not used referen-tially; the other two, *food* and *stuff,* both occurred in paraphrases as he tried to circumvent his inability to recall *cookie.* (Although the word *cookie* is written on the cookie jar, he could not speak it; it was a pe-culiarity of H.W.'s condition that he could not read aloud, although he could read silently with com-prehension at normal speeds.) H. W. was remarkable for being so clearly unable to produce nouns when trying to express himself, while at the same time showing good comprehension.

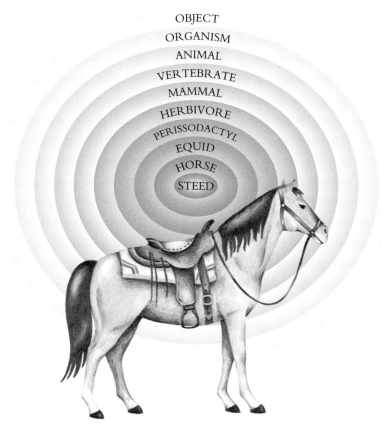

Hierarchically related nouns demonstrate class inclusion. As the terms become more generic, they denote progressively larger classes.

inclusive categories of animals. The relation among terms is transitive (all steeds are objects) and asymmetric (not all horses are steeds, not all equids are horses, not all perissodactyls are equids, and so on); transitive asymmetric relations lead to hierarchical systems.

Such facts about the organization of the internal lexicon call for an explanation, but the explanation is not obvious. Introspection is no help. People can be aware of words, or of the meanings of words, but no one can be consciously aware of the complex organization of lexical memory. The hierarchical structure of noun meanings, for example, is not experienced directly, but must be inferred indirectly from observations that would be hard to understand if that part of the mental lexicon were organized in any other way.

But first, is it true that nouns ARE hierarchically organized in the mental lexicon? The hierarchy might be some artificial arrangement of terms invented for the convenience of taxonomists and file clerks, rather than something that everyone internalizes as part of mastering a language. Fortunately, the psychological reality of subordinate-superordinate semantic relations can be demonstrated. One persuasive demonstration involves comparative adjectives. What is wrong with these sentences?

> *A monkey can be more active than an animal.*
> *A gun is less dangerous than a weapon.*
> *Fruit tastes better than grapes do.*
> *A car is more convenient than an automobile.*
> *People are funnier than anybody.*

The absurdity is obvious. A comparative construction cannot be used to compare something with itself; the paradigm of such absurdities would be

> *I am younger (shorter, funnier, wiser, more arrogant . . .) than I am.*

The sentences above show that this reflexive constraint on comparatives extends beyond a thing and itself: A comparative adjective cannot be used between a noun and any of its hyponyms (subordinates) or superordinates. A monkey cannot be more or less than an animal because a monkey IS an animal. If you think guns are less dangerous than weapons, you must not know that guns ARE weapons. And so on.

The interesting point is that any rule blocking such constructions, however it is stated, must apply to whole sets of hierarchically related terms—*rifle, firearm, gun, weapon, implement, object* would be a "set of hierarchically related terms," for example. Otherwise said, whole sets of hierarchically related terms must have sufficient psychological integrity to serve as the objects of such constraints. Moreover, these constraints operate automatically and without reflection; the absurdity of these sentences does not come as the conclusion of some abstract syllogism that must be painstakingly reasoned through. The unacceptability of such constructions is recognized immediately, which means that these hierarchically related terms must be closely associated in lexical memory.

Further evidence for the hierarchical semantic structure of noun meanings is found in their use in anaphora. An anaphoric noun can be co-referential with an antecedent hyponym. For example:

> *A gun lay on the table beside the guard, who checked nervously that the*
> *weapon was within easy reach.*

Note that the weapon mentioned in the second clause is (most likely, although not necessarily) the gun introduced in the first clause: The hyponym *gun* is (probably) the antecedent of the anaphoric noun *weapon*. The point is that *gun* and *weapon* can be co-referential only because a gun IS a weapon. And their co-referentiality can be appreciated only because their semantic relationship is recognized immediately by the reader. Replace *weapon* with *key* or *phone* and no anaphor is possible.

The psychological reality of the hierarchical structure of noun meanings can be demonstrated in still other ways, but most people accept the point without any demonstrations. The hard questions have to do with why this structure exists and what consequences follow from it.

How to Use Memory Economically

Why are noun meanings organized hierarchically in the mental lexicon? One explanation is based on the economy of memory that it allows.

The story goes like this. Each word is characterized by certain distinguishing features—attributes, parts, uses—that must be stored in lexical memory (see Chapter 8). A hierarchical organization makes it possible to store those features more efficiently. If the word W_h is a hyponym of the more generic word W_g, then the list of distinguishing features for word W_h will include all of the distinguishing features for word W_g. Features that the two words have in common will be stored with W_g, so as long as the hyponym and its superordinate are closely associated, these shared features need not be stored again with W_h; they can be retrieved from the superordinate as needed. For example, since *oak* is a hyponym of *tree*, the distinguishing features of oaks include all the distinguishing features of trees; that is, oaks have all the features of trees, plus a few more that distinguish oaks from other kinds of trees. Therefore, only those features unique to oaks must be stored with *oak*; the features that oaks have by virtue of being trees can be recovered easily as long as *oak* is automatically recognized as a hyponym of *tree*.

This account assumes that a hyponym inherits the properties of its superordinates. The fact that an oak has acorns is information stored directly with *oak*, but the fact that an oak has a trunk is inherited from *tree*. Moreover, the inheritance of features is transitive: The fact that an oak has cell walls of cellulose is inherited from *plant*, because oaks are trees, trees are plants, and all plants have cellulose cell walls. The logic here is syllogistic:

All oaks are trees.
All trees are plants.
Therefore, all oaks are plants.
All plants have cellulose cell walls.
Therefore, all oaks have cellulose cell walls.

How are different properties of, for example, an oak stored in the mental lexicon?

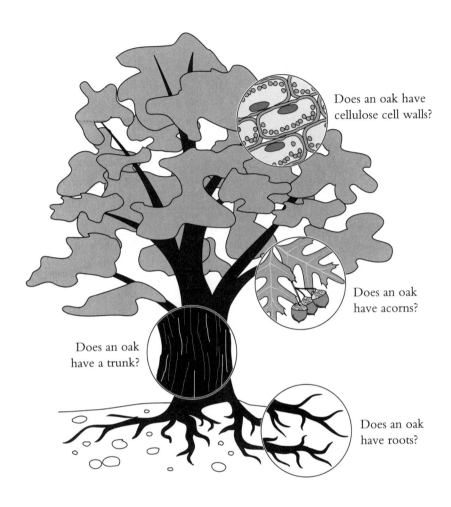

Does an oak have
cellulose cell walls?

Does an oak
have acorns?

Does an oak
have a trunk?

Does an oak
have roots?

The claim is not that a person must consciously run through this syllogism to answer the question, "Do oaks have cellulose cell walls?" The syllogism is merely a formal demonstration that a lexical memory organized in the manner suggested contains all the information needed to answer such questions.

The way that inheritance is supposed to work can be illustrated as follows. Suppose that your friend tells you, "I have a terrier named Rex." And suppose further that this is the first time you have ever heard of Rex. Nevertheless, you already know a great deal about Rex. You know that it is a small, furry quadruped that likes meat and barks and has a muzzle and a short tail and a stomach and much else. You do not need to ask pointed questions about each of these features because your information about Rex is simply inherited from your information about terriers. Similarly, when you first learned that W_h was a name for a kind of W_g, you did not need to ask pointed questions about the features that it inherited from W_g.

Since a major virtue of inheritance systems is that they save memory space, it is worth considering just how economical they really are. Some rough calculations are possible, based on an imaginary idealized model inheritance system (IMIS, for short). Let IMIS be a lexical hierarchy with 5 levels and a constant branching factor of 5. Thus there will be a total of $(1 + 5 + 25 + 125 + 625) = 781$ words in IMIS. Assume further that it takes 4 features to distinguish each word. Then IMIS must store $4 \times 781 = 3,124$ features. For comparison, if the same hierarchy stored every feature of a word with that word—if no inheritance of features were possible—the same 781 words would require 4 features at the top level, 5×8 features at the second level, 25×12 features at the third, 125×16 at the fourth, and 625×20 at the bottom level, for a total of 14,844 features, 79 percent of which would be redundant (that is, the 4 features that characterize the top level are stored not once, but 781 times). And the greater the number of levels, the greater the relative economy of IMIS. This comparison is idealized, of course, but it explains why scientists prefer inheritance systems for storing large databases in the memory of a computer.

Caution is recommended, however. The fact that inheritance systems use memory economically is no proof that the mental lexicon for nouns is organized in that manner. Some psychologists believe that people's memory for words and their meanings cannot be organized in this efficient manner. There are just too many facts that a simple inheritance theory cannot explain.

Consider the question, "Do oaks have roots?" If you introspect as you answer that question, either you will find nothing to report—the answer appears as fast as the question is understood—or you will experience mental imagery of tree roots: of an uprooted oak tree, or a cutaway diagram of tree roots underground, or whatever. In either case, you feel that you are answering the question on the basis of information about tree roots, not on the basis of the roots of some generic conception you may have of an abstract plant. Those introspections, to the extent that they mirror your mental processes in answering the question, argue for the redundant storage of feature information with every term it characterizes.

One way to test the inheritance hypothesis is to ask people simple questions whose answers can be retrieved from lexical memory and to measure how much time they need to find those answers. For example, if people are asked, "Does a collie have long hair?" the inheritance hypothesis predicts that they should answer on the basis of information stored under *collie*. If asked, "Does a collie have a muzzle?" they should answer on the basis of information stored under *dog*. And if asked, "Does a collie have a liver?" they should answer on the basis of information stored under *animal*. The early experiments that tested these comparisons found that it does indeed take people extra time to move from *collie* to *dog* to *animal* to find the information needed to answer the three questions. These results were considered strong support for an in-heritance system, since if all the features of collies were stored under *collie,* response times to all three questions would be the same.

No sooner were these results published than other psychologists began to criticize their generality. For example, a more complete taxonomy for collies would involve mammals: *collie → dog → mammal → animal.* So response times to questions about the mammalian features of collies should be intermediate between those for dogs and those for animals. In fact, however, questions like "Is a collie a mammal?" took longer to answer than they should have. Appar-ently, differences in the familiarity of categories play an important role in determining response times, a role that is unexplained by a simple inheritance theory.

Another reason to question whether inheritance systems provide an ade-quate model for lexical memory is that category instances are inherently un-equal. For example, robins, chickens, and ostriches are all birds, but robins are more typical birds than are chickens or ostriches. When people are asked to say yes or no as quickly as possible to questions about such categories, they will

Some birds are more typical birds than others are.

"Can a squirrel move?" is answered faster than "Does a squirrel have ears?" or "Does a squirrel have a backbone?"

respond yes significantly faster to "Is a robin a bird?" than to "Is an ostrich a bird?" Nothing in the theory of simple inheritance systems would account for such differences.

When people are asked to describe their conceptions of animals, some features are mentioned far more frequently than others. For example, *can move* is a frequently mentioned feature of *animal,* but *has ears* is seldom mentioned. And when asked to respond yes or no as quickly as possible to questions, people say yes to "An animal can move" significantly faster than to "An animal has ears." It is generally the case that when a feature shows high production frequency in the descriptions, it will also yield fast verification response times—no matter how many hierarchical levels intervene between the word and the level from which the property would be inherited. Such evidence seems to contradict any strong form of the inheritance hypothesis.

If lexical memory is not an inheritance system, then what could it be? An alternative hypothesis at the opposite theoretical extreme is complete redundancy: the assumption that features are stored in memory with every word that they help to differentiate, so they can be retrieved directly, rather than derived by inference. Some features are more strongly associated with a word than are others, and those differences in associative strength explain the differences in response times to questions. But this purely redundant system is as implausible as a pure inheritance system. For example, surely no one believes that *has a backbone* is stored separately with every word denoting a vertebrate organism. There are indefinitely many such features that people can verify; it is absurd to think that all of them have been explicitly stored in memory with the words they characterize.

What the psychological experiments demonstrate is that some features are probably stored with more than one word in an inheritance system. They do NOT prove that all applicable features must be stored with every word. If lexical memory for nouns were totally redundant, the semantic relation of hyponymy would not play such an important and immediate role in language comprehension. In other words, there are independent reasons for believing in a hierarchical structure with some inheritance of features, regardless of the outcome of any given reaction time experiment. Response times to questions about category membership are affected by many complex factors other than the levels of a lexical hierarchy. Working out the details of a lexical memory system that will permit partial redundancy and support rules of inference remains one of the challenging problems for scientists studying this aspect of lexical knowledge.

Basic Concepts

Lexical memory for the meanings of nouns incorporates some form of the inheritance principle, although not the kind of idealized inheritance system that would be maximally efficient. So the question becomes: How far, and in what way, does lexical memory depart from the most efficient system?

A plausible speculation is that some part of the familiarity effect (see Chapter 7) consists of associating redundant information with familiar, frequently used words. In this view, a newly acquired or seldom used lexical concept would inherit the distinguishing features of its superordinates, but, as its familiarity grew through frequent use, those features that were originally inherited would come to be associated with it directly. If this speculation is correct—if highly familiar words have many redundant features directly associated with them—it explains, at least in part, why questions involving familiar concepts can be answered faster than comparable questions involving unfamiliar concepts.

Assume, therefore, that lexical memory is a hybrid compromise between efficiency of storage and efficiency of retrieval. The basic design is that of an inheritance system, but frequently used paths develop shortcuts; information that is at first retrieved inferentially comes by frequent association to be stored redundantly.

As areas of redundancy develop in lexical memory, the system becomes subject to certain general constraints on redundant systems. In the comparison of an imaginary idealized model inheritance system (IMIS) with a completely redundant memory system, it was obvious that redundant systems become increasingly inefficient as the number of levels increases. It is an interesting fact, therefore, that few sets of hierarchically shared names have more than six or seven levels. Where more than that are found—*steed,* for example, illustrates a hierarchy with at least ten levels—some of the levels are likely to involve technical concepts that are not part of the everyday core vocabulary. In principle, there is no reason a lexical hierarchy could not have any number of levels, so the fact that there is a practical limit could be interpreted as an accommodation to memory limitations.

Since the number of levels is limited, the number of nouns in a hierarchy also tends to be limited. In other words, the noun lexicon is characterized by a number of hierarchies, each headed by a separate generic concept, called a unique beginner. For example, an {*act, action*} concept—curly brackets still mark lexical concepts—might head a hierarchy of nouns referring to things that people do; an {*animal, creature*} concept might head a hierarchy of nouns referring to all the different kinds of animal; an {*artifact, product*} concept might head a hierarchy of nouns referring to all the different human-made objects; and so on. Each one of these hierarchies would have from five to ten distinguishable levels. It is relatively easy to list possible unique beginners for English—act; animal; artifact; attribute; body part; cognition; communication; event; feeling; food; group; location; motive; natural object; person; natural phenomenon; plant; possession; process; quantity; relation; shape; state; substance; time—where to stop gets a bit hazy. But the important point is that unique beginners are the most generic concepts in a language; each unique beginner can be taken as the head of a different semantic field.

Comparing IMIS with a totally redundant system also demonstrates that the repetition of high-level features with every hyponym is particularly inefficient. An obvious economy, therefore, would be to reduce the number of high-level features. For convenience of calculation, IMIS introduced four new distinguishing features at each level, but this assumption is quite unrealistic. Most lexical hierarchies have a level, somewhere in the middle, where most of the distinguishing features are assigned. Linguistic anthropologists refer to this as the base level of the noun lexicon, and to the concepts at this level as basic concepts.

Base-level terms are the words that children learn first and that people are most likely to use when asked to name objects or pictures of objects. For lexical concepts at the base level, people can list many distinguishing attributes, parts, and uses. Above the base level, descriptions are necessarily brief and general. Below the base level, little is added to the features that characterize basic concepts. For example, if people are asked to list the distinguishing features of *furniture,* there is little more to say than that articles of furniture serve to make a room habitable. *Furniture* does not elicit any properties, shapes, or specific uses. If people are asked about *chair,* however, they have much more to say: It has a general shape with a seat, back, and legs; it is used

One Hundred Universal Lexical Concepts

1. *I*	26. **root**	51. **breasts**	76. **rain**
2. *thou*	27. **bark**	52. **heart**	77. **stone**
3. *we*	28. **skin**	53. **liver**	78. **sand**
4. *this*	29. **flesh**	54. *drink*	79. **earth**
5. *that*	30. **blood**	55. *eat*	80. **cloud**
6. *who*	31. **bone**	56. *bite*	81. **smoke**
7. *what*	32. **grease**	57. *see*	82. **fire**
8. *not*	33. **egg**	58. *hear*	83. **ash**
9. *all*	34. **horn**	59. *know*	84. *burn*
10. *many*	35. **tail**	60. *sleep*	85. **path**
11. *one*	36. **leather**	61. *die*	86. **mountain**
12. *two*	37. **hair**	62. *kill*	87. *red*
13. *big*	38. **head**	63. *swim*	88. *green*
14. *long*	39. **ear**	64. *fly*	89. *yellow*
15. *small*	40. **eye**	65. *walk*	90. *white*
16. **woman**	41. **nose**	66. *come*	91. *black*
17. **man**	42. **mouth**	67. *lie*	92. **night**
18. **person**	43. **tooth**	68. *sit*	93. *hot*
19. **fish**	44. **tongue**	69. *stand*	94. *cold*
20. **bird**	45. **claw**	70. *give*	95. *full*
21. **dog**	46. **foot**	71. *say*	96. *new*
22. **louse**	47. **knee**	72. **sun**	97. *good*
23. **tree**	48. **hand**	73. **moon**	98. *round*
24. **seed**	49. **belly**	74. **star**	99. *dry*
25. **leaf**	50. **neck**	75. **water**	100. **name**

The linguist Morris Swadesh constructed lists of concepts he judged to be so basic that every language would have words for them. His first list had two hundred concepts, but many of them proved unsatisfactory when he studied languages outside the Indo-European family. This list of one hundred items was then selected. The fifty-four nouns are in boldface; of these, the base-level terms for most English-speaking people would include person, fish, bird, dog, tree, sun, moon, star, water, stone, path, mountain, *and perhaps a few others.*

for sitting; and so on. *Chair* is a base-level word. Go further down to *armchair* and people will add arms, a minor addition to the basic concept. *Dog, horse, gun,* and *tree* are examples of other base-level terms in English.

By reducing the number of distinguishing features associated with concepts at the top of the lexical hierarchy, the cost of introducing redundancy can be greatly reduced. The price, of course, is that the top of the hierarchy becomes vacuously general. For instance, it is possible for a theorist to put an empty concept like *entity* at the very pinnacle of the nouns, then to make *object* and *idea* the immediate hyponyms of *entity,* and so on down to more specific concepts—and in that way to pull all nouns together in a single hierarchy. Such exercises give a certain ontological satisfaction, but the generic concepts at the top convey little semantic information; if a language had no words for these concepts, they would not be missed.

So the cost of redundant features can be controlled by introducing unique beginners that have few defining features. But the underlying design of the noun lexicon is still an inheritance system. The economies of inheritance are not exploited fully, but they provide a general plan for this part of the mental lexicon and facilitate the rapid growth of vocabulary.

Precisely where various distinguishing features should be attached to the inheritance system thus becomes a delicate theoretical decision. *Has wheels,* for example, cannot be attached to *vehicle,* because boats and sleds are vehicles that do not have wheels. If a category labeled *wheeled vehicles* (for which English has no special word) is created, it will include not only cars, trucks, trains, and the like, but also bicycles, baby buggies, skateboards, wheelbarrows, and much else; if the membership becomes too diverse, it might be necessary to rethink the decision to fill the lexical gap with *wheeled vehicle.* The alternative would be to make *has wheels* a feature of everything that has wheels and not try to achieve a generalization that would permit inheritance of that feature.

The integration of part-whole hierarchies into inheritance systems poses complex questions for a lexical semanticist. Not only can a part serve as a feature used in defining several different nominal concepts, but the part's name itself is a nominal concept that must have a place in the inheritance system and can have parts of its own. For example, *wheel* not only plays a defining role as a part-feature of wheeled vehicles, but a wheel—like a lever, screw, wedge, or pulley—is also a simple machine; *wheel* is a hyponym of *machine.* Moreover, a wheel can have parts: a tire, a rim, spokes. So *wheel* is in two hierarchies at the same time, one an inheritance system for machines and the other an inclusion hierarchy formed by wholes and their parts. This degree of complexity is common for complicated human artifacts and for names of body parts.

Building a theoretical representation of lexical memory at this level of detail requires considerable adjustment of the associations among levels and the attachment of features to concepts. It is reasonable to suppose that similar adjustments must be achieved by human learners as their vocabularies grow, but precisely how the incorrect information is unlearned and correct information substituted for it is still poorly understood.

Polysemy

A polysemous word has two or more meanings. Most people feel that there is something untidy about polysemy, because it invites misunderstanding: A well-planned language would avoid it in the interests of greater clarity and precision. To eliminate polysemy, however, would make the vocabulary a rigid system, unable to adapt to unanticipated situations or preoccupations. If the supply of different words were unlimited, of course, a one-word : one-idea vocabulary might be conceivable; English comes closer to that goal than most languages do. Spoken Chinese, on the other hand, is enormously polysemous by Western standards, yet the Chinese people get along with it quite well. Apparently, polysemy is not as severe a handicap as it might seem at first glance.

The nature of polysemy is best appreciated by considering specific examples. Take the English word *board. Board* has different meanings as a noun and as a verb. Even as a noun, however, *board* is still polysemous; {*board, committee*} and {*board, plank*} are but two of several uses to which it is put. In appropriate contexts, this polysemy can result in ambiguity. A sentence like

> *He hoped the boards would meet.*

can be understood with either reading of *board,* but only because there are also two senses of the verb *meet.* In most contexts, polysemous words are unambiguous—in the jargon of lexical semantics, context "disambiguates" polysemous words. When the two senses are in different grammatical categories—*board* as a verb and *board* as a noun, say—the syntactic context can provide the differential clue. The more difficult cases arise when the two senses are in the same grammatical category. How people manage to disambiguate polysemous words in understanding grammatical discourse is one of the more challenging problems of psycholinguistics, but it lies beyond the scope of this volume. Here it is sufficient to know that polysemy is not the threat it is sometimes said to be.

Polysemy serves as a reminder (if one is needed) that the lexical hierarchies that theorists represent by inheritance systems are really hierarchies of lexical concepts, not hierarchies of words. The word *board* meaning {*board, committee*} is a hyponym of the concept {*social group, group of people*}; the word *board* meaning {*board, plank*} is a hyponym of the concept {*lumber, sawed wood*}; the word *board* meaning {*board, blackboard, chalkboard*} is a hyponym of the concept {*writing surface*}; and so on. Each *board*—call them $board_1$, $board_2$, and so on—expresses a different lexical concept and is located in a different inheritance system. In another language, each *board* might be expressed by a different word.

Different languages allocate their polysemy differently. Any bilingual dictionary will provide detailed lists of these differences. For example, the English noun *board* translates into German as *das Brett* for {*board, plank*}, but as *der Ausschuss* for {*board, committee*}. There is no single German word that expresses exactly the same range of meanings that *board* expresses. Learning a second language heightens one's sensitivity to the subtleties of polysemy in both languages.

Indeed, these differences among languages are so common that exceptions are surprising, but similarities do exist. For example, approximately two-thirds of the different languages that have been compared have a single word that can express both {wood} and {tree}, and one-third merge {hand} and {arm} under a single word. These nomenclatural relations reflect common ways of perceiving and categorizing things in the world.

Polysemy plays a role in lexical change. It is common for a word's meaning to be extended when a term is needed for some new referent, but the new referent must be perceived as related in some manner to the old referent. For example, if a people who spoke a language that had a word *W* for {tree} came to need a word for {wood}, and if they perceived trees as the source of wood, they might well extend *W* to refer to {wood}, too. Cecil H. Brown, a linguistic anthropologist who has pursued comparative studies of polysemy, observes that the "development of polysemy typically entails extending a term for a high salience referent to a related referent of low salience."

For example, Brown surveyed the words used to refer to {wind} and {air} in 221 different languages. Of the two, {wind} is initially the more salient; all 221 languages had a term for {wind}, whereas only 137 had a term for {air}. But 77 languages had a polysemous word to express both {air} and {wind}. These figures support an account of lexical evolution as a reflection of increasing technical sophistication. Winds are directly perceptible, but an appreciation of air requires greater understanding. So it is not surprising that {wind} is initially the more salient concept. When the concept of {air} emerges, the existing term for {wind} can be extended to include it. A relation is perceived between the two—wind is the flow of air—so polysemy is a simple solution to a terminological need. And if {air} becomes still more important, this polysemous state may be replaced by a separate term for {air}.

With the help of the *Oxford English Dictionary*, a story illustrating this general scenario can be told about the polysemous English word *board*, although the exact details are lost in the mists of history. Sometime long ago *bord* referred to a piece of lumber sawed thin with a wide surface. Since these pieces of wood made useful surfaces for working and eating, *bord* was extended to express a concept that has since become familiar as *table;* expressions like *aboveboard, sideboard,* and *bed and board* still echo this use. The word was next extended to the table at which a council was held, and from there to the company of persons who sat around the council table, whence it is still used in expressions like *board of directors, board of health,* or *school board.*

Tracing the histories of words is an acquired taste, but those who have it pursue it with a passion. Every word has a story; documenting it, filling the gaps with plausible speculations, can become an absorbing occupation. Some of the fascination comes from the fact that these stories are often so surprising, so unexpected. That is to say, it is not necessary to know the etymology of a word to know what it means or how it is used, but that very independence is part of the appeal. Who would have expected to find a fragment of human history in a common noun?

■   ■   ■

One way that people cope with experience is by categorizing it, and the categories that are important to a group of people shape the words that they use. The result is a hierarchical structure of lexical concepts, in which a word's meaning can be identified by its place in the hierarchy. This organization provides a framework on which new concepts can be hung—a framework made sturdy by the multiple relations, both morphological and semantic, that hold it together, yet open enough to allow extensions to accommodate new insights and new interests.

▶ *This pair of hands can be verbally discriminated by means of the category of words called adjectives, which express values of attributes—in this case, size.*

▼ *This network representing the contrasted terms big and little (and their respective synonyms) illustrates the fundamental role of antonymy, direct and indirect, in organizing adjectives within the mental lexicon.*

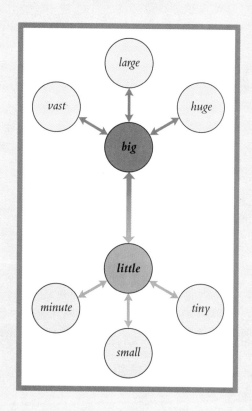

CHAPTER

Drawing Distinctions

To categorize is to disregard differences. A house and a barn are different things, but when they are classified together as instances of the concept labeled *building,* their differences are put aside. An ability to classify is an important component of the human ability to cope with experience, and a large segment of the vocabulary of any language—the nouns—is dedicated to standardizing the categories that are chosen as important. But ignoring differences is not always the most intelligent response to a situation. There are times when it is necessary to notice differences and draw distinctions between individuals or events. All higher animals have this discriminative ability, but its scope in human adaptation is greatly enhanced by the further ability to assign words to important distinctions.

Language serves many purposes, one of which is to communicate information. Other purposes are more fun, but serious people emphasize communication. And to emphasize communication is to emphasize reference: If the participants in a discussion cannot agree on what they are talking about, they will never realize the benefits of exchanging information. For that reason, linguistic devices that discriminate among possible referents come to be particularly important.

A proper noun usually denotes an individual thing—there is only one Princeton University, for example—so its referential intent can be reasonably clear. But confusion can arise with common nouns. Common nouns designate classes of objects or events, not specific instances. English provides a variety of syntactic devices to individuate a specific member of such a class. For example, to designate a particular car, you can use a relative clause (*the car that the truck hit*), or a prepositional phrase (*the car in the driveway*), or a genitive apposition (*your father's car*), or adjectival modification (either attributively, *the small car*, or predicatively, *the car is small*). All of these syntactic devices presuppose that the objects or events in question have certain features—histories, locations,

Even the eggplant has multiple dimensions of variability, and each dimension maps onto an adjectival attribute in English.

owners, appearances, parts, uses, whatever—and that those features can be used to distinguish one instance from another. The words that best serve to draw such distinctions are words in the syntactic category known as modifiers: adjectives and adverbs. Here again, the organization of a large part of the mental lexicon derives from a basic device that the human mind uses to manage experience and learn from it.

Dimensions of Meaning

Take some simple object—a cup, say. The word *cup* seems unambiguous, yet it fails to specify whether any particular cup is big or little, full or empty, white or brown, clean or dirty, paper or porcelain, here or there. These attributes can become important when it is necessary to distinguish one cup from another. A cup has size (both height and width, and the sides have thickness), color (hue, brightness, saturation), weight, temperature, shape, volume, hardness, elasticity. A cup has value, cost, age, usefulness, suitability, location, accessibility, portability, pleasantness. The list of attributes can go on and on. Any of these attributes can be used to distinguish one cup from another.

Attributes must be attributes OF something. That is to say, different attributes pertain to different kinds of things; people can discriminate many attributes other than those required to distinguish one cup from another. A cup is not ordinarily said to be ambitious, intelligible, aggressive, persuasive, powerful, or thoughtful—a list of irrelevant attributes would be longer than the list of relevant ones. What a person knows about any common noun includes the attributes of its referents, the attributes that determine which modifiers are appropriate to use in designating particular instances.

Some theorists think of attributes as dimensions. In that case, the N attributes of a given referent define an abstract N-dimensional space (a hyperspace); any particular instance can be thought of as a point in that space, its location given by its value on each dimension. Note that nouns are used to name attributes, but modifiers specify values of those attributes. The size (noun) of the cup, for example, can be large or small (modifiers), its height (noun) can be tall or short (modifiers), and so on. Each modifier specifies the position of a referent along a particular dimension; the full set of modifiers specifies a particular location in the N-dimensional space; differences between referents are given by their different locations in that space. Of course, not every value of every referent on every dimension needs to be specified; ordinarily a small subset will be enough to resolve any particular confusion between candidate referents. But the point is that modifiers provide an elaborate multidimensional system for distinguishing one object or event from another, and so facilitate agreement on what is being talked about.

In Indo-European languages, modifiers are an open class; new words can be introduced to express values of new attributes. But that freedom does not

Illustrating the effect of varying two attributes of an object. In this case, height and width generate the following lexical designations, from upper left to lower right: vase, cup, bowl.

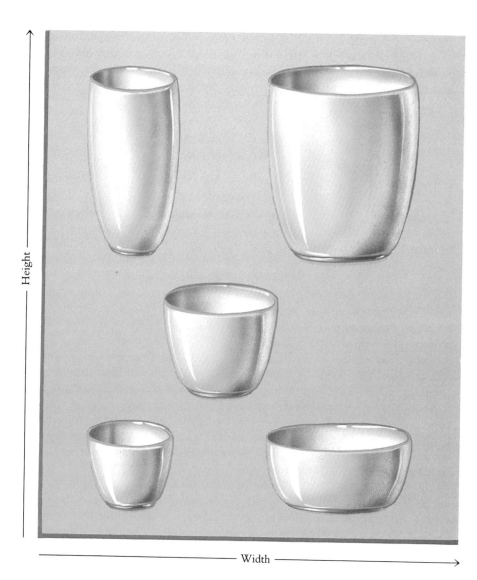

exist in every language. Some languages (Swahili is an example) have a class of words that can be called adjectives, but it is a closed class with a limited number of members—usually between eight and about fifty. Other languages have no adjectives at all, but express adjectival meanings primarily by nouns or by verbs.

Languages in which adjectives form a closed class shed suggestive light on the attributes you would choose if you were choosing very few. From one of these languages to the next, the range of meanings that the adjectives express is remarkably consistent. They usually include adjectives giving values of size, color, age, and worth; some also include adjectives for values of position, hardness, kindness, or speed. A paradigm example is Igbo, a Kwa language spoken in West Africa. It has only eight adjectives, which state values for four attributes; they translate into English as *big/little, light/dark, old/new,* and *good/bad.*

In English, of course, the variety of adjectives is unlimited. When the stock of pure adjectives runs thin, there are many affixes available to turn nouns into adjectives: *-y (flowery), -ly (leisurely), -like (childlike), -ful (wonder-ful), -some (burdensome), -ish (foolish), -en (silken).* Even constructions like *a meat-and-potatoes restaurant* or *a just-pretend-I'm-not-here observer* are acceptable in English (they would be unthinkable in French).

English adjectives are complicated, and getting the different varieties straight is a good way to start a discussion of the semantics of modification.

Predicable Adjectives

A predicable adjective is one that can be used in the predicate of a sentence. For example, *wealthy* is a predicable adjective because it can be used predicatively in such sentences as *The man is wealthy.* A few English adjectives can be used only predicatively; *afloat,* for example, can be used predicatively in *The boat is afloat,* but not attributively, as in *the afloat boat.* But most adjectives can be used attributively—*the wealthy man.* The important point to understand is that many adjectives cannot be used predicatively. For example, *the previous owner* is admissible, but *the owner is previous* is not; *the natal day* is admissible, but *the day is natal* is not. Adjectives that cannot be used predicatively are called nonpredicable adjectives.

The distinction between predicable and nonpredicable adjectives is complicated by the fact that many adjectives can be both. The adjective *mechanical* is an example: *A mechanical device* is a device that is mechanical, so one use of *mechanical* is predicative; but *a mechanical genius* should not be a genius who is mechanical, so *mechanical* has a second use that is nonpredicative. *Nervous* provides another example: *a nervous patient* versus *a nervous disorder.* Sometimes the distinction can be ambiguous: Out of context it is not clear whether *dramatic criticism* refers to criticism of drama or to criticism that is dramatic.

Linguists have provided several criteria that can be used to distinguish predicative from nonpredicative uses:

1. Predicable and nonpredicable adjectives cannot be combined conjunctively (with *and, or,* or *but*): *The rude and civil engineer* can only be a joke.

2. Nonpredicable adjectives partition the head nominal into subclasses: *criminal lawyer, corporate lawyer, divorce lawyer, trial lawyer,* and so on. These subclasses are not gradable: *The quite corporate lawyer* or *a very divorce lawyer* are unacceptable.

3. Predicable adjectives can be nominalized, but nonpredicable adjectives cannot be. For example, the predicative use of *nervous* in *the nervous patient* admits such constructions as *the patient's nervousness,* but its nonpredicative use in *the nervous disorder* does not—*the disorder's nervousness* is distinctly odd.

By all three criteria, nonpredicable adjectives behave as if they were nouns being used as modifiers. For example, in *garden party* the noun *garden* is used as an adjective; like a nonpredicable adjective, the nominal adjective does not conjoin, is not gradable, and cannot be nominalized:

1'. Predicable adjectives and adjectival nouns cannot be combined conjunctively: *the large and garden party.*

2'. Adjectival nouns are not gradable: *the highly garden party.*

3'. Adjectival nouns cannot be nominalized: *the party's gardenness.*

In short, nonpredicable adjectives can be considered stylistic variants of modifying nouns. In dictionaries, the definitions of nonpredicable adjectives are usually introduced by some phrase such as "of or pertaining to ———."

Numbers are a class of nonpredicable adjectives. Note that *the expensive and six books* is unacceptable, as are *the extremely six books* and *the book's sixness.* Of course, one does encounter such apparently predicative uses as *The apostles were twelve,* but that statement combined with *Peter was an apostle* does not lead to the conclusion that *Peter was twelve.* Although English has many nonpredicable adjectives, when people speak of adjectives it is almost always the predicable adjectives that they have in mind. The following discussion, therefore, is limited to predicable adjectives; hereafter, *adjective* will mean *predicable adjective* unless otherwise noted.

Antonymy

Hyponymy is basic to the organization of nouns in the mental lexicon, and from that transitive asymmetric relation the inheritance hierarchies are generated (see Chapter 9). Adjectives, however, are organized differently; it is not clear what it would mean to say that one adjective "is a kind of" some other adjective. Instead of hyponymy, the basic semantic relation organizing adjectives is antonymy.

The psychological role of antonymy first became obvious from results obtained with word association tests. When the probe word in such a test is a familiar adjective, the most common response from adults is another adjective—almost always the antonym of the probe. For example, when *hot* is the stimulus, *cold* is the most frequent response; when *cold* is the stimulus, *hot* is the most frequent response. This mutuality of association is a salient feature of data for adjectives; it led psychologists to an early appreciation of the importance of antonymy.

It would be helpful, therefore, to have a clear definition of this important semantic relation. Unfortunately, antonymy is not easily defined. The general idea is one of contrast or opposition along some given dimension, but words can contrast or stand in opposition to one another in a variety of ways. At a minimum, the following six types of antonyms have been distinguished in the literature on this subject:

1. Contradictory terms (*perfect/imperfect*)

2. Contrary terms (*white/black*)

3. Reverse terms (*constructive/destructive*)

4. Contrasted terms (*rich/destitute*)

5. Relative terms (*brother/sister*)

6. Complementary terms (*question/answer*)

From a cursory examination of this list it is obvious that no simple linguistic test will accommodate all these different kinds of opposition. Yet native speakers of English have little trouble recognizing antonyms when they encounter them.

The problem of defining antonymy is simplified by limiting the discussion to adjectives, since that move eliminates relative and complementary antonyms, which are antonymous nouns or verbs. The remaining four categories can be accounted for in terms of a few commonsense assumptions about the semantic role that adjectives play in English. The following ideas have already been introduced:

A1.   Adjectives express values of attributes.

A2.   Attributes are bipolar.

A3.   Attributes can be gradable (continuous) or ungradable (dichotomous).

According to A1, *x is Adj* means that there is an attribute A such that $A(x) = Adj$; that is, *Adj* is the value of the function $A(x)$. For example, *The chair is heavy* means that there is an attribute *Weight* such that *Weight(chair)* = *heavy*.

A2 implies that antonyms are labels for the opposing ends of a bipolar attribute: *The feather is light* means that *Weight(feather)* = *light*—toward the pole of the Weight dimension opposite the pole labeled *heavy*. Of course, A2 is false on a strict interpretation. Some attributes seem to be trichotomous (*solid/liquid/gaseous*) and some may have an even greater polarity (*red/green/yellow/ blue*). But A2 assumes that such complications are exceptional and that bipolarity is the general rule. It is the bipolarity of attributes that makes it so natural to think of them as dimensions.

C. K. Ogden on Oppositions

The British psychologist Charles Kay Ogden (1889–1957) is best known for his 1930 book *Basic English,* in which he proposed an international auxiliary language derived from English by simplifying its grammar and reducing the vocabulary to 850 words. Far less well known is the short monograph that he published two years later, *Opposition: A Linguistic and Psychological Analysis,* in which he analyzed various types of opposition between pairs of English words. Ogden saw classification and opposition as the two basic methods available to lexicographers for defining words, and he feared that the importance of opposition was being neglected. "Most controversial discussion in which practical problems of definition tend to arise," he wrote, "turns on questions of degree and contrast, as much as on differentia and hierarchy." And questions of degree and contrast, he noted, involve oppositions.

Charles K. Ogden.

Two types of opposition were fundamental for Ogden. He called them Scale and Cut—oppositions between the two extremes of a scale (*long* and *short,* for example) and oppositions between the two sides of a cut (*inside* and *outside,* for example). But different Scales and Cuts have different properties, which led him to a complex notation for representing different types of oppositions.

The practical reason for Ogden's concern with opposition was that approximately 20 percent of his list of 850 Basic English words could be paired. By eliminating opposites and a few other terms, he was able to reduce the list of Basic words from 850 to 500. He calculated that the time saved by this reduction—a couple of hours per person spent in memorizing vocabulary—was, when multiplied by the world's population, like saving the entire productive lives of thousands of people.

According to A3, there are two kinds of attributes, gradable and non-gradable. *Weight,* for example, is a gradable attribute whose values range over a continuum between *heavy* and *light,* whereas *sex* is an ungradable attribute that takes two values, *male* and *female.* A3 is really too vague to falsify. Sometimes the distinction between gradable and ungradable is unclear, and any adjective that has comparative and superlative forms can appear to be graded. But since the majority of hard-working adjectives in English are graded, the distinction is more logical than practical.

For the vast majority of adjectives, these three assumptions suffice to account for the observation that antonymy is basic to the semantics of adjectives: The semantic role of adjectives is to express opposite values of (gradable or ungradable) bipolar attributes. Each of the four types of antonymous adjectives can be understood in these terms; consider them in turn.

Begin with the distinction between (1) contradictory and (2) contrary terms. This terminology originated in logic, where two propositions are said to be contradictory if the truth of one implies the falsity of the other, and the falsity of one implies the truth of the other: *Caesar is dead* implies that *Caesar is alive* must be false, and vice versa. Logicians distinguish contradictories from contraries, where two propositions are contrary if only one of them can be true, but both can be false: *That is hot* and *That is cold* cannot both be true of the same "that," but both can be false. So *hot* and *cold* are contrary terms.

One problem with this logical distinction is that the definition of contrary terms is not limited to opposites. It can be applied so broadly as to be practically meaningless. For example, *That is a tree* and *That is a dog* cannot both be true, but both can be false, so *dog* and *tree* are also contrary terms. Assumptions A1 through A3 ignore this logical distinction and assume instead that gradability is basic. What a logician would call contradictory terms are simply values of nongradable attributes; contraries are gradable.

The same assumptions account for (3) reverse terms, which signify acts or states that reverse or undo one another. Reverse terms are usually antonymous verbs, but they do occur as deverbal adjectives (*tied/untied*). Reverse adjectives are simply values of ungradable attributes; mutual exclusivity derives from the special relation of reversibility.

Which leaves to be discussed: (4) contrasted terms.

Indirect Antonyms

If antonyms are defined as pairs of labels for opposite poles of an attribute, then pairs like *dry/moist* and *vigilant/careless* are clearly antonyms. How do they differ from other antonyms? The most obvious difference is that they are not primary associates of one another; compare them to *dry/wet* and *careful/careless.*

For ease of discussion, the contrasted terms can be called indirect antonyms, as distinguished from the so-called contradictory, contrary, and reverse terms, which can be called direct antonyms. This grouping reduces the variety of antonymous adjectives from four types to two: direct versus indirect antonyms. Then the question becomes: Why is a distinction needed between direct and indirect antonyms? Why do native speakers of English feel that the relation between *dry/moist* is different from that between *dry/wet*? Why are *vigilant/careless* felt to be somehow less antonymous than *careful/careless*?

The rationale for this distinction begins with the observation that many adjectives do not have direct antonyms. What is the direct antonym of *musty*, for example? A contrasting term is *fresh*, but the direct antonym of *fresh* is *stale*. To call *fresh/musty* indirect antonyms is to suggest that the conceptual contrast between *fresh* and *musty* is mediated by the semantic similarity between *musty* and the direct antonym *stale*. Similarly, the conceptual contrast between *dry* and *moist* is mediated by the synonymy of *moist* and *wet*; *vigilant/careless* is mediated by the synonymy of *vigilant* and *careful*; and so on.

Thus, the rule is that the direct antonym of an adjective A_1 that is similar in meaning to adjective A_2 is the indirect antonym of adjective A_2. This rule merits an additional semantic assumption:

> **A4.** Adjectives lacking direct antonyms are synonyms of adjectives that have direct antonyms.

In other words, both synonymy and antonymy are required to characterize the semantic structure of adjectives.

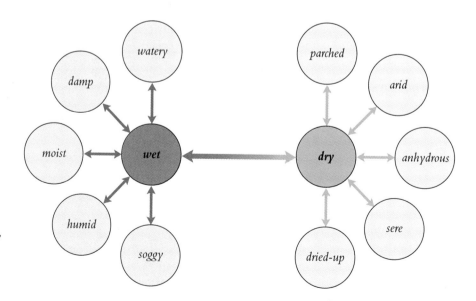

Two clusters of adjectives having similar meanings are related by the direct antonymy of wet *and* dry. *Within each cluster, the adjectives are related by similarity of meaning.*

The general picture that emerges from these four assumptions is that predicable adjectives are organized in the mental lexicon in clusters of synonymous (or near synonymous) terms, and that pairs of clusters are held together by bipolar attributes whose opposite ends are labeled by direct antonyms that provide foci for the clusters. Or, to state it the other way round, associated with each member of a directly antonymous pair is a cluster of other adjectives with similar meanings. For example, *wet* and *dry* are direct antonyms; clustered around *wet* are *moist, damp, soggy, waterlogged,* and so on, while clustered around *dry* are *arid, baked, parched, dehydrated,* and so on.

Gradation

In addition to antonymy and synonymy, a third semantic relation is added to the adjective system as a consequence of the gradability of bipolar attributes. For example, there are differences between *big* and *huge* and between *small* and *tiny*. These quantitative differences between terms that express similar values of an attribute are differences in gradation. Gradation is not entirely lexical, however. It is partially lexicalized, but most grading is expressed by suffixation or adverbial modification.

Gradable adjectives come in three flavors: *some, more,* and *most,* otherwise known as the positive, comparative, and superlative degrees. Comparatives and superlatives of monosyllabic adjectives are formed by adding *-er* or *-est,* which was the Anglo-Saxon rule for all adjectives. This rule also applies to many bisyllabic adjectives, but it is not reliable. It applies to *tender* but not to *proper,* for example, and to *able,* but not to *hostile,* so the terminal sounds are not a reliable guide. These are matters that speakers of English simply have to memorize.

When the morphological rule does not apply, *more* and *most* are used. A natural five-point scale results when *less* and *least* are added:

least desirable, less desirable, desirable, more desirable, most desirable

Psychologists who make frequent use of rating scales tend to avoid this natural terminology, however, probably because *least* and *most* are understood to designate unique instances, not classes of instances. A psychologist would probably prefer something like

highly undesirable, undesirable, indifferent, desirable, highly desirable

where the interpretation is less relativistic. That is to say, the least desirable option may not be undesirable, and the most desirable need not be desirable. Sir Winston Churchill, for example, could agree that democracy is not a good form of government and still conclude that it is the best there is.

Quantifiers

*Q*uantifiers are a special class of adjectives. Three of them are particularly important: *all, some,* and *no*. These three played a central role in Aristotelian syllogisms and have fascinated logicians ever since. For example,

> All men are mortal.
> Some Greeks are men.
> Therefore, some Greeks are mortal.

The conclusion that some Greeks are mortal does not logically imply that some Greeks are not mortal, although that is how it would be understood in everyday speech. In logic it follows that if all men are mortal, then some men are mortal, but in everyday speech it would be considered misleading to say that some men are mortal if you knew that they all are. That is only one of the discrepancies between logic and ordinary language.

As an aid to reasoning with these words, the English logician John Venn (1834–1923) introduced the use of circles to represent the sets of things involved—Greeks and men, in this example. Unfortunately, the same statement can be true of more than one Venn diagram.

These three adjectives form a closed logical system. With the negative operator NOT, they can be defined in terms of one another. For example:

All men are mortal.
≡ It is NOT the case that *some* men are NOT mortal.
≡ *No* men are NOT mortal.

Or:

Some Greeks are men.
≡ It is NOT the case that *all* Greeks are NOT men.
≡ It is NOT the case that *no* Greeks are men.

And so on. The combinatorial possibilities are truly endless.

The quantifiers of natural languages are much richer than the quantifiers of logic. In English, for example, there are also such quantifiers as *every, any, many, more, nearly all, most, not many, few, each, only, other, both*—and perhaps others, as well as the more specialized *the* and *a/an*, plus the specific numerals *one, two three,* . . . and *all three, all four,* . . . (but not *all two*). How formal logic might be extended to represent all these important quantificational concepts is a subject that only experts should debate. It is obvious, however, that these words are not ordinary predicable adjectives.

Not all Greeks are men.
Not all men are Greeks.
Some Greeks are men.
Some men are Greeks.

All Greeks are men.
All men are Greeks.
Some Greeks are men.
Some men are Greeks.

All Greeks are men.
Not all men are Greeks.
Some Greeks are men.
Some men are Greeks.

Venn's diagrams. Not only are several statements true of the same diagram, but the same statement (Some Greeks are men, for example) can be true of several diagrams.

Some grading is lexicalized. For example, the clusters of adjectives involved in the *hot/cold* polarity provide a lexicalized grading from fire to ice:

> *torrid, scalding, fiery*
> *HOT, sweltering, tropical*
> *warm, toasty, heated*
> *tepid, temperate, lukewarm*
> *cool, chilly, bracing*
> *COLD, frosty, wintry*
> *frigid, ice-cold, frozen*

Lexical gradation is the exception in English, however, not the rule, Only a few attributes allow it; size, brightness, age, and value (important attributes in any language) provide good examples.

Most clusters consist of adjectives that modify limited classes of nouns. For example, both climates and lips can be wet or dry, but *arid climate* and *parched lips* are preferable to *arid lips* and *parched climate*. How the different adjectives in a cluster relate to one another and to the nouns they modify is a complex and subtle topic.

Markedness

Attributes underlying antonymous pairs usually have an orientation. In 1967 the German linguist Manfred Bierwisch published an important analysis of German adjectives in which he pointed out that not all spatial adjectives can take measure phrases. For example,

> *Der Zug ist zehn Wagen lang (The train is ten cars long)*

is acceptable; the measure phrase *zehn Wagen* (*ten cars*) describes how long the train is. But when the antonym is used:

> *Der Zug ist zehn Wagen kurz (The train is ten cars short)*

the result is not acceptable in either language (unless it has already been established that the train is short in the sense that some cars are missing).

The antonymous pairs, *lang/kurz* in German and *long/short* in English, illustrate a phenomenon known as markedness. The primary member (*lang, long*) is unmarked and can take a measure phrase; the secondary member (*kurz, short*) is marked and does not take measure phrases without special preparation. Note that it is the unmarked member that lends its name to the attribute (*Länge, length*). In Bierwisch's terminology the primary pole of the attribute is positive and the other negative. Or, to revert to the idea of dimensions in a hyperspace, one end of each dimension (the end expressed by the unmarked member of the antonymous pair) is anchored at the point of origin of the space.

Not all unmarked adjectives take measure phrases. Nevertheless, markedness is a general linguistic phenomenon that seems to characterize all direct antonyms. In nearly every case one member of an antonymous pair is primary: more customary, more frequently used, less remarkable. It is the default value, the value that would be assumed in the absence of information to the contrary. And it is the member normally used in asking questions: *How long is it? How big were they?* Unmarked adjectives include *long, big, bright, pleasant, comfortable, good, strong, happy, healthy, legal, public,* and so forth—a perfect world for Pollyanna.

How can you tell which member of any given pair of antonyms is marked? A few cases are puzzling, but for the vast majority of pairs the marker is plain to see. *Unpleasant* carries the prefix *un-* as an explicit marker; *impatient* is marked by *im-, illegal* by *il-,* and so on. *Un-* is the most productive of these negative affixes. But even the common Anglo-Saxon adjectives whose antonyms are not marked morphologically usually have a clear orientation; such uncertain pairs as *wet/dry* or *hot/cold* are exceptions. For example, if a language has modifiers, it will have an adjective that can be translated as *good.* Many languages, however, do not have a word for *bad,* which is expressed as *not good.* But no language is known that lacks a word for *good* and expresses that concept as *not bad. Good* is the unmarked member in all known languages.

The fact that most antonyms are formed by the addition of a negative affix is a reminder that antonymy, like synonymy, is a semantic relation between words, not a semantic relation between concepts or meanings. Synonymy is a relation of similarity of meaning among words: Any two or more words that can express the same meaning are said to be synonyms. Antonymy is a relation of opposition of meaning between words: Antonymy is frequently the semantic change that accompanies the addition of the negative *un-* prefix. (Recall the necessary element of semantic change, or change in meaning, associated with the derivational rules established in Chapter 6, and the fact that the domains of such rules are always actual words.) In this respect, antonymy (and synonymy) differ from hyponymy and meronymy, which are semantic relations between concepts.

Note that this feature of antonymy is responsible for the organization into direct and indirect antonyms. Two clusters of adjectives that express opposite meanings cannot all be direct antonyms of one another because an adjective can have only one direct antonym. For example, *big* and *large* express very similar meanings, as do *little* and *small,* but the meaning {*big, large*} is not the antonym of the meaning {*little, small*}. Instead, the words *big/little* form one pair of direct antonyms, and *large/small* form another. *Large/little* are indirect antonyms, conceptually opposed but unpaired.

Color Terms

Color commands a lexicon of its own: English has more than three thousand color terms. The color lexicon has received so much attention, and seems to be organized so particularly, that something special must be said about it.

First, the color terms of English serve both as nouns and as adjectives. As nouns, they have a clear hierarchical structure: For example, a scarlet is a red, a red is a color, and a color is a visual attribute. *Scarlet,* along with *crimson* and *vermilion,* are secondary color terms; *red, green, yellow, blue, black,* and *white* (and sometimes *brown, olive, orange, purple, violet, pink,* and *gray*) have been called basic color terms. Unlike most nouns, however, color terms when used as adjectives are predicable adjectives. But the usual pattern of direct and indirect antonymy that is observed for other predicable adjectives does not hold for color adjectives. Only one attribute is clearly described by direct anto-

The variety of color terms in a language seems to depend on the sophistication of the society's color technology. English allows discrimination of thousands of colors.

nyms: lightness, whose values are expressed by *light/dark* or *white/black.* Students of color vision can produce evidence of an opposition between red and green and also between yellow and blue, but the names of those color pairs are not treated as direct antonyms in lay discourse. The secondary color terms can be viewed as groups of similar adjectives clustered around a basic color term, but antonymy does not play a central role.

In brief, color terms are not a good example either of a noun hierarchy or of adjective oppositions. Rather, the semantic organization of color terms is given directly by the dimensions of color perception: hue, lightness, and saturation. These dimensions define an abstract color solid, and every color that the eye can recognize is located somewhere in that solid. The achromatic colors—white, gray, black—form a graded scale of lightness running through the center of a circle of hues, providing the vertical dimension of the color solid. Saturation gives the location of the color between achromatic center and the highly saturated colors on the perimeter.

The color solid is not a concrete object available for inspection; it is a conceptual structure, a representation of the theory of color perception. Color terms are defined by mapping them onto the color solid—by giving their focus and boundaries on the solid. The focus for the word *yellow,* for example, is the most typical, highly saturated yellow on the perimeter of the solid. Other colors immediately adjacent to that focal yellow will also be called *yellow;* yellow is a region in the color solid. But the farther you move away from that focus, the less confident you will be that the color should be called *yellow.* The point at which the majority of people would stop calling it yellow and start calling it something else is the boundary of the yellow category. In general, judgments of focal colors are relatively stable and independent of the language you happen to speak, but judgments of category boundaries are variable and depend on what other color terms you are allowed to use.

Psychological experiments have shown that any chromatic color can be described by using combinations of only four terms: *red, yellow, green,* and *blue.* These four colors are the so-called psychological primaries. Orange, for example, can be described as 50 percent red and 50 percent yellow. In these experiments, however, no color was found that was described either as a combination of red and green or as a combination of yellow and blue. Red/green and yellow/blue are opponent processes; the visual system has evolved in such a way that light can excite either a red or a green response (but not both) and either a yellow or a blue response (but not both). That fact is represented conceptually by placing red opposite to green on the hue circle and yellow opposite to blue. Lexically, it is represented by the absence of any color terms that would be defined as, say, *reddish green* or *bluish yellow.*

Not all languages are blessed with as many color terms as English; the variety of color words seems to correlate with the sophistication of the technology. It has been noted that color terms tend to appear in a fixed order. In some languages there are only two words that can be used to designate colors; they translate into *light/dark* or *white/black.* The first chromatic adjective to be

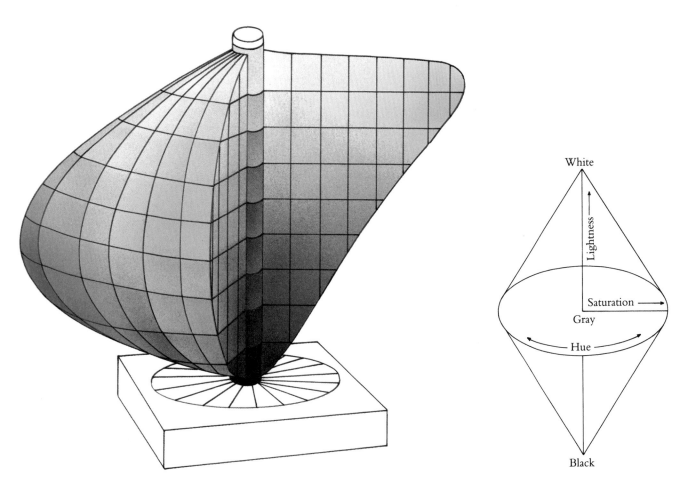

The color solid as seen from the blue-green side. Each point in this three-dimensional space represents a separate color.

added is a term for focal *red.* Many languages have only those three color terms. One of the puzzles that has received much attention is the existence of many languages with five basic color terms that translate as *black, white, red, yellow,* and a fifth term that refers to both blue and green. But no known languages have a primary color term for brown, pink, gray, purple, violet, or orange without also having terms for all of the six landmark colors. It is as if color terminology began with a conventional adjective, but then developed along lines determined more by perception than by linguistic principles as the need for greater precision grew.

One qualification of this generalization is that in some cultures the domain of color may not be as completely abstracted from surfaces as it has been in technologically advanced countries. For example, the Hanunóo people in the Philippines use their words for red and green to signify desiccated and succulent, respectively. A shiny wet brown-colored section of newly cut bamboo is *malatuy,* a color term that would usually be translated into English as *green.*

Selectional Preferences

Adjectives are selective about the nouns they can modify. A cup can be tin and a dog can be obedient, but not vice versa. It is as if common nouns denote bundles of attributes, and only those adjectives can be used that state values of attributes in that bundle. This generalization is systematically violated in the figurative use of language, but it seems to describe the normal or expected state of the world.

Evaluative adjectives—for example, *good/bad, pleasant/unpleasant, clean/dirty*—can modify almost any noun at all, but other kinds of adjectives have more restricted domains of application. Charles E. Osgood, an experimental psychologist at the University of Illinois who was one of the founders of the modern field of psycholinguistics, conducted extensive studies of this question. He began with fifty rating scales defined by pairs of antonymous adjectives and asked people to rate each one of twenty nominal concepts (nouns or noun phrases) on all fifty of the rating scales. For example, *nurse* might be rated closer to *good* than to *bad* on the *good/bad* scale; closer to *active* than to *inactive;* near the middle on *angular/rounded;* and so on through the fifty scales. He found consistent patterns of correlation between the scales: Concepts that were rated *good* were also rated *nice* and *clean;* concepts that were rated *weak* also tended to be rated *cowardly,* and so on.

Osgood found that EVALUATION accounted for the most variance in the ratings; all of the nominal concepts could be rated meaningfully on the evaluative scales. Next most important were the scales rating POTENCY (*strong/weak, brave/cowardly*) and those rating ACTIVITY (*active/passive, fast/slow*); these adjectives cannot modify all nouns, but they are appropriate for nouns denoting animate beings. Ratings on these three kinds of scales were not correlated, so together they defined a three-dimensional space in which Osgood could plot the various concepts that his subjects had rated. Osgood interpreted positions in this space as indicators of the affective value of the concepts. For example, the concepts of *sleep* and of *gentleness* lie close together in that space; these words have different meanings, but the same adjectives can be used to modify them, and Osgood judged them to have similar emotional connotations.

It would seem, therefore, that every common noun has evaluative attributes and that animate nouns have attributes of potency and activity. Beyond those highly general dimensions of meaning, however, each noun has its own bundle of attributes.

It is a common observation that the values expressed by adjectives depend critically on the head nouns that they modify. A horse, for example, has an expected size, and that expectation determines the interpretation of such phrases as *a large horse* or *a small horse.* To say that a pony is a small horse and that a canary is a small bird does not mean that ponies and canaries are the same size. Linguists have usually assumed that the meaning of the head noun must include information about the expected (or default) values of its referent. This fact implies that a noun's meaning cannot be JUST a bundle of attributes; normal values for at least some attributes must also be part of the meaning of a noun. Then the adjective simply modifies that expected value up or down: A large horse is larger than the expected size for horses; a tall snowman is a snowman that is taller than the expected height of snowmen; and so on. But why a tall snowman built by a basketball team is clearly much taller than the tall snowman built by a kindergarten class can be explained only in terms of general knowledge, not specifically lexical knowledge.

■   ■   ■

No single theory can account for all the different semantic structures that coexist in the mental lexicon. Hierarchical inheritance systems can represent the semantic relations between nouns; hyperspaces are handy for thinking about the organization of modifiers in the mental lexicon. But how are these representations related? Presumably, adjectives provide features for distinguishing among the nouns: The glittering hyperspaces defined by bipolar attributes hang on the hierarchy of nominal concepts like ornaments on a Christmas tree.

The more deeply semantic structures are explored, the more complex they seem. And the most complex words of all still lie ahead.

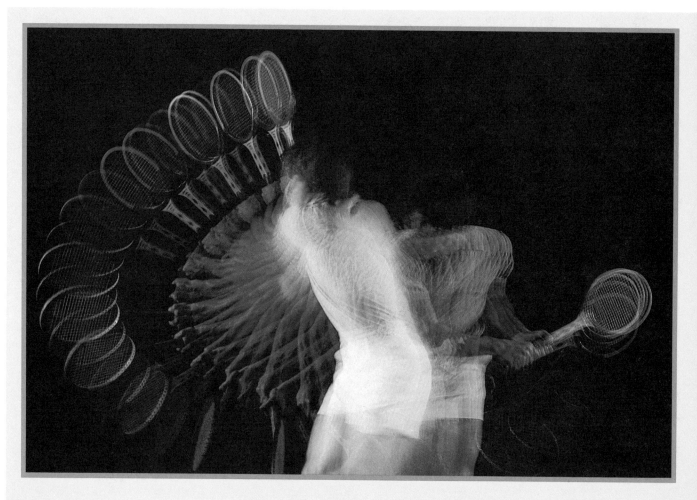

▲ *When nouns collide—or otherwise interact—verbs come into play.*

▶ *Verbs make sentences possible, linking actors and actions according to the structural rules of syntax. This parse tree, a graphical representation of the sentence* The player hit the ball with the racquet, *is a step toward making those rules explicit.*

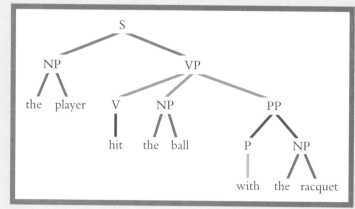

Making Sentences

*T*he general scenario that children follow in mastering their first language is universal. All children, all languages—the developmental sequence is roughly the same. But in the midst of generality there is diversity: diversity in opportunity to learn, diversity in rate of learning, diversity in style of learning. Some children start as namers. They will wander around a playroom looking at things and saying, almost to themselves, "Doll," or "Car," or "Book," quietly practicing these associations with little attention from their adult caretakers. At the opposite extreme are the controllers. For them, speech is a means to an end. "More!" they demand. "Up!" they call, reaching with upstretched arms. They scream "Unh, unh!" as they strain toward something they want. Their vocabulary may be small, but their power is enormous. Vocal noises control people, and these children play it to the hilt.

Children who fall exclusively into one category or the other are rare, but they exemplify two separate developments that are hard to disentangle in an average child. It is as if two separate streams were flowing, one filled with reference, the other with action. In some children one stream starts stronger than the other, but eventually the two must merge: Reference must provide names for participants in the action. Children need a little time to discover how this combination is accomplished in the particular language that they have been born into, but eventually they all master it, for the coupling of actors and actions is the essence of human language.

In its purest form, what they learn is known as predication. For example, the sentence *The baby cried* combines a reference to a baby with the action of crying. The combination accomplishes something that neither the name of the actor, *the baby,* nor the name of the action, *cry,* could do alone. This extra something that predication accomplishes can be described in different ways. A linguist might say that the sentence has a subject and a predicate; that *the baby* is the subject and that *cried* is what the sentence says about its subject. A logician might say that the sentence affirms a statement or proposition in which *cry* is predicated of *the baby.* A mathematician might liken CRY to a function and *baby* to an argument of that function: CRY(*baby*) = *true,* analogous to SQUARE(3) = 9. A psychologist might emphasize that the declarative sentence, unlike its parts in isolation, is something that another person can agree or disagree with. But however it is said, all recognize that predication adds something vital to the sum of its parts.

The words that have this power to incorporate names into assertions are called verbs. Schoolchildren are taught that verbs are where the action is, and it is indeed true that the most typically verbal verbs are action verbs, like *run* or *hit* or *climb.* But, contrary to common belief, action does not characterize all verbs: *Sleep, know, love, contain, own,* and many others are also verbs, although no overt physical action is involved. Such verbs are sometimes called stative verbs, because they describe states of affairs, rather than actions; in English, the verb *to be* combines with adjectives to express a wide range of states of affairs. Stative verbs and *be* + adjective constructions contribute to the characterization of situations, not actions. Yet the common notion that sentences describe the actions of actors is so basic that, grammatically, stative verbs are used the same way active verbs are. Moreover, the actor-action model for predication is characteristic of all Indo-European languages. The important point is not that verbs express actions, although many do, but rather that verbs are the words that make sentences possible.

Classification and discrimination are fundamental psychological mechanisms that enable intelligent animals like dogs or monkeys to recognize familiar situations. It is also true that intelligent animals can learn to associate appropriate actions with familiar situations—a great deal of intelligent behavior can be characterized in terms of such situation-action pairs. But what is missing in those animals, or only dimly anticipated, is the dimension that predication adds to human thought. Since it is verbs that make possible this intellectual

The most typically verbal verbs are action verbs.

advance, the semantic structure of verbs in the mental lexicon must come close to the center of what the analysis of words can reveal about the human mind.

A Little Syntax

All languages draw a distinction between nouns and verbs, although it is subtler in some than in others. And all languages combine words from those categories to form acceptable sentences. But the building blocks of language are not thrown together haphazardly. Each language has its rules for combining words, and those rules must be followed if grammatical sentences are to result. *The baby cried* is a sentence because it follows the rules for forming sentences in English, but *cried baby the* does not follow the rules and so is not a sentence. The rules for combining words to form grammatical sentences in a language are called the syntax of that language.

Everyone who speaks a language fluently knows the syntax of that language, but it is an odd kind of knowledge. They know the rules in the sense that they can follow them and can recognize departures from them. But if you define "knowing a rule" as being able to state the rule explicitly, they do not know them. Fluent speakers are like ball players who know how to throw and catch, but who could never solve the differential equations of motion to extrapolate the flight of the ball. The problem is to make their implicit knowledge explicit.

Scholars tried for centuries to make the rules of syntax explicit and communicable, but syntax is surprisingly complex. Much of what was taught as syntax were prescriptive rules, the dos and don'ts of good usage. Not until the twentieth century did a descriptive science of syntax begin to emerge, and then it was logicians and mathematicians who showed the way. When logic and mathematics came to be seen as artificial languages, some of the implicit design features of all languages were pushed forcefully into view. And when modern computers stimulated the invention of artificial languages for programming, the value of such abstract descriptions became apparent. Concepts so basic that no human being would need to have them explained had to be explained to computers. Not only did the importance of these fundamental ideas become clear, but ways were developed to express them precisely and to test their consequences. Linguists borrowed these logical ideas, adapted them to natural languages, and so redefined the science of linguistics. The idea of "language in general" was extended beyond the realm of languages spoken by human beings. It is now possible to think of grammars—that is, syntactic theories of natural languages—as special cases of a syntactic theory sufficiently general to describe anything, natural or artificial, that you might want to consider a language.

Acquiring this new set of tools enabled linguists to state their problems more precisely, but it did not solve them. It was still necessary to discover what makes natural language a special case, and that has proved difficult. Artificial languages are intellectual toys. They are designed for a limited range of applications, the rules can be conveniently simple, and the vocabulary can be sanitized of all ambiguity. Natural languages, on the other hand, must be ready to express anything and everything. Their rules are complex beyond reasonable explanation, and the resolution of ambiguity is a continuing requirement. Linguists now understand better what the problem is, but there is still much about the syntax of natural languages that is not well understood.

Given the intrinsic complexity of the subject, it would be tempting to ignore syntax. After all, as long as the discussion is limited to single words in isolation, syntactic rules do not apply. But an understanding of words would be shallow indeed if nothing were known about the ways that they combine in sentences. What is most needed is at least a partial understanding of how verbs organize phrases into sentences; to ensure that the examples are intelligible, the discussion will begin with English syntax.

First, what do syntactic rules look like? Take, for example, the rule that imposes a subject-predicate structure on English sentences. One familiar notation, introduced by Noam Chomsky in 1956, uses a syntactic rewriting rule of the form

S1.   S → NP VP

which says that a sentence (S) can be analyzed into, or rewritten as, a noun

Artificial Languages

An artificial language can be described in the same terms as a natural language—both have a vocabulary of symbols, a grammar for combining symbols into admissible strings, rules for determining meaningful combinations of strings, and the possibility of interpretation in other domains. The major difference is that people invent artificial languages for specific purposes, whereas natural languages evolved to serve a wide and unpredictable variety of human needs.

Two kinds of artificial languages can be distinguished, according to whether their purpose is to facilitate communication or calculation. Esperanto, for example, is an artificial language intended for use in international communication: Its vocabulary consists as far as possible of words common to the major European languages. Basic English is another artificial international language: It was created by simplifying the grammar and reducing the vocabulary of natural English. None of these products of linguistic engineering have caught on as international languages. Ironically, however, many of the artificial languages

Gottfried Wilhelm von Leibniz.

invented to aid reasoning—logical, mathematical, and programming languages—HAVE been accepted internationally.

The modern idea of creating a language to think with probably

originated with Baron Gottfried Wilhelm von Leibniz (1646–1716), the German mathematician and philosopher who was one of the great geniuses of all time. One among Leibniz's many accomplishments was to lay the groundwork for mathematical logic. Throughout his life he worked to discover a kind of universal language, which he called *Characteristica Universalis,* that would enable people to think the way mathematicians calculate. "If we had it," he wrote, "we should be able to reason in metaphysics and morals in much the same way as in geometry and analysis." His hope that a properly designed language would enable people to replace controversy by calculation was probably the most optimistic view of artificial languages ever put forward by a serious intellect.

Today mathematical logic is well developed, but it has contributed little to reduce the scope of public controversy. Progress in understanding such artificial languages, however, has done much to clarify the logical structure of natural languages and to define what might be meant by a formal theory of language in general.

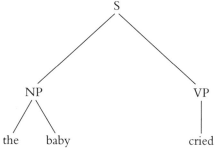

A parse tree showing the grammatical structure of the simple sentence the baby cried. *The sentence node (S) immediately dominates the noun phrase (NP) and the verb phrase (VP); NP immediately dominates the words* the *and* baby.

phrase (NP) followed by a verb phrase (VP). For example, if S is *The baby cried,* then NP is *the baby* and VP is *cried:*

$$[_S[_{NP}\text{the baby}] [_{VP}\text{cried}]]$$

Notice that S1 is stated in terms of syntactic categories, whereas "subject" and "predicate" are syntactic relations. If syntactic categories are taken as the elements in terms of which syntactic rules are to be stated, then additional definitions are needed for these important relations: A subject is an NP immediately dominated by S, and a predicate is a VP immediately dominated by S.

It is hard to think of a syntactic rule more fundamental for English than S1. It is so fundamental that it does not have to be taught: Any student capable of understanding an explanation of S1 would already know it implicitly. Indeed, S1 is so fundamental that it can be overlooked entirely—unless you are trying to write a completely explicit, formal description of some language, a description sufficiently detailed to be understood even by a computer.

Here the topic is predication, so the part of this syntactic structure to be examined is the verb phrase, VP. The syntactic complexity of the English verb phrase was analyzed by Chomsky in 1965 in a seminal monograph, *Aspects of the Theory of Syntax* (Cambridge, Mass.: MIT Press), that set the terms in which syntax would be discussed for at least the next quarter century. In *Aspects,* Chomsky introduced two concepts, strict subcategorization and selectional restrictions, that are critically important for understanding how a person's lexical memory might be organized in the service of predication.

Subcategorization

Because English verb phrases come in a great variety, a corresponding variety of rewriting rules is needed for VP, including such examples as

S2a.	VP → V	$[_S[_{NP}\text{she}][_{VP}[_V\text{cried}]]]$
S2b.	VP → V NP	$[_S[_{NP}\text{she}][_{VP}[_V\text{hit}][_{NP}\text{the ball}]]]$
S2c.	VP → V NP NP	$[_S[_{NP}\text{she}][_{VP}[_V\text{gave}][_{NP}\text{the boy}][_{NP}\text{the ball}]]]$
S2d.	VP → V NP PP	$[_S[_{NP}\text{she}][_{VP}[_V\text{put}][_{NP}\text{the ball}][_{PP}\text{in the basket}]]]$
S2e.	VP → V that S′	$[_S[_{NP}\text{she}][_{VP}[_V\text{said}]\text{that}[_{S'}\text{the baby cried}]]]$

The various versions of S2 list only required companions of the verbs. Other constituents exist, of course, that are neither required nor excluded by the choice of the verb. For instance, a locative prepositional phrase (PP)—such as *in the house*—can be inserted almost anywhere in English.

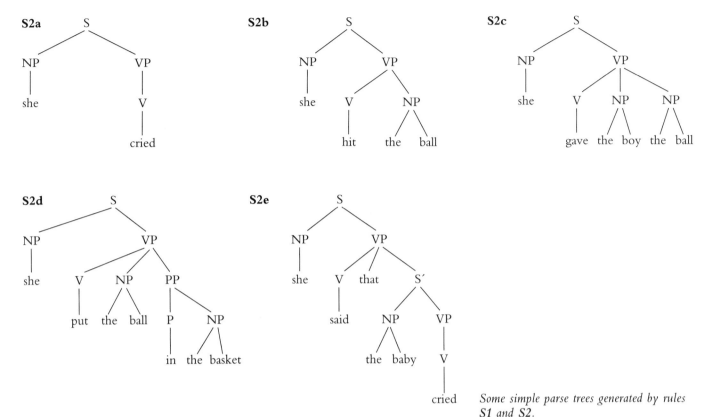

Some simple parse trees generated by rules S1 and S2.

When S1 and S2 are combined, they generate a phrase structure that can be indicated by labeled parentheses, as above, or can be represented graphically as a parse tree. Further rules for rewriting NP and PP would add further details to the structure. At the bottom of the parse tree are the words to be spoken; there are no rules for rewriting the words, so they are the terminal symbols of this method of analysis.

Notice that different kinds of verbs follow different rules. Rule S2a is the rule for intransitive verbs (*weep, die, elapse*), verbs that do not take an object. Rule S2b is for transitive verbs (*drop, invent, discern*), verbs that can take an object NP. Rule S2c is for doubly transitive verbs (*sell, give, send, teach*), verbs that can take both a direct and an indirect object NP. Rule S2d is for verbs like *put* or *place* that require an object NP followed by a locative prepositional phrase PP. Rule S2e is for communication or cognitive verbs (*say, believe*) that take another sentence (S') as the complement of the verb. And there are still other classes of verbs that can be described in similar formulations. The important idea here, however, is that it is necessary in English to classify verbs on the basis of the kinds of sentence constituents with which they occur.

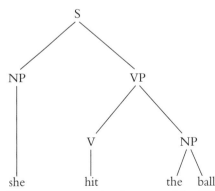

The parse tree previously generated by S1 and S2b, aligned to show the words of the sentence as the terminal symbols of the analysis.

Noam Chomsky and *Syntactic Structures*

*A*vram Noam Chomsky was twenty-seven years old in 1957 when *Syntactic Structures* opened what has since become known as the Chomskyan revolution in linguistics. That short monograph used three simple models to summarize several years of highly technical research. Each model was a generative grammar—

it consisted of a set of explicit rules for generating grammatical sentences. The three grammars differed with respect to the complexity of the rules that they contained.

The first, called "finite state grammar," had rules of the form $S \rightarrow Sx$ (the string S can be rewritten as S followed by x) for adding a linguistic element x to the right

end of an existing string S. That model, which had been studied explicitly by communication engineers and implicitly by behavioral psychologists, was quickly shown to be insufficiently powerful for the syntactic analysis of English and other natural languages.

The second, called "phrase structure grammar," had rules for

Noam Chomsky.

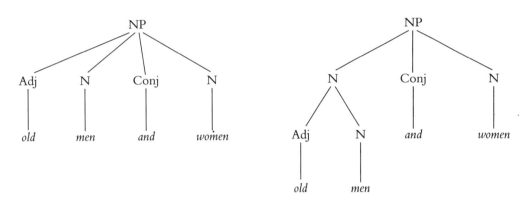

Alternative parses accounting for the ambiguity of the noun phrase old men and women.

inserting linguistic elements at any point in an existing string. That model, which most linguists had followed implicitly, if not explicitly, allowed rules of the form $S \rightarrow A\ B$ (where A and B can also be rewritten), as well as rules of the form $A \rightarrow x$, where x is a terminal element (a linguistic element for which there is no rewriting rule: a word, for example). A phrase structure grammar assigns a structural description to the strings of words that it generates—it "parses" the sentence—and so makes it possible to explain why phrases like *old men and women* have more than one interpretation.

Chomsky incorporated phrase structure rules into his own theory of grammar, but argued that such rules are still not powerful enough to capture the syntactic structure of natural languages. And so he proposed a third model, called "transformational grammar," which has rules that permit the phrase structure components to be reordered. Transformational rules enable a grammar to characterize relations such as those between the sentences *She is here, Is she here?* and *Where is she?*—which would otherwise require three different sets of phrase structure rules for their derivation.

Transformational grammars can be too powerful. It has been shown that an unrestricted transformational grammar is equivalent in power to a universal Turing machine, which can compute any computable function. To say that a language can be generated by a universal Turing machine is like saying that it can be written in ink. How transformational rules might be avoided—or, if they are accepted, how plausible constraints on their power might be formulated—has, in one way or another, motivated much of the subsequent debate on the theory of syntax.

"Verb" is a syntactic category, so these verb classes are subcategories. Chomsky called rules like S2 "strict subcategorization rules" and included information about the subcategories in the lexicon. What this means is that along with these words in lexical memory is stored not only their pronunciation and meaning and the fact that they are verbs, but also the kinds of constituents that they co-occur with. For example, the verb *die* is intransitive, so it would be assigned a subcategorization feature showing that it has no object NP:

$$die \; [\text{V}, + \text{—}]$$

In this notation, the "V" means that it is a verb, the "+" means that the feature applies to the word, and the dash "—" indicates where the verb occurs relative to the other constituents. The verb *hand,* to take a more complex example, is doubly transitive, so it would be assigned the following subcategorization feature:

$$hand \; [\text{V}, + \text{—} \; \text{NP NP}]$$

These two subcategorization features are enough to ensure that *she died* and *she handed the boy a book* are acceptable, but that *she handed* and *she died the boy a book* are unacceptable.

Some verbs seem to have more than one subcategorization feature. The verb *move,* for example, can occur both intransitively, *she moved,* and transitively, *she moved the chair,* so it requires at least two subcategorization features:

$$move \; [\text{V}, + \text{—}, + \text{—} \; \text{NP}]$$

Of course, intransitive *move* and transitive *move* can be regarded as separate lexical entries having slightly different meanings, in which case each lexical entry could be assigned to a single subcategory. A purely syntactic theory, however, would not be concerned with semantic distinctions.

Subcategorized NPs serve logically as arguments, with the verb as the function. In contrast to these (obligatory) arguments, there are other NPs that play more specialized roles and are known as (optional) adjuncts. For example, in *She handed the boy a book in the library,* the NPs *the boy* and *a book* are arguments of the verb, but the PP ($\rightarrow$ Prep NP) *in the library* is an adjunct that serves to locate the event.

Chomsky's formulation of strict subcategorization focused attention on a significant problem, but his proposed solution has run into difficulties, some of which he pointed out himself. For one thing, it presupposes the existence of VP as a sentence constituent, a condition that is not satisfied in all languages. Moreover, it is redundant to specify subcategorizations twice, first in syntactic rewriting rules like S2 and a second time in the subcategorization features assigned to each verb. This dual representation seems to imply that in some language other than English the two might be different, but that is clearly not what was intended. Since the dually represented information cannot be eliminated from the lexical entries for each verb, the natural impulse is to eliminate it from the rewriting rules, thus making the rewriting component much simpler. But if each verb is listed separately in the lexicon, each verb could call for its own peculiar set of arguments; it is no longer obvious how general syntactic rules for whole subcategories of verbs should be formulated.

How this problem of redundancy should be resolved is unclear, but some theorists have looked to semantics for an answer. If it could be shown that verbs with similar subcategorization features also share similar meanings, a different basis for generalizations across subcategories would be available. It remains to be seen, however, how the notions of subcategorization and of semantic role can best be formulated to accommodate both syntactic generality and lexical specificity.

Selectional Restrictions

In *Aspects* Chomsky also proposed a second kind of feature to be associated with each verb—a selectional feature. A subcategorization feature may call for an NP, but not just any NP will work. For example, the sentence *Sincerity frightens the boy* is acceptable, but *The boy frightens sincerity* is not; *frighten* requires an animate object NP. Chomsky proposed that the lexical entry for *frighten* should include the information that the subcategorized NP refers to something having the feature [+animate]. Then the subcategorization feature in the lexical entry for *frighten* could be represented:

$$\text{\textit{frighten} } [\text{V}, + - \text{NP}_{[+\text{animate}]}]$$

But this is redundant, of course, because only nouns can have animate or inanimate referents. The subcategorization feature could be stated more economically as

$$\text{\textit{frighten} } [\text{V}, + - [+\text{animate}]]$$

This notation shows how the subcategorization feature can be derived from the selectional restriction, which might have certain theoretical advantages, since selectional features are more general than subcategorization features. Subcategorization features are normally assigned only for the predicate phrase, whereas selectional restrictions apply to subject NPs as well as to predicate NPs: *The girl elapsed* is odd because *elapse* must take an inanimate subject having the feature [+duration]. Presumably, this information is stored in lexical memory for the verb *elapse*. Moreover, selectional features can also be assigned to adjectives—*tall,* for example, can only modify a noun that refers to something having the feature [+vertical] (see Chapter 10)—whereas there are no subcategorization features for adjectives.

In his initial proposal, Chomsky regarded selectional restrictions as rules of syntax, which means that sentences such as *Noise frightened the chair* would be classified as ungrammatical. Subsequently, however, by general agreement, selectional features were dropped from the syntactic component and added to the semantic component. Under a semantic interpretation, *She frightens the clock* is not ungrammatical; it is simply meaningless—or semantically anomalous, to use the terminology generally preferred for such violations of selectional restrictions.

"Meaningless" is less well defined than "ungrammatical," of course, and large gray areas exist. For example, *talk to* ordinarily demands a human object, but people do talk to animals and even to inanimate objects. And figurative language is characterized by violations of selectional restrictions that are nonetheless intelligible. A study of why certain selectional restrictions are more easily violated than others would be a complex undertaking. Some workers have suggested that these constraints might better be called selectional preferences, since preferences are easily violated.

Subcategorization assumes that information is stored in the lexical entry for the verb, but selectional restrictions assume that information is stored with the verb and also with the nouns. If, say, the verb *marry* demands arguments that are marked [+human], then it must be possible to determine which nouns are so marked. Indeed, some theorists have argued that the noun lexicon is organized in terms of the verbs and adjectives that can be predicated of different nouns. For example, the basic semantic distinction between [+animate] and [−animate] nouns derives from the fact that *live* and *die* and *is alive* can be predicated of one class of nouns but not of the other. That is to say, selectional restrictions reflect some of the most fundamental conceptual distinctions you can draw about the world.

Semantic Components of Verbs

When a verb has two different subcategorizations, does it necessarily have two different meanings? Consider an example. In the language of American baseball, the verb *walk* can be used either intransitively, as in *The batter walked,* or transitively, as in *The pitcher walked the batter.* These two uses of *walk* are certainly related; both sentences can be used to describe the same event. But are they synonymous? Consider the differences. In *The batter walked,* the meaning of *walk* is that the batter did something: moved from being at bat to being on first base. In *The pitcher walked the batter,* the meaning of *walk* is that the pitcher did something: caused the batter to move from being at bat to being on first base. (Note that pitchers can walk a batter intentionally, but batters cannot walk intentionally.) Transitive *walk* incorporates a notion of causality that is missing from the intransitive use. The distinction may be subtle, but it is real. A semantic theory should have some way to represent such distinctions, and that is the need that componential analysis tries to fill. In the baseball context, transitive *walk* can be analyzed into (at least) two semantic components: intransitive *walk* plus a causal component. Neither *walk* incorporates an intentional semantic component, however—intention must be expressed explicitly.

Analysis into semantic components is possible throughout the verb lexicon. The best known example is probably the one proposed in 1968 by the Chicago linguist James McCawley. He analyzed the verb in *Brutus killed Caesar* by parsing the sentence into a series of sentences:

$$S \rightarrow \text{Brutus caused } S'$$
$$S' \rightarrow \text{become } S''$$
$$S'' \rightarrow \text{not } S'''$$
$$S''' \rightarrow \text{alive Caesar}$$

Or, as others have represented this analysis, using a notation that designates functions with small capital letters:

CAUSE (*Brutus,* BECOME (NOT (ALIVE (*Caesar*))))

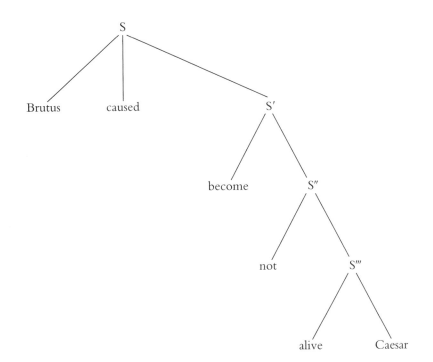

The semantic decomposition of the verb kill *in the sentence* Brutus killed Caesar *is here represented by a parse tree.*

Auxiliaries

Some linguists believe that the number of syntactic categories available is limited and that the categories found in any particular language will always be a subset selected from that number. Nouns and verbs are selected by every language; beyond those two syntactic categories, however, differences begin to appear and theorists begin to disagree. When is a linguist justified in saying, for example, "THIS category of words in language L_1 plays the same syntactic role that THAT category plays in language L_2"? It is not easy to state rules for matching syntactic categories across languages, so even linguists who agree that there is a universal list can disagree about its membership.

The category of words known as auxiliaries is an example. Auxiliaries are words that are adjoined to verbs and serve to express such features as modality, tense, or aspect. Not every language has auxiliaries—many languages use affixes instead. But even languages that do have lexicalized verb adjuncts use them so differently that a skeptic might easily doubt the existence of any universal category of auxiliaries.

English and German, for example, are historically related, yet their auxiliary systems are very different—the auxiliaries of Modern German are closer to those of Old English than they are to those of Modern English. Some linguists think that the progressive simplification of English inflectional morphology made it difficult to distinguish the subjunctive from the indicative mood, so contingent or nonfactual expressions had to be marked lexically by such modal auxiliaries as *should, would, may, might*. Whatever the cause, English underwent considerable change in a relatively short time, resulting in an auxiliary system different from any other.

Modern English has a small closed class of auxiliaries. Recall the Bear Family's exasperation when they came home:

"Somebody *has been sitting* in my chair!"

The main verb is *sit;* the aspectual auxiliaries *have* and *be* express the temporal shape of the action of the verb—the present perfect progressive in this example. They might equally well have said

"Somebody *must have been sitting* in my chair!"

Here the modal auxiliary *must* is added, indicating that *Somebody has been sitting in my chair* is regarded as a necessary inference on the basis of the evidence. The Bears could have provided an even fuller example if they had said

"My chair *must have been being sat* in by somebody!"

The final auxiliary *be* marks the passive voice. In English, auxiliaries are often called auxiliary verbs (or helping verbs), although nonverbs are auxiliaries in some languages.

Modal auxiliaries pose special problems for translators and for people learning English as a second language. The general idea is that modals fall into three groups on the basis of meaning:

Meaning	Modal	Periphrase
possible/permissible	*can, could, may, might*	*is able to, was able to*
necessary/obligatory	*must, should*	*has to, had to, ought to*
predictive/volitional	*shall, will, would*	*is going to, was going to*

Problems arise in distinguishing the epistemic meanings (possible, necessary, predictive) from the deontic or root meanings (permissible, obligatory, volitional) of these words. A speaker's ground for using modals in the epistemic sense is some factual theory; ground for using the deontic sense is some ethical or moral code. *You must go to church,* for example, can mean either that the speaker has a theory about your habitual behavior (the epistemic meaning) or that the speaker feels you are under some ethical or moral obligation to attend (the deontic meaning). The distinction is important because when events contradict the epistemic interpretation, the speaker should be corrected; whereas when the deontic interpretation is violated, you should be corrected.

The interaction of modal auxiliaries and negation can also be confusing in English. For example, *He can go* and *He must go* have clearly different meanings, but add negation and the difference disappears—both *He cannot go* and *He must not go* mean that it is necessary/obligatory for him to stay.

The important point about English modals is that they mark inferential statements. To use one is to claim to have ground (epistemic or deontic) for drawing the inference on which your statement is based. Thus, if you are indoors when your friend says, "It must be raining," you can plausibly ask, "Why do you think so?" But if the two of you are standing together in a downpour, your friend's statement will seem a bad joke—in those circumstances, claims to have ground for saying that it is raining are not required.

The importance of context. In some situations, It must be raining *indicates that the speaker has ground for drawing an inference; in this one, it can be understood only as a joke.*

In either notation, McCawley's analysis of *Brutus killed Caesar* can be read as *Brutus caused Caesar to become not alive*. At the time, McCawley believed that this compound conceptual structure is generated whenever a sentence expressing this meaning is produced; before the sentence is uttered, however, *killed* is inserted in its place. This belief, which was part of a theory that came to be known as generative semantics, was influential during the 1970s and is still advocated, in one form or another, by some computational linguists.

Analysis into semantic components need not be tied to any particular theory of syntax, however. It is still useful for understanding similarities and differences in meaning between different words or between different uses of the same word. Consider the verb *move*, for example. A dozen different meanings of *move* could be distinguished easily, but concentrate on four relatively central meanings:

1. *To change location,* used intransitively, as in *The boat moved through the water*

2. *To change orientation* without changing location, used intransitively, as in *The deck moved under his feet*

3. *To cause something to change location,* used transitively, as in *He moved the bag of food into the galley*

4. *To cause something to change orientation,* used transitively, as in *He moved the wheel in a clockwise direction*

(Prepositional phrases are added to these illustrative sentences to make it easier to judge their acceptability.)

Note that the four defining phrases effectively decompose these four meanings into semantic components. The notion of change occurs in all four; the notions of location, orientation, and causation are each used in two definitions. The four senses can be written:

1. MOVE$_1$(*boat*) = CHANGE (LOCATION (*boat*))

2. MOVE$_2$(*deck*) = CHANGE (ORIENTATION (*deck*))

3. MOVE$_3$(*he, bag*) = CAUSE (*he,* CHANGE (LOCATION (*bag*)))

4. MOVE$_4$(*he, wheel*) = CAUSE (*he,* CHANGE (ORIENTATION (*wheel*)))

These formulas seem to make simple definitions difficult, but there is a bold idea behind them.

The idea is that all the thousands of different meanings that words express can be reduced to a relatively small set of semantic primitives, a set of universal concepts that cannot be further analyzed, but simply must be accepted as given to all human beings alike. If someone did not comprehend these semantic primes, there would be no way to explain them in terms of simpler ideas. The concepts represented by the functions CAUSE, BECOME, NOT, CHANGE, LOCATION, and ORIENTATION are candidates for such universal status.

When componential analysis is pursued systematically through the verb lexicon, it is found that two kinds of semantic components are required. One kind can be called core concepts, since they are part of the meaning of every verb in their semantic field. For example, MOVE is a core concept for verbs of motion; SEE is central to verbs of visual perception; POSSESS to verbs of possession; CONTACT to verbs of touching; MAKE to verbs of creation; and so on. The core concepts that enter into the analysis of verb meanings are themselves always verbs. Different theorists postulate different sets of core verbs, but there are probably no more than twenty of them in English.

In contrast to core components are the elaborative semantic components, sometimes called semantic operators because they can be thought of as operating on the core concepts. For example, the concept of negation, NOT, is a necessary component of the meanings of many verbs in different semantic fields, yet NOT is not a verb and there is no semantic field of negation verbs. Similarly, there does not seem to be a semantic field of verbs of causation; CAUSE turns up in every field, where it provides a standard elaboration of core concepts: cause to move, cause to see, cause to possess, and so on. Another elaborative concept is MANNER, which provides a different modulation of the core concepts: manner of moving, manner of seeing, manner of possessing, manner of contacting, manner of creating, and so on.

Treating these elaborative concepts as semantic components, on a par with core concepts, is awkward, however. The temporal shapes of actions denoted by verbs are particularly difficult to incorporate as a semantic component. For example, *depart* and *arrive* are elaborations of MOVE, but the temporal shape—starting versus stopping—that distinguishes them from one another and from verbs like *travel,* which do not incorporate the idea of starting or stopping, does not lend itself easily to description as a semantic component.

Most psycholinguists have assumed that a componential theory has psychological implications, that the process of understanding a verb must involve decomposing it into the semantic primitives that define it. To understand *Brutus murdered Caesar,* for example, it would be necessary to decompose *murder* into INTENTIONALLY CAUSE TO BECOME NOT ALIVE. Such decomposition is a cognitive process, and cognitive processes take time; therefore, the more components a verb has, the longer it should take to understand it. All experimental attempts to detect this time difference have failed, however. It is still possible that componential semantic analysis serves a psychological function at the time verbs are first learned—componentially simple verbs may be easier to learn—but it appears that semantic decomposition is not a necessary part of understanding verbs in everyday usage.

An alternative analysis does not try to explain everything in terms of universal semantic components, but looks instead at semantic relations between verbs. In discussing nouns and modifiers in Chapters 9 and 10, extensive use was made of semantic relations: synonymy, antonymy, and so forth. Similar semantic relations can be identified between verbs.

Semantic Relations Between Verbs

To describe the structure of the noun and modifier lexicons, a number of semantic relations were needed: synonymy, antonymy, hyponymy, meronymy. In approaching the structure of the verb lexicon, a natural way to begin is by asking whether these same semantic relations hold between the concepts expressed by verbs. Some obviously do. Synonymy and antonymy, for example, apply to verbs as well as to nouns and adjectives. As for hyponymy and meronymy, there are superficial similarities and deep differences. The differences are worth exploring because they raise interesting questions about verbs.

Hyponymy in the Verb Lexicon

Some verbs seem more generic than others. For example, *move* describes a wider range of activities than does *walk,* and *walk* is more general than *strut.* It would seem, therefore, that there must be verb hyponyms. How can this possibility be tested?

The sentence frame used to test hyponymy between nouns, *An x is a y,* is not suitable for verbs, because it requires that *x* and *y* be nouns: *A strut is a walk* treats *strut* and *walk* as nouns, not verbs. When this sentence frame is used with verbs in the gerundive form, *Strutting is walking,* it comes closer to testing the semantic relation between verbs, but most native speakers of English feel that there is something odd about it. People who are perfectly comfortable with statements like *A robin is a bird* or *A hammer is a tool* are likely to pause over the acceptability of such statements as *Strutting is walking* or *Lisping is talking.* When pressed, they say that they feel the superordinate should be qualified in some way.

What qualification is needed? A simple solution is to introduce the notion of MANNER: *Strutting is a manner of walking.* Or, to ensure that the words in the test frame really are verbs: *To strut is to walk in a certain manner.* This leads to a general test: When two verbs can be substituted into the sentence frame *To x is to y in a certain manner,* then *x* can be said to be a verb hyponym of *y.*

This solution requires two comments. First, in componential theories of lexical semantics, MANNER is considered to be a semantic component of the verbs. Componentially, MANNER is a non-verbal component of a verb; it is theoretically awkward to decompose verbs into nouns. Here it is introduced as a semantic relation between verb meanings, which avoids that particular awkwardness. Second, since the hyponymic relation between nouns does not involve MANNER at all, it cannot be the same relation as the one between verbs. To avoid confusion, a different term is used for the relation between verbs; that is, *strut* will not be said to be a "verb hyponym" of *walk;* rather, it will be called a troponym (after *tropos* manner or fashion + *nym* name). In summary:

V1. When two verbs can be substituted into the sentence frame *To V_1 is to V_2 in a certain manner,* then V_1 is a troponym of V_2.

To leap is to jump in a certain manner.

Troponyms can be related to their superordinates in various ways, subsets of which tend to cluster within a given semantic field. Among contact verbs, for example, many troponyms are conflations of the verbs *hit, cut,* and *fasten,* with nouns denoting instruments or materials; for example, *hammer, club, knife, saw, cable, tape.* Thus, *To hammer is to hit in some manner,* or *To tape is to fasten in some manner,* and so forth. Troponyms of communication verbs often encode a speaker's intention or motivation for communicating, as in *beg, persuade,* or *flatter.*

Although troponymy results in a hierarchical structure for verbs similar to the hyponymic structure for nouns, there are important differences. Verbs tend to have a shallow, bushy structure; in most cases, the number of hierarchical levels does not exceed four. Moreover, within a semantic field, not all verbs can be grouped into a single hierarchy, under a single unique beginner. Motion verbs, for example, have at least two top nodes, one being the concept of motion in place {*move, make a movement*} and the other being the concept of moving through space {*move, travel, displace*}. Verbs of possession can be traced up to the three verbs {*give, transfer*}, {*take, receive*}, and {*have, hold*}; for the most part, their troponyms encode ways in which society has ritualized the transfer of possessions: *bequeath, donate, inherit, usurp, own, stock,* and so on. Many communication verbs involving language, such as *announce, petition,* or *hail,* can be classified as troponyms of verbs denoting the basic speech acts: *tell, ask, command,* and so forth. Only verbs of change seem to have a single common superordinate, *change.*

Meronymy in the Verb Lexicon

Like hyponymy, meronymy is a relation well suited to nouns, but less well suited to verbs. That is to say, the part-whole relation for verbs is different from the part-whole relation for nouns, but the differences are subtle enough that some care is required to demonstrate them.

To test whether one word is a meronym of another, the test frame *An x is a part of a y* is normally used. Since *part* is itself a noun, both *x* and *y* should be nouns for the resulting sentence to be acceptable. Verbs can be substituted into the frame, however, if their gerundive forms are used. But making that substitution leads to some unexpected consequences. Consider the following sentences:

> A. *Weighing is a kind of measuring.*
> B. *Measuring is a part of weighing.*
>
> C. *Weight is a kind of measure.*
> D. *Measure is a part of weight.*

The only difference between the first and second pairs of sentences is that the gerundive verbs in the first pair are replaced by nouns in the second pair. Most people accept both sentences A and B, which use the related verbs *to weigh* and *to measure* (although A sounds better if *manner of* is substituted for *kind of*). When the nouns *weight* and *measure* are substituted for their verb counterparts, however, C remains acceptable, but D becomes definitely odd.

Sentence D should be odd; if *x* is a kind of *y*, you do not ordinarily expect *y* to be a part of *x*. *Hammer* is a kind of *tool*, but *tool* is not a part of *hammer*. Yet that is precisely what can be accepted when *x* and *y* are verbs. B is the puzzler. Clearly, the *is-a-part-of* test frame is not interpreted the same way for verbs as for nouns. The challenge is to try to figure out what semantic relation must hold between two verbs for people to accept claims that one is a part of the

John Austin and the Performative Verbs

For his colleagues who believed that meanings depend on truth conditions, the Oxford philosopher John Langshaw Austin (1911–1960) posed the following question: What are the truth conditions of the sentence, "I hereby bet you that it will rain tomorrow"? Austin's claim was that the sentence is meaningful, yet it does not have truth conditions because it does not make an assertion. Such sentences do not SAY something, they DO something—this one offers a wager. Instead of stating the truth conditions for such sentences, the analyst must state their felicity conditions: the conditions under which they will perform the intended act felicitously.

Austin noted that English has hundreds of verbs that can be used to do things: *appoint, bet, challenge, demand, invite, order, promise, request, warn,* and on and on. Austin called them performatives because they can be used to perform something. One test for whether a verb is a performative is whether the first person singular can be used with *hereby.* "I hereby ask you . . ." is acceptable, so *ask* is a performative verb, but "I hereby persuade you . . . " is unacceptable, so *persuade* is not.

"I hereby christen you ————" The traditional spurt of champagne punctuates the performative sentence naming the World War II battleship, South Dakota.

As Austin and his colleagues pursued the study of performative verbs, it became clear that all sentences, even those intended to state simple facts, are performative implicitly, if not explicitly. For example, in any conventional communication context, "The sun is shining" will be understood to mean *I hereby assert that the sun is shining,* in the same way as "Pass the salt" will be understood to mean *I hereby request that you pass the salt.*

Thus, from Austin's interest in this special class of verbs grew the theory of speech acts, which takes as basic to all language not whether what is said is true or grammatical, but what act the speaker intended to perform by saying it.

No single English verb means to carry a baton *or* to run in a relay race. *Since these two verb phrases are related as if they were lexicalized, they can be regarded as lexical gaps in English. That is to say, if verbs for them were introduced (*to carbat *and* to runlay, *perhaps) they would fit into the general semantic structure of other English verbs. Note first that* to carry a baton *is not a troponym of* to run in a relay race—*it does not mean* to run in a relay race *in a certain manner. However, most people will agree that* carrying a baton *is a part of* running in a relay race *and will reject the idea that* running in a relay race *is a part of* carrying a baton. *This judgment, that* to carry a baton *is a meronym of* to run in a relay race, *reflects the fact not only that* running in a relay race *entails* carrying a baton, *but also that the two activities are coextensive in time. In short, the semantic relation between* runlay *and* carbat *would be just the same as the semantic relation between* drive *and* ride.

other. What are you thinking of when you agree that measuring is a part of weighing? The answer, like most things about verbs, is complicated.

Some verbs can be taken apart, but not in the same way as nouns; parts of verbs are not analogous to parts of nouns. Acceptable statements about part-whole relations between verbs always involve temporal relations between the activities that the two verbs denote. One activity or event is part of another activity or event only when it is part of, or a stage in, its temporal realization.

Some activities can be broken down into sequentially ordered subactivities. For example, *eat at a restaurant* can be broken into *enter, sit, read, order, eat, pay,* and *leave.* But such sequentially complex activities are seldom lexicalized in English: No single English verb means *eat at a restaurant, clean an engine, get a medical checkup,* and so on. Moreover, the analysis into lexicalized subactivities that is possible for these verb phrases is not available for most simple verbs in English. Consider the relation between the verbs *ride* and *drive. Riding* and *driving* are carried on simultaneously—the two activities are temporally coextensive. Yet most people will accept *Riding is a part of driving* and will reject *Driving is a part of riding,* even though neither activity is a sequentially ordered subactivity of the other. So it is not always an analysis into sequentially ordered subactivities that people have in mind when they judge that an is-a-part-of sentence relating verbs is acceptable. *Riding* and *driving* are semantically related because when you drive a vehicle you necessarily ride in it.

The differences between pairs like *ride* and *drive, snore* and *sleep,* and *succeed* and *try* are due to the temporal relations between members of each pair. The activities can be simultaneous (as with *ride* and *drive*); one can include the other (as with *snore* and *sleep*); or one can precede the other (*try* and *succeed*). All the

pairs have in common that engaging in one activity necessitates either engaging in, or having engaged in, the other activity. For each pair of verbs, a kind of generalized entailment relation holds between them.

Lexical Entailment

Entailment, or strict implication, is a logical relation defined for propositions, not for words. A proposition P is said to entail a proposition Q if and only if there is no conceivable state of affairs that could make P true and Q false. The notion of entailment can be adapted, however, and used to refer to the relation that holds between two verbs V_1 and V_2 when the statement *Someone V_1* entails *Someone V_2*. Thus, *snore* entails *sleep* because the statement *He is snoring* entails *He is sleeping;* the second statement necessarily holds if the first one does. When there is any danger of confusion, this adaptation of logical entailment can be called lexical entailment. If a verb V_1 lexically entails another verb V_2, then, unless V_1 and V_2 are synonyms, it cannot be the case that V_2 lexically entails V_1. Negation reverses the direction of lexical entailment; *not sleeping* entails *not snoring*, but *not snoring* does not entail *not sleeping*.

Lexical entailments include the different relations illustrated by the pairs *ride-drive, snore-sleep,* and the backward presupposition holding between *succeed-try*. It also includes verb pairs related by a result or purpose relation, such as *fatten-feed* and *smooth-rub*. The relations subsumed under lexical entailment can be distinguished on the basis of the temporal relations that the members of the verb pairs bear to one another.

Verbs that are related by entailment can be classified exhaustively into mutually exclusive categories on the basis of temporal inclusion. A verb V_1 is said to include a verb V_2 if there is some stretch of time during which the activities denoted by the two verbs co-occur, but no time during which V_2 occurs and V_1 does not. If there is a time during which V_1 occurs, but V_2 does not, V_1 will be said to properly include V_2.

Consider the three different kinds of entailment relations that are possible. The first kind is the backward presupposition holding between such verbs as *succeed* and *try* or *parole* and *arrest*. A second category consists of pairs like *snore* and *sleep* or *buy* and *pay: Snore* entails *sleep* and is properly included by it; *buy* entails *pay* and properly includes it. Still a third category consists of pairs like *lisp* and *talk* or *limp* and *walk,* where the first verb in the pair entails the second and the two are mutually inclusive, or temporally coextensive. This categorization yields a simple generalization:

V2. If the verb V_1 entails the verb V_2, and if a relation of temporal inclusion holds between them, then the relation between the two verbs can be cast in the form of a part-whole statement.

Some verb pairs that are related by entailment and temporal inclusion are also related by troponymy: *Lisp* and *talk,* for example, satisfy V2, as do *traipse* and *walk.* Traipsing entails walking, the two activities are temporally coextensive (one must necessarily be walking while one is traipsing), and walking can be said to be a part of traipsing. But *to traipse* is also *to walk in a certain manner; traipse* is a troponym of *walk.*

By contrast, a verb like *snore* entails and is included in *sleep,* but is not a troponym of *sleep;* snoring is not a manner of sleeping. Similarly, *get a medical checkup* entails and includes *visit the doctor,* but is not a troponym of *visit the doctor;* and *buy* entails *pay,* but is not a troponym of *pay.* The verbs in these pairs are related only by entailment and proper temporal inclusion; the implication is that verbs related by entailment and proper temporal inclusion cannot be related by troponymy.

V3. For two verbs to be related by troponymy, the activities they denote must be temporally coextensive.

One can sleep before or after snoring, buying includes activities other than paying, and visiting the doctor is not temporally coextensive with getting a medical checkup, so even though these pairs are related by entailment, none of them are related by troponymy. Note, incidentally, that if the entailment relation in such pairs is stated as *to V_1 entails to V_2,* the relation of temporal inclusion may still go in either direction; that is, either one of the two activities may properly include the other. Thus, *snore* entails *sleep* and *sleep* properly includes *snore,* whereas *buy* both entails and properly includes *pay.*

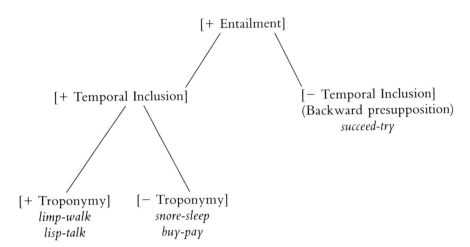

A graphical representation of the relations among three kinds of English verb pairs.

Analysis of the semantic organization of nouns reveals a complex interaction between hyponymy and meronymy. Among the verbs there is an equally complex interaction between troponymy and temporal inclusion. The two interactions are similar enough that any tidy language engineer would surely have used the same solution for both. But not so. Nouns and verbs are so different, semantically as well as syntactically, that they must be organized differently.

■   ■   ■

Because they make predication possible, verbs are arguably the most important word family of all. They are also the most complicated. Not only do they cover a variety of semantic fields—motion, possession, change, communication, perception, and the like—but by incorporating adverbs, prepositions, and nouns by conflation, they come to share the semantic characteristics of those other word families.

It is a remarkable fact that this complex conceptual structure, this intellectual cathedral, grows organically—and almost unnoticed—in the mind of every child.

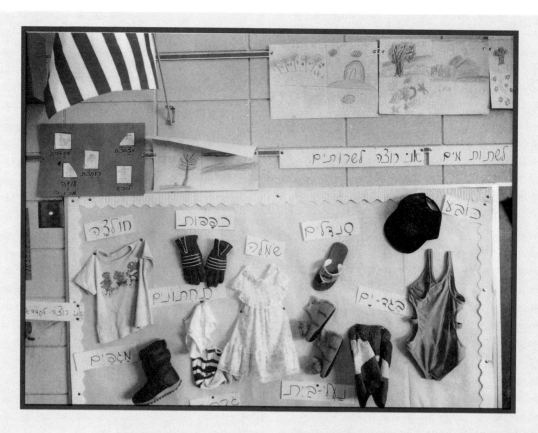

▲ Schoolchildren learn thousands of new words per year—entries in the mental lexicon that prompt its constant reorganization.

▶ Learning vocabulary is far more than learning dictionary definitions, as every child discovers when struggling to use new words in sentences that provide appropriate contexts.

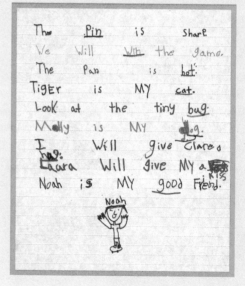

CHAPTER

The Growth of Vocabulary

When adults set out to learn a new language, they understand what is in store. They realize that they will have to learn a new phonology, a new grammar, a new vocabulary, a new style of expression. They accept the fact that they will spend many hours every day for years before they become fluent. But they also expect that they will be able to rely on teachers to explain, in their first language, everything they need to know about the second.

For infants it is very different. They have no language in which they can be told what they need to learn. Yet by the age of three they will have mastered the basic structure of their native tongue and will be well on their way to communicative competence.

Students of language acquisition have, by and large, found the child's rapid mastery of syntax to be the most amazing aspect of this accomplishment, more striking than, say, the slower process of vocabulary acquisition. Word learning is not easy—it can take a lot of time and effort—but that learning process seems simpler and easier to understand; parents can generally provide some guidance to understanding unfamiliar words, whereas few have any comparable access to their knowledge of the rules of syntax. Nevertheless, the ability of children to conform to syntactic rules is only slightly more amazing than their robust proclivity to learn new words.

After the age of six or seven years, the most obvious change in a child's linguistic competence is the growth of vocabulary. It has been estimated (see Chapter 7) that the average high school graduate in the United States knows some 60,000 root words. Some know more, some know fewer—vocabulary tests are a standard way of assessing individual differences in intelligence. But if this average can be taken as representative, it says something important about children's ability to learn words. If the average high school graduate is seventeen years old, the 60,000 root words must have been acquired over a period of sixteen years. So the average rate of acquisition is 3,750 root words per year, or better than ten new words every day.

Numerical estimates of the increase in vocabulary are impressive, but they give only a superficial picture of what is really going on. At the same time the new words are being added, lexical knowledge, the knowledge underlying vocabulary, is being reorganized. Children begin to see relations among words they have already learned, and those relations make it possible to reorganize their lexical knowledge into a more abstract, patterned system—into the kind of mental lexicon described in these pages. Clearly, a learning process of great complexity goes on at an impressive rate in every normal child.

First Words

Most children have begun to utter words by the middle of their first year. Perhaps "words" is not the right term; some observers prefer to call them utterances that are both words and sentences simultaneously. If they are indeed words, it should be possible to decide whether they are nouns, verbs, modifiers, or particles. But the first wordlike utterances occur alone, without syntax, and there can be no syntactic categories before there is syntax. In any case, these pregrammatical utterances continue for several months, during which time some parents try to keep a written log of all the "words" their child knows. Before the list becomes 100 items long, however, the child will have begun to combine them into longer utterances, and the number of new words will be growing so fast that a parent can no longer recognize which words are new and which are old.

No one teaches children ten words every day. It seems necessary to assume that children are born with a special talent for this kind of learning. Some valuable hints as to how they do it were uncovered by Elsa Bartlett and Susan Carey while they were working together in an experimental nursery school at The Rockefeller University in New York. These developmental psychologists were observing how young children go about the business of learning color names. First, they established that a group of three-year-olds did not know the color olive. Most called it green, some called it brown. Bartlett and Carey then taught the children a nonsense name for olive—a name that they would not have heard anywhere else. They took two cafeteria trays and painted one tray olive and the other blue.

Each three-year-old child, individually, was told casually, "Hand me the chromium tray. Not the blue one, the chromium one."

The child would hesitate and perhaps point to the olive tray. "This one?"

"Yes, that one. Thank you."

A week later, with no further instruction, the children were again asked to name the colors. When olive was presented, they paused. They did not remember what it had been called, but now they knew that this color was not called green or brown. A single exposure was enough to begin a reorganization of their color lexicon.

This simple experiment was followed up by a series of more carefully controlled studies that confirmed two important conclusions about how children learn words. First, to learn a word and enter it into the vocabulary matrix, a child must be able to associate its sound with its meaning. Mastering the mechanics of uttering and recognizing a word is one kind of learning; mastering the concept that the word expresses is another kind; associating one with the other is still a third. After their experience with the trays, the children knew that olive has a special name—it is not called green or brown—but they did not remember the particular utterance that was associated with that perceived color. Many repetitions may be required before the sound of a new word becomes familiar and repeatable, and many more before it is associated with the correct referent.

Second, a child's appreciation of the meaning of a word seems to occur in two stages, one rapid and the other much slower. Children are quick to notice new words and to assign them to broad semantic categories. After hearing the nonsense name *chromium* used just once to differentiate the tray, the three-year-olds assigned it to the semantic field of color names. Children are able to keep such semantic fields separate even before they know what the individual words mean. When asked the color of something, they may respond with almost any color term at random, but they never answer *big* or *six* or *doll*.

The slow stage begins when the child starts to work out distinctions among words within a large semantic category. A child who has correctly assigned several terms to the color domain still must learn the differences and relations among those terms. This process of sorting out similarities and differences within a semantic field ordinarily takes much longer than the first stage and may never be completely finished. Some adults, for example, can correctly assign *sycamore* and *hickory* to the semantic field of names of trees, but have not learned what trees they refer to and could not identify them on sight. At any given time, many words will be in this intermediate state in which they are familiar and roughly categorized, but are not yet distinguished from one another.

Attentive parents frequently observe that their children tend to overgeneralize the meanings of new words. A small child learning the word *apple,* for example, may use it to refer to a tomato. The usual explanation is that *apple* is thought to denote a certain list of attributes—say, round, red, and of a certain size—and confusions occur because the list is incomplete. Without further qualification, those attributes define ripe tomatoes as well as ripe apples. The opposite error, undergeneralization, also occurs, but it is not as easily observed. Special questioning is needed to bring it out. For example, a child who thinks that being round, red, and of a certain size defines *apple* might refuse to use *apple* to refer to green or yellow apples. The only way to discover whether this is the case is to show the child a green or yellow apple and ask what it is called.

Semantic theories that decompose word meanings into universal components find overgeneralization easy to explain. If comprehension depends on appreciating semantic components, and if young children are innately prepared to recognize a basic set of those components, then it is reasonable to assume that learning the meaning of a word proceeds by associating more and more of those basic concepts to a word until its meaning is finally fixed. For example, *apple* might refer first to anything round, later to anything round and of the right size, still later to anything round, red, and of that size; and so, attribute by attribute, the meaning of the word would simply accumulate in the child's mind. As more semantic components are added, the meaning eventually converges on the correct, adult concept of apples.

Overextensions

Child's word	First referent	Extensions	Possible common property
Bird	Sparrows	Cow, dogs, cats, any moving animal	Movement
Mooi	Moon	Cakes, round marks on window, round shapes in books, tooling on leather book covers, postmarks, letter O	Shape
Fly	Fly	Specks of dirt, dust, all small insects, his own toes, crumbs, small toad	Size
Koko	Cock crowing	Tunes played on a violin, piano, accordion, phonograph, all music, merry-go-round	Sound
Wau-wau	Dogs	All animals, toy dog, soft slippers, picture of old man in furs	Texture

Source: deVilliers & deVilliers, 1979.

Overextension in the use of words occurs among children when their understanding of a word's meaning is incomplete. A child who thinks that anything round, red, and of a certain size is an apple will call a ripe tomato an apple.

Underextension also occurs, but is harder to observe. A child who thinks that anything round, red, and of a certain size is an apple may fail to use the word for green or yellow apples. But to discover underextension, it is necessary to ask the child what such apples are called.

Not everyone believes that children learn the meanings of words by adding more and more semantic features. Critics are troubled by the fact that many errors that should be observed if this theory were correct do not seem to occur. For example, not only is a verb like *jump,* which is complex from a componential point of view, mastered just as easily as the simpler verb *move,* but there seems to be no stage at which the word *jump* is overgeneralized to refer to simpler movements. To state the objection in more general terms, there is no reason to suppose that the semantic components that serve as definitional primitives will also serve as developmental primitives. One alternative would be to search for the primitives of semantic development. Another is to assume that children learn word meanings as unanalyzed wholes.

Whether or not young children instinctively perform semantic analyses may be debatable, but there is agreement that in the beginning they do not perform morphological analyses. A young child's initial bias is to suppose that each concept has its own distinct phonological representation—to expect that the vocabulary matrix will have a one-to-one mapping. For example, *know* and *knew* may both be familiar to a child who then learns that the past tense is formed by adding -*ed,* at which point *knowed* (and sometimes the doubly past *knewed*) appears spontaneously in the child's speech. Productive use of the -*ed* inflection indicates that morphological analysis is beginning, with the corollary indication that the morphological relation between *know* and *knew* had gone unnoticed before that time.

Another example is provided by the reversative *un-* verbs. The first of these verbs that a child learns—*untangle, unfasten, unbuckle, uncover*—are treated like unanalyzed monomorphemic units. Before about age three-and-a-half, there is no evidence that *un-* is recognized as an independent morpheme. But then the analysis is appreciated, and *un-* begins to appear productively in front of many different verbs. Melissa Bowerman, a developmental psycholinguist, reported this exchange with her four-year-old daughter, Christy:

> Christy asked her mother why the pliers were on the table.
> M: "I've been using them for straightening the wire."
> C: "And unstraighting it?" [=bending]

Since the adult reversatives are *bend* and *unbend,* it is unlikely that Christy had heard anyone say *unstraighting.* At the age of four Christy had performed the morphological analysis and was using *un-* in a highly productive manner. But before that time the reversatives had been unanalyzed wholes.

The slow phase of word learning continues long after the association between the spoken word and its meaning is formed. At around three to four years, children begin to reorganize how they think about the words that they have been learning. Once a child has acquired a core vocabulary and a basic knowledge of syntax, this covert reorganization becomes particularly important, and vocabulary growth develops a deeper and subtler character. Some children seem to do more of this in-depth analysis than others do, and some certainly feel freer than do others to incorporate the discovered patterns into their own speech. But all children have started this reorganizational process long before they start school.

Ostension

Adults often explain a word to children by pointing to instances. This teaching method, called ostension (or ostensive definition), is so simple and effective that the puzzle it poses can easily be overlooked.

For example, when an adult points to a rabbit and says, "That's a rabbit," how does the child know that *rabbit* refers to the whole animal and not to some attribute, some part, some posture, activity, developmental stage, or orientation of the rabbit? Or to a combination of these? Or even to some aspect of the act of pointing? It is usually assumed that coupling "That's a rabbit" with a variety of rabbits will cancel out irrelevant features, but that procedure opens up the further possibility that *rabbit* might refer to the sequence of instances, or to their number or timing. In short, there is simply not enough information in such demonstrative gestures to eliminate all the hypotheses that are logically consistent with the available evidence.

Children are quick to grasp the referents that adults have in mind because they are born with a bias to consider some possibilities and to ignore others. The bias begins with the fact that children and adults have the same kind of perceptual apparatus. For both children and adults, objects and shapes stand out as coherent figures against a background—when an adult points to something, the child can assume that the adult intends to refer to the same perceptual whole that the child is perceiving. Assigning priority to the perceptual whole greatly reduces the variety of possibilities that a child must consider.

The problem, of course, is that parts, attributes, and relations often ARE defined ostensively. If children assume that an unfamiliar noun is likely to refer to a perceptual whole, not to its parts or attributes, how can they understand ostensive definitions of anything else? Suppose that a child has just mastered the fact that a rabbit is called "rabbit." The adult now points to the same object and says, "That's an ear," or "That's white," or "That's an animal." Why doesn't the child conclude that *rabbit, ear, white,* or *animal* are synonyms, all used to refer to the same perceptual whole?

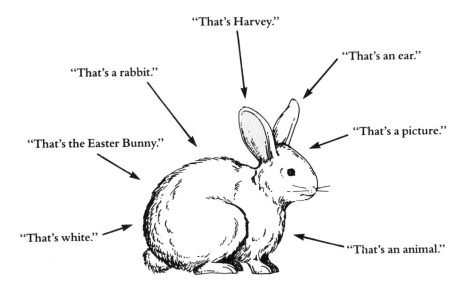

How do children sort this out?

The answer has to do with how children think about labels. Young children regard a thing's name as an inherent property of the thing. "Snake," they will tell you, "is a long word." For a thing to have two names would be as confusing as for it to have two shapes or two lengths. Ellen M. Markman and her colleagues have shown that young children tend to assume that each object has one and only one name; she calls it the child's assumption of exclusivity.

So a young child's assumptions work as follows. The first noun associated with an object is assumed to be its name (by the priority of the perceptual whole), and subsequent nouns must refer to something else (by the assumption of exclusivity). What that "something else" will be poses still another puzzle.

How can an adult point at one thing (a rabbit, say) to refer to something else (a color, perhaps)? To discuss such indirect ostensions, it is necessary to distinguish between P, the thing pointed at, and R, the thing referred to. That distinction was forcefully illustrated by the linguist Geoffrey D. Nunberg, who used the example of a waitress pointing at a ham sandwich while saying, "He's sitting at table twenty." Little knowledge of restaurants is required to understand that the sandwich (P) and "he" (R) are two different things—two things that are associated by virtue of a function, *the R who ordered P*. Nunberg argues that a theory of ostension must explain how listeners' knowledge of P enables them to identify R. He proposes that there is always a function, called the referring function, that relates P and R in such a way that when the value of P is given (ostensively), the value of R can be inferred. When an adult points to the rabbit and says, "That's an ear," the adult has judged that the child knows enough to understand the referring function PART: *The ear (R) is a part of the rabbit (P)*. Similarly, the adult who points and says, "That's an animal" is using the referring function TYPE: *The rabbit (P) is a type of animal (R)*. And so on through many other possible referring functions.

It is a remarkable fact that young children are able to choose appropriate referring functions. Or, to state the matter more cautiously, it is remarkable how well adults can judge what referring functions young children will be able to understand. Where it starts is presumably with the distinction between proper nouns and common nouns. When an adult points to a rabbit and says, "That's Harvey," P and R are identical. But when the adult points and says, "That's a rabbit," the ostension is indirect; the child is expected to understand the referring function INSTANCE: *This object (P) is an instance of the class of rabbits (R)*. Not long after children understand INSTANCE, they can understand PICTURE: "That's a rabbit" is understood to mean *This object (P) is a picture of a rabbit (R)*.

Because superordination plays a central role in organizing lexical memory for nouns, experimental studies have been conducted with the referring function TYPE. For example, Sandra Waxman and Rochel Gelman presented a puppet to three-year-old children and then showed them pictures of a dog and a horse and a duck, while telling them: "This puppet only likes things like a dog or a horse or a duck." Then the children were handed a dozen pictures of

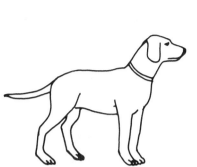

Can very young children understand the semantic relation of superordination? Presented with a puppet, three-year-olds were shown these standard pictures and told either that "This puppet only likes things like this" or "This puppet only likes dobutsus." When asked to choose from other pictures the things that the puppet liked, children who thought they were learning the meaning of dobutsus *selected only animal pictures, whereas the other children did not.*

animals, foods, and articles of clothing and asked to select things that the puppet liked. Under those conditions, the children did not consistently assign all the animal pictures to the puppet and set aside all the pictures of foods and clothing; given a free choice, the three-year-olds did not assume that the puppet liked nothing but animals. But then Waxman and Gelman repeated the experiment exactly, except that now the children were told: "This puppet only likes dobutsus. I don't know what dobutsus are, but this puppet only likes things like a dog or a horse or a duck." After this minor change—introducing the novel word *dobutsu* (the Japanese word for *animal*)—the children gave the puppet only animals.

Young children do not spontaneously group things categorically, but they will do so when they are learning new words. Adding a verbal label led the children to believe that they were in a word-learning situation, so they interpreted the experimenter's act of demonstrating the dog, horse, and duck (P) as referring indirectly to the dobutsus (R). The children defined the novel word by the referring function TYPE: *The dog, horse, and duck (P) are types of dobutsu (R)*. When the relevance of taxonomic relations was indicated, the three-year-olds had no difficulty in selecting the appropriate referring function.

Reading and Vocabulary

Children in the United States are expected to learn to read and write during the first three or four years of elementary school. At first they read and write only words that they have learned before starting school, but by about the fourth

Being taught to read in second grade.

grade they begin to see written words that they have never heard anyone use in conversation. At this point, American educators assume that something special must be done to help children learn these unfamiliar words.

One possibility is to provide special coaching: phonological drills and conceptual clarifications. But that kind of teaching, even when well done, is slow and painful. No more than 100 or 200 words can be taught that way during a school year. Since learning runs so far ahead of teaching—some 3,750 words learned in a year compared with 200 taught—it is hard to avoid the question: How do schoolchildren learn so much more than they are taught?

For children who can read, many new words are picked up from context by a process that psychologists call incidental learning. That is to say, children can learn words at school the same way they learned them at home: by observing how they are used in intelligible contexts. The principal difference is that the academic environment depends more on written than on spoken contexts. It is widely recognized that the best way to facilitate vocabulary growth in schoolchildren is to encourage them to read as much as possible.

Learning words by reading them in context is effective, but not efficient. Some contexts are uninformative. Some are even misleading. For reading to have any substantial effect on vocabulary, a word must be encountered several times—which means that a great deal of reading must be done.

How much is a great deal? Some rough calculations are instructive. A child who spends fifty minutes of every school day reading at, say, two hundred words per minute, would read one million words in a hundred-day school year. That may sound like a lot, but it is not enough. A million running words of prose will typically contain no more than fifty thousand distinct word types, representing roughly ten thousand root words or "word families." School texts would probably contain fewer than ten thousand, but even with that much diversity it is unlikely that more than a thousand would be totally unfamiliar lexical items. Since several encounters with a new word are required in order to master it, it is clear that reading one million words per year is insufficient. It is not surprising, therefore, that children who read little or nothing outside of school generally do poorly on vocabulary tests.

It might seem that one way to shortcut all this reading would be to look up unfamiliar words in a dictionary. But reading a dictionary is itself an acquired skill. In about the fourth grade, therefore, most American schools begin to teach what are called dictionary skills: spelling, alphabetization, pronunciation, parts of speech, a little morphology and etymology. The goal is to teach children how to find unfamiliar words in a dictionary and, having found them, how to understand what they read there.

One trouble with this approach is that most healthy, right-minded children have a strong aversion to dictionaries. And with good reason, for after a long and tedious search they often misunderstand what they have found. For example, one fifth-grader looked up *stimulate* in her school dictionary and then wrote the sentence, *Mrs. Morrow stimulated the soup,* because she found "stir up" among the definitions. Another wrote *Me and my parents correlate,* because he found that the definition of *correlate* was "be related one to the other." Perhaps such errors could be reduced if the authors of children's dictionaries were more aware of the strategies that children adopt when using them.

Observations of how children use dictionaries illustrate what has been called a simple substitution strategy: Find a familiar word, assume that it is a synonym of the unfamiliar word, then substitute the unfamiliar word into contexts where the familiar word could have been used. The substitution strategy is not limited to dictionary use; something similar occurs when children learn new words by reading them in context. For example, one group of fifth-graders read the sentence, *The king's brother tried to usurp the throne,* and then produced such sentences as *The blue chair was usurped from the room, Don't try to usurp that tape from the store, The thief tried to usurp the money from the safe,* and so on. They had gathered from the sentence they read that *usurp* means *take,* so they wrote sentences using *take* and substituted *usurp* in its place.

This learning strategy looks much like overgeneralization. Just as younger children may overextend *apple* because they know only part of its meaning, so a partial definition of *usurp* resulted in its being overextended. That is to say, if *usurp* is incompletely defined as *take,* it can be predicated of anything that can be taken: chairs, tape, money, whatever. Thus, the substitution strategy can be

Dictionary definition	Child's abstraction from definition	Child's sentence
correlate 1. be related one to the other: *The diameter and circumference of a circle correlate.* 2. put into relation: *Try to correlate your knowledge of history with your knowledge of geography.* v., correlated, correlating.	be related	Me and my parents correlate, because without them I wouldn't be here.
meticulous very careful or too particular about small details. *adj.*	very careful	I was meticulous about falling off the cliff.
redress 1. set right; repair; remedy: *King Arthur tried to redress wrongs in his kingdom.* 2. reparation; setting right: *Any man deserves redress if he has been injured unfairly.* v., n.	remedy	The redress for getting well when you're sick is to stay in bed.
relegate 1. send away, usually to a lower position or condition: *to relegate a dress to the rag bag.* 2. send into exile; banish. 3. hand over (a matter, task, etc.). *v.*	send away	I relegated my pen pal's letter to her house
tenet opinion, belief, principle, or doctrine held as true. *n.*	true	That news is very tenet

Puzzling sentences are often written by schoolchildren when their understanding of an unfamiliar word is incomplete. Here are examples from some children in the fifth and sixth grades. The dictionary definitions that they consulted make clear what was going on. A child will frequently extract some familiar word from a definition, think of a sentence containing that word, and substitute the unfamiliar word in the written sentence.

viewed as a later stage in the development of a word-learning process employed by preschool children.

The more interesting question, however, is how the children abstracted the concept of *take* from the context *The king's brother tried to ——— the throne.* The search for an answer to that question entails a closer look at contexts and the information they contain.

For a child's vocabulary growth, reading one million words per school year is not enough.

Meanings and Definitions

Most discussions of how children learn new words presuppose two propositions: first, that to learn a word is to learn its meaning, and second, that a word's meaning is given by its definition. Taken together, these propositions underlie the common opinion that to learn a word is to learn its definition. This adds up to a view of word learning that can have several practical consequences. For example, those who hold this opinion will advise students to study dictionary definitions to learn new words. They will test students' vocabularies by challenging pupils to provide definitions or to match words with defining phrases. If they also believe that definitions are semantic decompositions, they will assume that children learn new words by assembling their semantic components one or two at a time.

And they will be puzzled that people who know a word often have trouble giving an acceptable definition for it. People may be able to describe what someone would be talking about when he or she used the word, but that description falls far short of a real definition. Composing good constructive definitions is an art, and like any art it rests on native talent polished by interminable practice. Without special training, most people have trouble defining words whose meanings they know perfectly well. Some refuse to try. Others give inadequate or incorrect definitions. A few protest that they do not understand the task: One person who was asked to define *crime* responded, "I don't know what 'crime' means. I know a lot about crime and criminals. Is that what you mean by a definition of 'crime'?"

At first glance, this ineptness in providing definitions might appear to be another instance of implicit linguistic knowledge. Just as a syntactician says that people implicitly know and respect rules of syntax that they are unable to state explicitly, so the lexical semanticist might say that people implicitly know and respect definitions that they are unable to state explicitly. But there are reasons to believe that this explanation is not available to a lexical semanticist. Consider a counterexample.

Lay people find some words easier to define than others. As a general rule, the more specific a word is, the easier it is to formulate its definition. For example, it is easy to define *pony* as a small horse, but it is more difficult to define *horse*—and more difficult still to give a good definition of *animal*. Again, *rise* can readily be defined as to move upward, but *move* is more difficult; *move* may be defined as to change location or orientation, but the definition of *change* is still more challenging. Apparently, the words that express semantic primitives are the words needed to define less generic words, but the primitives themselves are given; they do not need definitions. That claim, however—that the meanings of the most basic words are understood immediately, not through definitions, either explicit or implicit—must confound anyone who believes that to know a word is to know its definition. The claim that people can know definitions implicitly may be true, but it does not explain how it is possible to know the semantic primes immediately without any definitions at all.

Meanings and Contexts

If knowing words is more than a matter of knowing their definitions, then what more is it? A possibility that has been proposed many times is that to know a word is to know how to use it. Usually these proposals define "use" in terms of the purposes that language can serve; language is "used" to communicate information, to command assistance, to entertain, to pray, to express emotion, to persuade—the list of uses goes on and on. In this view, the meaning of any particular utterance depends on the goal the person hoped to achieve by uttering it. Long lists of speech acts that make different uses of language have been drawn up and analyzed in detail. The pragmatic theories that emerge from those analyses are undeniably instructive, but they are more concerned with the uses of language than with the uses of words. When word use is the point in question, the answer must be sought in terms of the contexts in which the word can be used.

The presuppositions behind this alternative account of word learning are, first, that to learn a word is to learn how to use it, and second, that learning how to use it is a matter of learning the contexts in which it can occur. Taken

Context and Event-Related Potentials

An electroencephalogram (EEG) is a record of voltage fluctuations, popularly known as brain waves, that are generated by the electrical activity of cells in the brain and picked up by electrodes placed on the scalp. The EEG is the summation of many processes that are going on in the brain at the same time; however, it is possible to obtain records of specific activities by a procedure known as computer averaging. Recordings are time-locked to the repeated presentation of a stimulus; after many records are averaged together, the random background fluctuations will cancel out and only the effects of the stimuli will be left. The resulting average shows the event-related potential (ERP) that is produced by stimuli of that type.

In 1980 at the University of California at San Diego, Marta Kutas and Steven Hillyard discovered that semantically anomalous words produce a large negative wave in the ERP, starting about 200 milliseconds after the presentation of the word and peaking at 400 milliseconds—a wave that has since become familiar as the "N400." Short sentences were displayed on a computer screen one word at a time, and the ERP was recorded as the last word appeared. For example, participants might read, *I like my coffee with sugar and* ———, where the final word

could be either *cream,* which is the most predictable continuation, or *dog,* which is semantically anomalous. If the average ERP for sentences with highly predictable terminal words is taken as the baseline, then sentences ending with anomalous words show a large N400.

Control experiments established that the N400 is not a simple startle reaction; changing the typeface, for example, surprised the readers but did not produce the N400. Grammatical errors—*As the turtle grows its shell also grow*—do not produce the N400. Nor is it a response to falsity; reading *A robin is not a vehicle* produced much the same N400 as did *A robin is a vehicle.* The reaction depends on

the meaning, but the less probable the continuation is, the greater the N400 will be.

One plausible interpretation of these observations is that the N400 component of the ERP measures the extent to which the terminal word has been primed by the antecedent context. That is to say, if a sentence context closely matches the context representation of a word, the N400 will not occur. If a sentence context is plausible but improbable—*I like my coffee with sugar and cake,* for example—a moderate N400 will be observed. The maximal N400 occurs when the terminal word is one whose context representation is incompatible with the antecedent context.

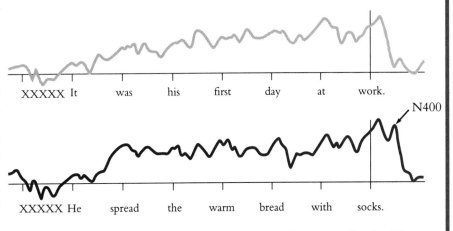

Average ERP waveforms recorded by Marta Kutas and Steven Hillyard while subjects read words one at a time from a computer screen. When the final word was semantically inappropriate, the N400 potential was observed.

together, these presuppositions add up to the opinion that to know a word is to know the contexts in which it can occur, a view that also has practical consequences. For example, those who hold this opinion will advise students to learn new words by reading and thinking about the contexts in which they occur. They will assess word knowledge by how skillfully a student uses words in appropriate contexts. If they also believe that semantic components are important, they will assume that children learn new words by first assigning them to appropriate semantic fields and then, later, working out the relations and regularities within each field according to the different contexts in which the words are used.

This formulation seems to neglect the critical importance of word meaning, but it does respect the fact that children are good at learning words from context. That is to say, if learning a word is learning how to use it, then hearing or seeing it used should be the best kind of practice. For that reason, if for no other, the role of context deserves serious consideration.

One place to begin is with the semantic relation of synonymy. Words are said to be synonyms if they have the same meaning, but "the same meaning" is what needs to be defined. Since it is difficult to assess the meaning of a word outside the context in which it is used, most semanticists prefer to phrase the definition of synonymy in terms of statements that have the same meaning, where "the same meaning" can be defined as having the same truth functions. Following a formulation usually attributed to Leibniz, two words can be said to be synonyms if one can be used in a statement in place of the other without changing the truth or falsehood of the statement. Or, to use a term favored by some linguists, two synonyms must have the same contextual distribution.

Thus, synonymy forges a link between meanings and contexts. But synonymy, strictly defined, is not a gradable semantic relation; two words either are synonyms or they are not. In practice, however, synonymy should be gradable; natural languages have few exact synonyms. Pairs like *glad* and *joyful,* for example, seem very close, yet they are not interchangeable in all contexts; you might talk about a *joyful gathering,* but a *glad gathering* is odd. Some semanticists have concluded that the term "synonymy" should be dropped—that it is impossible to do better than to say that two words have a greater or lesser degree of "likeness of meaning." Psycholinguists generally agree; they have largely abandoned "synonymy" in favor of "similarity of meaning," "semantic distance," or, more often, "semantic similarity."

This move introduces a continuous variable where before there was a dichotomy. Armed with semantic similarity, it is no longer necessary to decide whether, say, *snake* and *serpent* are exact synonyms. It is enough to say that native speakers of English judge them to be highly similar in meaning. Indeed, native speakers of English can construct a series of word pairs ordered for semantic similarity: *snake/serpent, snake/eel, snake/rat, snake/dog, snake/bush, snake/taxi, snake/charity,* for example.

When synonymy is generalized to semantic similarity, truth values are abandoned—in two-valued logics there are no intermediate truth values to go along with intermediate similarities. Substitutability need not be abandoned, however. Words with different but similar meanings can often be substituted for one another without changing a sentence into something that no one would be likely to use. Zellig S. Harris, for many years a distinguished professor of linguistics at the University of Pennsylvania, put the idea this way:

> If we consider words or morphemes A and B to be more different in meaning than A and C, then we will often find that the [contextual] distributions of A and B are more different than the distributions of A and C. In other words, difference of meaning correlates with difference of distribution.

In short, two words are judged similar in meaning to the extent that they share similar privileges of occurrence.

So the argument goes like this. To know a word is to know the contexts in which it can occur. Two words that can occur in many of the same contexts are judged to be similar in meaning. Therefore, if an unfamiliar word is observed to occur in contexts that would also accommodate some familiar word, the unfamiliar word will be judged to be similar in meaning to the familiar word. For example, on reading the sentence, *The king's brother tried to usurp the throne,* the context of the unfamiliar *usurp* is recognized as suitable for several familiar verbs, one of the more likely being *take.* This rapid assessment of the general meaning of *usurp* will then be followed up by a slower phase during which the particular manner of taking is worked out.

It is assumed, therefore, that word knowledge must be organized in such a way that people can recognize immediately which contexts will accept a word and which will not. Otherwise speakers would not be able to insert words rapidly and appropriately into phrase structures and listeners would not be able to use context to improve their perception of speech. For convenience of discussion, this abstract representation of the contexts a word can take is called the word's *context representation.* This terminology keeps the contextual origins of most lexical knowledge in plain view—to know how a word is used is to know the context representation of that word—and leaves room for more than semantic information in the characterization of word knowledge.

The simplest way to understand what information can be abstracted from contexts and included in a context representation is to consider specific examples.

1. *Collocations:* From *absolute zero* to *zygomatic arch,* English is studded with strings of words that occur together with far greater than chance probability. For example, *hermetically sealed* is probably the only use of *hermetically* that a student will encounter, so its entry in the mental lexicon could be:

hermetically [Adv, + —*sealed*]

This context would also be included in the context representation for *tightly.*

2. *Syntactic contexts:* Most syntacticians assume that along with each verb is stored a strict subcategorization (see Chapter 11). The verb *kill,* for example, can occur only in such contexts as

$$kill \ [V, \ + \ \text{—}NP]$$

where it is followed by a noun phrase (NP) representing the object of the verb. This part of a context representation plays an important role in many syntactic theories.

3. *Semantic contexts:* Contexts also provide selectional restrictions—information about constraints on the arguments that a given predicate can take. For example, syntax says that *kill* takes an object NP, but semantics says that the NP should denote an animate object. The hierarchical organization of the noun lexicon can be derived in large outline from the verbs and adjectives that can be predicated of them.

4. *Pragmatic contexts:* A large and heterogeneous variety of constraints on word use can be classified as pragmatic. For example, questions constrain answers; a responsive answer to *What do you want to eat?* should include a word denoting food. And anaphors should be superordinate to their antecedents: In *He saw a bomber; the plane was sitting on the runway,* the information is given that *bomber* is a hyponym of *plane.*

All of these different kinds of contextual information must be stored with each word in the mental lexicon. Taken together, they give so much information that some lexical semanticists have assumed that all the semantic properties of a lexical item are fully reflected in aspects of the relations that it contracts with actual and potential contexts. If the meaning of a word is nothing more than a product of its contextual relations, it is obvious that similarity of meaning and similarity of contexts must vary together.

But can an exclusively contextual description of the learning process be sufficient? One curious consequence of tying meaning so closely to context is that different parts of speech must correspond to basic differences in meaning. Since nouns, verbs, and adjectives are not interchangeable without destroying the syntax of a sentence, their meanings must be very different. For example, *weight, weigh,* and *weighty* seem similar in meaning, yet they are never interchangeable in contexts. It would seem that, after all the information that contexts contain has been abstracted, there is still a need for specifically semantic information to ground words on the bedrock of experience.

But context representations do not exclude semantic information. A confirmed contextualist could answer such questions with a broader definition of context. The contexts in which words occur need not be exclusively linguistic; the physical and social environments in which language is used are part of a larger context that also contributes to the learner's understanding of a word's meaning.

The definitional and the contextual accounts of word learning are two views of the same thing. They differ principally in what they take to be the figure and what the background. A definitional approach makes the word the figure and its contexts the background; a contextual approach makes the contexts the center of attention and leaves the word in the background. The definitional approach seems the natural one to anybody familiar with definitions and dictionaries, but the contextual approach is a necessary reminder that there is much more to learning a word than learning its definition.

■ ■ ■

Sharing a common vocabulary.

No two people learn exactly the same words, but if people do not have many words in common, they cannot communicate effectively or work together efficiently. A language with a common vocabulary, more than any other shared knowledge, defines a social group and gives it a basis for cultural coherence.

Children come into this world with a keen interest in words and a natural talent for acquiring them. The responsibility to understand those gifts and nurture them is not limited to teachers, but concerns everyone who hopes for a future filled with brighter, better-informed citizens. A primary goal of formal education should be to ensure that all members of the national community share a common vocabulary—a vocabulary in which important issues can be clearly phrased, in which questions can be asked and answers debated. Of all the fascinating facts and ideas about words, none are of greater practical importance than those pertaining to the growth of a common vocabulary.

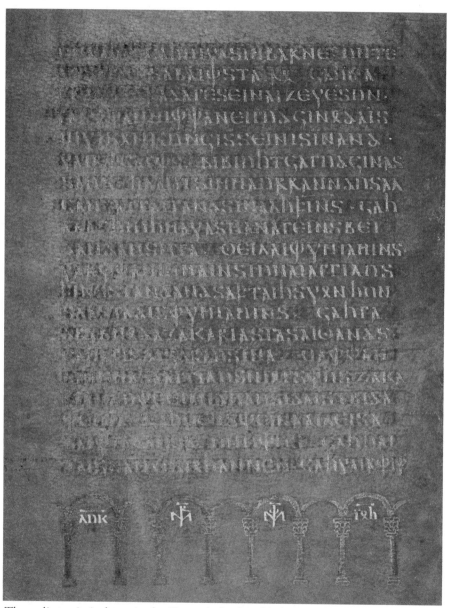

The earliest principal text in the Germanic family of Indo-European languages—which includes English—is the Gothic Bible translated by Bishop Ulfilas around A.D. 350. The Codex Argenteus, this copy of his work, dates from the fifth or sixth century.

A Final Word

The preceding pages illustrate a particular way of doing science, a way that searches for a framework, a coordinate system within which objects of interest can be understood in terms of their locations relative to one another. Thus, words acquire meaning by virtue of their locations in concrete situations here and now, by virtue of their locations in the syntactic and rhetorical structures of a discourse, and (of central interest here) by virtue of their locations in the lexical-conceptual structures of human memory.

To those who expect science to begin with a search for physical causes, systems thinking can be vaguely unsettling. Or unsettlingly vague. Even when a systems account makes sense of the facts, questions about causation remain unanswered. Why this system, rather than some other? To a reductionist, a systems account is not an explanation; it is something to be explained. But reductionistic accounts of human institutions or human language seem doomed to failure. When human behavior is reduced to patterns of energy exchange in the physical world, nothing human remains—the result differs little from an analysis of the behavior of a colony of ants. Analyzing physical events to find explanations for social conventions is like analyzing air molecules to explain the wind.

Those who hope for historical explanations in terms of first causes also tend to find systems thinking disappointing. Most accounts of complex systems say nothing about when or how the systems first arose. For example, despite brilliant efforts to trace the history of languages, chronological accounts of their origins are almost pure speculation; those who have searched for historical sources have found only abandoned linguistic structures. As far back as the mind can extrapolate, languages were as complicated as they are today. The languages of modern industrialized nations have larger vocabularies, of course, but the systematic structure of language has remained invariant.

This way of doing science—the systems approach to problems of intricately structured complexity—emerged during the nineteenth century and flowered in the twentieth. Probably its ultimate expression is the modern computer. A computer not only IS a system, it can become any system that you are clever enough to define precisely. A computer is a laboratory in which the feasibility and coherence of any hypothetical system can be explored—rapidly. But the development of this way of doing science did not await the invention of computers; some who practice it still think that high technology is an invention of the devil. Anthropologists and sociologists who would never go near a computer still create theoretical frameworks. They see their task as one of characterizing the coherent systems that give meaning to the values and conventions that enable people to live together as a society. And the modern science of language provides a prototype of systems thinking, a model for those studying other social phenomena; yet computers are little used by the leading linguistic theorists.

It remains true, nevertheless, that one way to test your understanding of a system is to build your own. If you knew how to program a computer to comprehend natural languages, you would indeed have a good theory of language systems. Of course, a computer that can understand and answer human speech has been a staple of science fiction for many years, but it is still far from a practical reality. Translation was one of the first applications of computers to linguistic problems, and the dismal failure of those early attempts was eloquent testimony to how much about human language was still not adequately understood. In the thirty years since then, much progress has been made, but the robot that uses language like a human being is still out of reach.

Getting a computer to speak and understand speech is not a single problem. It is several problems wrapped into one, and some are easier than others. For example, how to make a computer generate speechlike sounds was a relatively simple problem, but how to make a computer recognize spoken words as people do turned out to be much, much harder. Simulating the lexical-conceptual system is particularly thorny. Computers have been programmed to deal intelligently with miniature problems where the lexicon can be limited to a few hundred words, but so far no one has extended those results to the full vocabulary of English.

Why is it so hard to model the lexicon? Several answers are possible, but take just one as an example. Consider the problem posed by polysemous words. Imagine that some computer-based system is processing language when it encounters the sentence, *He drove a nail*. What is the device to make of the polysemous words *drive* and *nail*? In a miniature exercise with a small lexicon, the problem can be avoided by telling the computer only the relevant senses: *to exert physical force* and *a wire fastener*. In a device intended for general use, however, the computer would also know other senses: *to operate* and *a horny sheath*. So the better informed device must solve the

Polysemy Problem: Which senses of polysemous words are the most appropriate in given contexts?

People who know English resolve the potential ambiguity of *He drove a nail* so rapidly that they have trouble understanding what the problem is. So far, however, no general algorithm for solving the polysemy problem is known.

Why various seemingly plausible approaches to the polysemy problem have not worked is a technical subject of no great interest. The reason for introducing the polysemy problem at all here is not to solve it, but rather to show how important it is.

Suppose the problem had been solved. That is to say, suppose that lexical-conceptual systems were understood well enough that computer scientists could write programs to select the appropriate sense of a polysemous word on the basis of an examination of its context. The obvious consequence would be that a major obstacle to the development of language comprehension devices would have been removed. But what does that mean? What then could computers do that they cannot do now?

Consider this situation. A student who is reading an assignment hits an unfamiliar word. When a dictionary is consulted, it turns out that the word has several meanings. The student reconsiders the original context, testing each definitional gloss in turn, and eventually chooses a best fit. It is a slow process and a serious interruption of the real task of understanding the text. Now compare this situation. A computer is presenting a reading assignment to a student when an unfamiliar word appears. The student points to the word, and the computer, which is able to solve the polysemy problem, presents to the student only those meanings that are appropriate in the given context—as if a responsive teacher were sitting at the student's side. The desired information is presented rapidly, and the real task of understanding is not interrupted.

Or consider the thoughtful author who would like to avoid using words ambiguously in her own writing. It would be possible to give her a word processor that could flag every word that the machine could not disambiguate on the basis of its context. Where the computer could not solve the polysemy problem, the author could revise the manuscript to remove that problem for a reader.

Information retrieval provides still another example. Suppose you are a carpenter looking for information about a new kind of nail, and you ask an information retrieval system for all the articles it has with the words *nail* or *nails* in the title or abstract. With no better descriptor than that, you will retrieve unwanted articles about fingernails and toenails—which is known as the problem of false drops. So you revise your descriptor to *metal nail* and try again. Now you eliminate the horny nails, but you also eliminate a lot of articles about metal nails that did not bother to include the word *metal* in the title or abstract—which is known as the problem of misses. False drops and misses are the Scylla and Charybdis of information retrieval; anything that reduces one increases the other. Note that a computer that was able to solve the polysemy problem would select only those titles and abstracts in which the desired meaning was appropriate and so would increase the efficiency of information retrieval enormously.

In short, a variety of practical technological advances could be implemented if it were possible to solve the polysemy problem in some tidy and reliable way. The reason that the polysemy problem is important is that it lies at the very heart of the process of turning word forms into word meanings. Many of the limitations of computers in dealing with human languages arise from the fact that computers presently deal with word forms, whereas people talk and think in terms of word meanings. But the reason the polysemy problem is important is also the reason it is difficult. What is needed to find a general solution to the polysemy problem is neither a cause-effect explanation of polysemy nor an account of its chronological origins. Rather, it is a better understanding of the lexical-conceptual system.

The fact that computers find it so difficult to do what people do so easily says something about computers. And about people. And about the current state of psycholinguistics.

About computers, it says that the modern conception of what a machine can be and do has advanced dramatically. Most engineering proposals assume that a computer able to solve the polysemy problem will have rapid access to an enormous range and variety of information. But how that information should be stored and when it is to be retrieved are still under investigation.

About people, it confirms that language is uniquely human—only human beings have mastered the extended systems of relations that constitute a language. Indeed, the relational nature of the lexical component of language merits a brief review. Begin with the fact that for a noise or inscription to count as a word, it must express or communicate a concept: It must have a meaning. And for a noise or inscription to have a meaning, it must be part of a lexical-conceptual system. But a lexical-conceptual system is highly arbitrary:

- First, there is no necessary set of word forms that every language must use.

- Second, there is no universal catalogue of concepts that every language must express.

- Third, there is no intrinsic link between a word form and a word meaning: A form can have many meanings, and a meaning can be expressed by many forms.

- Fourth, for this highly arbitrary system to have any coherent structure, both the forms and the meanings must be defined in terms of their relations with other forms and meanings; a mental lexicon is a vast and intricately woven body of knowledge.

The polysemy problem cannot be solved unless that extensive mental lexicon is readily available. Human beings are not only innately prepared to acquire such relational systems, but are also uniquely able to exploit this relational knowledge in the production and comprehension of speech and writing.

About psycholinguistics, it suggests that polysemy, far from being a problem, may actually be an opportunity for research. Clearly, not enough is presently known about how people cope with polysemy to enable anyone to write specifications for a computer program that could do the same thing. But by analyzing carefully the conditions under which people are able (or unable) to resolve polysemy, it may be possible to learn more about the kinds of contextual information that are involved and how those contexts interact with stored lexical information. Polysemy offers a window on the association of form and meaning.

Words should not be studied in isolation, one at a time. The lexical component of any natural language is a relational system, not an alphabetical list, and should be studied as a system. For the fact is that the human mind creates meaning by establishing relations: Words—both word forms and word meanings—can play a representational role only in relation to other word forms and word meanings. What the study of words reveals about the mind is not a set of primitive concepts, not some universal set of innate ideas that every language must express, but rather the general mental operations of relating and structuring by means of which words—the fundamental units of human language—are differentiated and given significance.

Not until 1824, when Jean-François Champollion published his translation of the royal proclamation carved on this black basalt stone, were Egyptian hieroglyphics (top)—used for three millennia—and their associated demotic script (middle) deciphered. The Greek version at the bottom was the key. The inscription, from 196 B.C., was discovered by Napoleon's troops at Rashid (Rosetta), Egypt, in 1799.

A LEXICAL CHRONOLOGY

The following, arranged in chronological order, are some of the more important developments and publications that have influenced scientific studies of words.

1690   John Locke argues that word meanings have necessary and sufficient conditions.

1755   Samuel Johnson writes his famous modern monolingual dictionary of English.

1779   Christian Kratzenstein devises resonators that produce vowels.

1786   Sir William Jones launches the search for Proto-Indo-European.

1811   Rasmus Rask publishes evidence for sound changes in Germanic languages.

1822   Jakob Grimm formulates sound laws for Germanic languages.

1824   Jean-François Champollion deciphers hieroglyphic text of the Rosetta Stone.

1828   Noah Webster publishes *An American Dictionary of the English Language*.

1833   H. Feldmann reviews reports of the vocabularies of thirty-three children.

1838   Morse code is introduced.

1848   Johannes Müller proposes the source-filter theory of speech.

1852   The first edition of Peter Mark Roget's *Thesaurus* appears.

1857   A proposal for a new dictionary is made that leads to the *Oxford English Dictionary*.

1861   Pierre Paul Broca localizes speech in the left hemisphere of the brain.

1874   Carl Wernicke describes sensory aphasias and lays a scientific basis for aphasiology.

1875   Karl Verner reformulates the sound laws to explain discrepancies.

1876   Alexander Graham Bell invents the telephone.

1877   Thomas Alva Edison invents the phonograph.

1878   Ferdinand de Saussure predicts the discovery of laryngeals in Proto-Indo-European.

1879   Sir Francis Galton publishes the first study of word associations.

1880   Wilhelm Wundt standardizes the word association experiment.

1884   James Murray publishes the first installment of the *Oxford English Dictionary*.

1885   James KcKeen Cattell shows that letters are easier to read when they form a word.

1888   The first version of the International Phonetic Alphabet (IPA) is published.

1892   Gottlob Frege distinguishes between sense and reference.

1901   Karl Marbe's law states that common word associations are faster than are uncommon ones.

1904	Carl Jung collects word association norms.
1905	Bertrand Russell proposes a theory of descriptions.
1905	Henri Binet and Theodore Simon include vocabulary questions in the *Metrical Scale of Intelligence*.
1906	Lee De Forest develops vacuum tubes as voltage amplifiers.
1906	Ferdinand de Saussure begins lecturing on the scientific foundations of linguistics.
1910	Word association norms for English published by G. H. Kent and A. J. Rosanoff.
1911	*The Handbook of North American Indians* by Franz Boas is published.
1921	Edward Sapir's *Language* presents an anthropological view of linguistics.
1923	C. K. Ogden and I. A. Richards's *The Meaning of Meaning* is published.
1926	M. E. Smith standardizes a vocabulary test for preschool children.
1928	The final installment of the *Oxford English Dictionary* is published.
1928	E. V. Condon gives an equation describing the distribution of word frequencies.
1929	Harvey Fletcher's *Speech and Hearing* summarizes research at the Bell Telephone Laboratories.
1930	C. K. Ogden proposes Basic English as an international language.
1931	Alfred Tarski defines truth for formalized languages.
1933	Leonard Bloomfield's *Language* presents a theoretical integration for linguistics.
1934	Karl Bühler's *Sprachtheorie* calls attention to deictic words.
1935	George Kingsley Zipf shows the relation of word frequency and word length.
1935	J. Ridley Stroop shows how automatic word recognition can interfere with color naming.
1938	L. L. Thurstone's factor analysis distinguishes word fluency and verbal comprehension.
1940	R. H. Seashore and L. D. Eckerson introduce dictionary sampling to estimate vocabulary size.
1944	Edward Lee Thorndike and Irving Lorge publish a frequency tabulation for words in written English.
1945	Tape recorders become available.
1946	John Mauchly and John Eckert, Jr., invent the electronic vacuum-tube computer ENIAC.
1947	Ralph Potter, George Kopp, and Harriet Green's *Visible Speech* introduces speech spectrograms.
1948	*The Mathematical Theory of Communication* by Claude Shannon is published.
1950	Heinz Werner and Edith Kaplan study the acquisition of word meaning from linguistic context.
1951	George Miller, George Heise, and William Lichten demonstrate the role of expectation in word perception.
1952	Michael Ventris deciphers Linear B.
1952	Charles Osgood's semantic differential maps concepts into a space defined by adjectives.
1953	Ludwig Wittgenstein argues that words have family relationships.
1954	Charles Osgood and Thomas Sebeok's *Psycholinguistics* names a new interdisciplinary field.
1955	John Austin lectures on how to do things with words.

1957	Noam Chomsky formulates transformational generative grammar.
1962	Minicomputers are introduced by the Digital Equipment Corporation.
1963	I. J. Gelb's *A Study of Writing* is published.
1963	Jerrold Katz and Jerry Fodor's semantic theory provides a basis for disambiguating words.
1964	James Deese describes the role of antonymy in organizing lexical memory for adjectives.
1965	Word processing is first introduced by IBM.
1965	Jeffrey Gruber's thematic relations analyze the semantic roles of words in sentences.
1967	Michael Gazzaniga and Roger Sperry show that either half of the brain can have its own lexicon.
1967	Manfred Bierwisch illustrates differences between marked and unmarked adjectives.
1967	Ross Quillian devises the first semantic network and proposes inheritance of attributes.
1968	James McCawley's analysis of lexical insertion rules initiates generative semantics.
1969	Allen Collins and Ross Quillian use reaction times to test Quillian's semantic proposal.
1969	Gerald Reicher shows how to demonstrate the word-superiority effect.
1970	Noam Chomsky proposes a lexicalist alternative to generative semantics.
1970	Herbert Rubenstein introduces the lexical decision task to study the subjective lexicon.
1971	David Meyer and Roger Schvaneveldt demonstrate priming of lexical decisions by related words.
1971	Samuel Fillenbaum and Amnon Rapoport use scaling methods to study the structure of lexical memory.
1972	Ray Jackendoff formulates semantic interpretation within a theory of generative grammar.
1972	Roger Schank offers conceptual dependency theory to explain how word meanings combine.
1976	Eleanor Rosch and colleagues provide psychological evidence for a level of basic concepts.
1976	Mark Aronoff formulates morphology within a theory of generative grammar.
1977	*Semantics* by John Lyons summarizes linguistic semantics.
1979	Hartvig Dahl publishes a frequency tabulation for words in spoken English.
1980	Marta Kutas and Steven Hillyard discover the N400 response.
1982	W. Nelson Francis and Henry Kučera's syntactically tagged count of English word frequencies appears.
1982	Paul Kiparsky's theory of lexical phonology characterizes morphological levels.
1986	*Lexical Semantics* by D. A. Cruse emphasizes the importance of context.
1987	Marcel Just and Patricia Carpenter incorporate lexical access and semantic analysis into reading theory.
1988	Positron emission tomography (PET) is used to localize lexical processes in the brain.
1989	The second edition of the *Oxford English Dictionary* becomes available on-line.

This 1985 sculpture, The Words We Have Spoken, *by Ian Hamilton Finlay, with Nicholas Sloan, renders a quotation from Louis-Antoine de Saint-Just, styled the "archangel" of the French Revolution. Saint-Just was guillotined in 1794 with Robespierre, to whose cause he had dedicated his passionate and eloquent idealism. Using stone, the artists have attempted to embody the contradictions of both the statement and the speaker.*

FURTHER READINGS

Every author is biased. Serious readers know to look for alternative points of view, and the following list should suffice to launch a scholarly search for them. The suggestions are grouped according to the chapters for which they are most relevant, but most of them will be found to contain material of much broader interest.

Chapter 1:   The Scientific Study of Language

Blumenthal, Arthur L. (1970). *Language and Psychology: Historical Aspects of Psycholinguistics.* New York: Wiley.

Jankowsky, Kurt R. (1972). *The Neogrammarians.* The Hague: Mouton.

Miller, George A. (1981). *Language and Speech.* New York: W. H. Freeman.

Osherson, Daniel N., and Howard Lasnik. (1990). *Language: An Invitation to Cognitive Science,* vol. 1. Cambridge, Mass.: The MIT Press.

Pinker, Steven. (1994). *The Language Instinct: How the Mind Creates Language.* New York: William Morrow and Co.

Chapter 2:   Units of Analysis

de Saussure, Ferdinand. (1959). *Course in General Linguistics.* Edited by Charles Bally and Albert Sechehaye, in collaboration with Albert Reidlinger; translated from the French by Wade Baskin. New York: Philosophical Library.

Sapir, Edward. (1921). *Language.* New York: Harcourt, Brace and Co.

Shannon, Claude E., and Warren Weaver. (1949). *The Mathematical Theory of Communication.* Urbana, Ill.: University of Illinois Press.

Chapter 3:   The Written Word

Gelb, Ignace J. (1963). *A Study of Writing,* revised edition. Chicago, Ill.: University of Chicago Press.

Just, Marcel A., and Patricia A. Carpenter. (1987). *The Psychology of Reading and Language Comprehension.* Newton, Mass.: Allyn and Bacon.

Pope, Maurice. (1975). *The Story of Decipherment: From Egyptian Hieroglyphic to Linear B.* London: Thames and Hudson.

Sampson, Geoffrey. (1985). *Writing Systems.* Stanford, Calif.: Stanford University Press.

Chapter 4:   The Spoken Word

Chomsky, Noam, and Morris Halle. (1968). *The Sound Pattern of English.* New York: Harper and Row.

Eimas, Peter D., and Joanne L. Miller. (1981). *Perspectives on the Study of Speech.* Hillsdale, N.J.: Lawrence Erlbaum Associates.

Lieberman, Philip. (1991). *Uniquely Human: The Evolution of Speech, Thought, and Selfless Behavior.* Cambridge, Mass.: Harvard University Press.

Chapter 5:   Word Families

Hudson, Richard. (1984). *Word Grammar.* Oxford: Basil Blackwell.

Schachter, Paul. (1985). Parts-of-speech systems. In Timothy Shopen (editor), *Language Typology and Syntactic Description. Volume 1. Clause Structure.* New York: Cambridge University Press. pp. 3–61.

Chapter 6:   Word Formation

Anderson, Stephen R. Where's morphology? *Linguistic Inquiry,* 13, 571–612.

Aronoff, Mark. (1976). *Word Formation in Generative Grammar.* Cambridge, Mass.: The MIT Press.

Di Sciullo, Anna Maria, and Edwin Williams. (1987). *On the Definition of Word.* Cambridge, Mass.: The MIT Press.

Gleitman, Lila R., and Henry Gleitman. (1970). *Phrase and Paraphrase: Some Innovative Uses of Language.* New York: Norton.

Marchand, Hans. (1969). *The Categories and Types of Present-Day English Word-Formation.* München: C. H. Beck.

Selkirk, Elizabeth. (1982). *The Syntax of Words.* Cambridge, Mass.: The MIT Press.

Chapter 7: The Mental Lexicon

Aitchison, Jean. (1994). *Words in the Mind: An Introduction to the Mental Lexicon*. Second Edition. Oxford: Basil Blackwell.

Carroll, David W. (1986). *Psychology of Language*. Monterey, Calif.: Brooks/Cole.

Fillenbaum, Samuel, and Anatol Rapoport. (1971). *Structures in the Subjective Lexicon*. New York: Academic Press.

Fromkin, Victoria A. (editor). (1973). *Speech Errors as Linguistic Evidence*. The Hague: Mouton.

Kintsch, Walter. (1974). *The Representation of Meaning in Memory*. Hillsdale, N.J.: Lawrence Erlbaum Associates.

Levelt, Willem J. M. (1989). *Speaking: From Intention to Articulation*. Cambridge, Mass.: The MIT Press.

Schvaneveldt, Roger W. (editor). (1990). *Pathfinder Associative Networks: Studies in Knowledge Organization*. Norwood, N.J.: Ablex.

Chapter 8: Word Meanings

Cruse, D.A. (1986). *Lexical Semantics*. New York: Cambridge University Press.

Jackendoff, Ray. (1983). *Semantics and Cognition*. Cambridge, Mass.: The MIT Press.

Kempson, Ruth M. (1977). *Semantic Theory*. New York: Cambridge University Press.

Landau, Sidney I. (1984). *Dictionaries: The Art and Craft of Lexicography*. New York: Scribners.

Lehrer, Adrienne. (1974). *Semantic Fields and Lexical Structures*. Amsterdam: North Holland.

Lyons, John. (1977). *Semantics*, 2 volumes. New York: Cambridge University Press.

Miller, George A., and Phillip N. Johnson-Laird. (1976). *Language and Perception*. Cambridge, Mass.: Harvard University Press.

Morton, Herbert C. (1994). *The Story of Webster's Third: Philip Gove's Controversial Dictionary and Its Critics*. New York: Cambridge University Press.

Chapter 9: Categorizing Experience

Lakoff, George. (1987). *Women, Fire, and Dangerous Things: What Categories Reveal about the Mind*. Chicago, Ill.: University of Chicago Press.

Smith, Edward E., and Douglas L. Medin. (1981). *Categories and Concepts*. Cambridge, Mass.: Harvard University Press.

Touretzky, David S. (1986). *The Mathematics of Inheritance Systems*. Los Altos, Calif.: Morgan Kaufman.

Chapter 10: Drawing Distinctions

Berlin, Brent, and Paul Kay. (1969). *Basic Color Terms: Their Universality and Evolution*. Berkeley, Calif.: University of California Press.

Bierwisch, Manfred. (1967). Some semantic universals of German adjectives. *Foundations of Language, 3*, 1–36.

Bolinger, Dwight. (1972). *Degree Words*. The Hague: Mouton.

Dixon, R. M. W. (1982). *Where Have All the Adjectives Gone?* Berlin: Walter de Gruyter.

Chapter 11: Making Sentences

Bresnan, Joan. (1978). A realistic transformational grammar. In Morris Halle, Joan Bresnan, and George A. Miller (editors), *Linguistic Theory and Psychological Reality*. Cambridge, Mass.: The MIT Press. pp. 1–59.

Chomsky, Noam. (1957). *Syntactic Structures*. The Hague: Mouton.

Chomsky, Noam. (1965). *Aspects of the Theory of Syntax*. Cambridge, Mass.: The MIT Press.

Gleitman, Lila R. (1990). The structural sources of verb meaning. *Language Acquisition, 1*, 3–55.

Pinker, Steven. (1989). *Learnability and Cognition: The Acquisition of Argument Structure*. Cambridge, Mass.: The MIT Press.

Chapter 12: The Growth of Vocabulary

Anglin, Jeremy M. (1977). *Word, Object, and Conceptual Development*. New York: Norton.

Brown, Roger. (1973). *A First Language: The Early Stages*. Cambridge, Mass.: Harvard University Press.

Keil, Frank C. (1979). *Semantic and Conceptual Development: An Ontological Perspective*. Cambridge, Mass.: Harvard University Press.

McKeown, Margaret G., and Mary E. Curtis (editors). (1987). *The Nature of Vocabulary Acquisition*. Hillsdale, N.J.: Lawrence Erlbaum Associates.

Slobin, Dan I. (1985). *The Crosslinguistic Study of Language Acquisition*. Hillsdale, N.J.: Lawrence Erlbaum Associates.

Wanner, Eric, and Lila R. Gleitman (editors). (1982). *Language Acquisition: The State of the Art*. New York: Cambridge University Press.

A Final Word

Lehrer, Adrienne, and Eva Kitlay, (editors). (1992). *Frames, Fields, and Contrasts: New Essays in Semantic and Lexical Organization*. Hillsdale, New Jersey: Lawrence Erlbaum Associates.

SOURCES OF ILLUSTRATIONS

Illustrations on pp. 69, 73, 74, 76, 78, 96, 132, 175 by Carlyn Iverson.

Illustrations on pp. 100, 123, 164, 165, 166, 194, 207, 241 by Ann Neumann.

Illustrations on pp. 160, 176, 181, 182, 243, 245 by Linda Krause.

Illustration on p. 236 (bottom) by Cordelia Johnson.

Other line drawings by Precision Graphics, which also contributed to the illustrations on p. 73 and p. 176; special thanks to Jim Dennison.

Frontmatter   *Frontispiece*: Ingeborg Lippman/Peter Arnold. *p. vi*: Paul Klee Foundation, Museum of Fine Arts, Berne; © 1990 by COSMOPRESS, Genf.

Chapter 1   *Facing p. 1*: (top) Smithsonian Photo No. 55,300. (bottom) Entropic Systems. *p. 3*: Kansas City School for the Deaf, Classroom, Kansas City, Mo., 1987; photo by Catherine Wagner; Fraenkel Gallery, San Francisco. *p. 4*: (top) American Philosophical Society. (bottom) John Scheiber/Stock Market. *p. 6*: E.T. Archive. *p. 7*: National Portrait Gallery, London. *p. 9*: After D. Crystal, *The Cambridge Encyclopedia of Language*, Cambridge University Press, 1987. *p. 10*: (top; bottom right) Det Kongelige Bibliotek, Copenhagen. (bottom left) Brüder Grimm-Museum Kassel. *p. 12*: University of Geneva Archives. *p. 13*: Trustees of the British Museum. *p. 15*: Smithsonian Photo No. 4305-a.

Chapter 2   *p. 20*: (left) Yale University Art Gallery, Collection Société Anonyme. (right) Royal British Columbia Museum, Victoria, B.C., Photo No. PN505. *p. 22*: Paul Klee Foundation, Museum of Fine Arts, Berne; © 1990 by COSMOPRESS, Genf. *p. 25*: After W. S-Y. Wang, The Chinese language, in W. S-Y. Wang (ed.), *Language, Writing, and the Computer*, Readings from *Scientific American*, W. H. Freeman, 1986; Chinese lettering by Litjiun Wong. *p. 27*: Canadian Museum of Civilization, Ottawa. *p. 29*: Nationalbibliothek, Vienna.

Chapter 3   *p. 38*: (top) The Fine Arts Museums of San Francisco, Achenbach Foundation for Graphic Arts. (bottom) Timothy Eagan/Woodfin Camp. *pp. 40, 41*: After J. D. Becker, Multilingual word processing, in *Language, Writing, and the Computer*. *p. 42*: (top) John Eastcott and Yua Momatiuk/Woodfin Camp. (bottom) David Burnett/Woodfin Camp. *p. 43*: Timothy Eagan/Woodfin Camp. *p. 45*: Metropolitan Museum of Art. *p. 46*: After I. J. Gelb, *A Study of Writing*, 2nd ed., University of Chicago Press, 1963. *p. 47*: Photo by Peter Kresan. *p. 48*: After Crystal, *The Cambridge Encyclopedia of Language*. *p. 50*: Trustees of the British Museum. *p. 51*: E.T. Archive. *pp. 52, 53, 54*: Ashmolean Museum, Oxford. *p. 55*: G. Sampson, *Writing Systems*, Stanford University Press, 1985. *p. 58*: (top) Granger Collection. (bottom) Grosvenor Collection, Library of Congress. *p. 61*: Yusuf Karsh/Woodfin Camp; Shavian orthography from Sampson, *Writing Systems*. *p. 62*: Martha Cooper.

Chapter 4   *p. 64* (left) Windsor Castle, Royal Library; © 1990 by Her Majesty Queen Elizabeth II. (right) John Laver, Centre for Speech Technology Research, University of Edinburgh. *p. 66*: Grosvenor Collection, Library of Congress. *p. 68*: After G. A. Miller, *Language and Communication*, McGraw-Hill, 1951. *p. 69*: After G. A. Miller, *Language and Speech*, W. H. Freeman, 1981. *pp. 70, 71*: After H. Dudley and T. H. Tarnoczy, The speaking machine of Wolfgang von

Kempelen, *J. Acoustical Society of America*, 22, 1950. *pp. 72, 73, 74, 75, 76*: After Miller, *Language and Speech*. *p. 77*: After M. Halle, The immanent form of phonemes, in W. Hirst (ed.), *The Making of Cognitive Science: Essays in Honor of George A. Miller*, Cambridge University Press, 1988. *p. 78*: After Miller, *Language and Speech*. *p. 80*: L. Lisker and A. Abramson. "The voicing dimension: Some experiments in comparative phonetics," *Proceedings of the Sixth International Congress of Phonetic Sciences*, Prague. © 1970 Academia, Publishing House of the Czechoslovak Academy of Sciences.

Chapter 5   *p. 88*: (top) Trustees, The National Gallery, London. *p. 91*: Tarasque Press, 1968. *p. 92*: Collection of Jasper Johns. *p. 96*: (top) Roger-Violett. *p. 97*: © 1972 by Lee and Felinger.

Chapter 6   *p. 102*: (top) Ric Ergenbright Photography. *p. 105*: Gernsheim Collection, Harry Ransom Humanities Research Center, University of Texas at Austin. *p. 116*: Craig Newbauer/Peter Arnold.

Chapter 7   *p. 120*: (top) © 1990 by Jasper Johns/VAGA New York; collection Mr. and Mrs. S. I. Newhouse, Jr. *p. 127*: After Miller, *Language and Speech*. *p. 129*: F. R. Vellutino, Dyslexia, *Scientific American*, March 1987. *p. 130*: Alexandra Avakian/Woodfin Camp. *p. 133*: S. E. Petersen et al., Positron emission tomographic studies of the processing of single words, *J. Cognitive Neuroscience*, 1(2). *p. 137*: National Portrait Gallery, London. *p. 139*: Metropolitan Museum of Art; Bequest of Charles Allen Munn, 1924. *p. 141*: K. M. Elisabeth Murray.

Chapter 8   *p. 144*: (top) K. M. Elisabeth Murray. (bottom) Oxford University Press: The Oxford Dictionaries. *p. 148*; *p. 149*: (left) Bettman Archive. *p. 149*: (right) The Austrian Ludwig Wittgenstein Society. *p. 155*: National Portrait Gallery, London. *pp. 156, 162*: Bettman Archive. *pp. 164, 165, 166*: After J. D. Bransford and N. S. McCarrell, A sketch of a cognitive approach to comprehension: Some thoughts about understanding what it means to comprehend, in W. B. Weimer and D. S. Palermo (eds.), *Cognition and the Symbolic Processes*, Erlbaum, 1974. *p. 168*: From *Language, Thought and Reality, Selected Writings of Benjamin Lee Whorf*, MIT Technology Press and Wiley, 1956.

Chapter 9   *p. 170*: (top) Michel Viard/Peter Arnold. *p. 172*: Harvey Lloyd/Peter Arnold. *p. 174*: Deutsches Museum, München. *p. 185*: After Miller, *Language and Speech*.

Chapter 10   *p. 190*: (top) John Garett/Tony Stone Worldwide. *p. 192*: D. Cavagnaro/Peter Arnold. *p. 198*: Bettman Archive. *p. 205*: Ernst Haas/Magnum.

Chapter 11   *p. 210*: (top) Bruce Curtis/Peter Arnold. *p. 213*: Ernst Haas/Magnum. *p. 215*: Deutsches Museum, München. *p. 218*: Jerry Brendt. *p. 225*: Bettman Archive. *p. 229*: Bruce Curtis/Peter Arnold. *p. 231*: Bettman Archive. *pp. 232, 233*: Globus Brothers/Stock Market.

Chapter 12   *p. 236*: (top) Hyman Brand Hebrew Academy, Classroom, Kansas City, Mo.; photo by Catherine Wagner; Fraenkel Gallery, San Francisco. *p. 246*: Erika Stone. *p. 248*: After G. A. Miller and P. M. Gildea, How children learn words, *Scientific American*, Sept. 1987. *p. 249*: John Eastcott and Yua Momatiuk/Woodfin Camp. *p. 251*: After M. Kutas and S. Hillyard, Event-related brain potentials to semantically inappropriate and surprisingly long words, *Biological Psychology*, 11, 1980. *p. 255*: Erika Stone.

Backmatter   *p. 256*: Uppsala Universitet Bibliotecket. *p. 262*: Bridgeman Art Library/Art Resource. *p. 266*: Photo by Antonia Reeve.

INDEX

Selected hardcover books in the Scientific American Library series:

ATOMS, ELECTRONS, AND CHANGE
by P. W. Atkins

DIVERSITY AND THE TROPICAL RAINFOREST
by John Terborgh

GENES AND THE BIOLOGY OF CANCER
by Harold Varmus and Robert A. Weinberg

MOLECULES AND MENTAL ILLNESS
by Samuel H. Barondes

EXPLORING PLANETARY WORLDS
by David Morrison

EARTHQUAKES AND GEOLOGICAL DISCOVERY
by Bruce A. Bolt

THE ORIGIN OF MODERN HUMANS
by Roger Lewin

THE EVOLVING COAST
by Richard A. Davis, Jr.

THE LIFE PROCESSES OF PLANTS
by Arthur W. Galston

IMAGES OF MIND
by Michael I. Posner and Marcus E. Raichle

THE ANIMAL MIND
by James L. Gould and Carol Grant Gould

MATHEMATICS: THE SCIENCE OF PATTERNS
by Keith Devlin

A SHORT HISTORY OF THE UNIVERSE
by Joseph Silk

THE EMERGENCE OF AGRICULTURE
by Bruce D. Smith

ATMOSPHERE, CLIMATE, AND CHANGE
by Thomas E. Graedel and Paul J. Crutzen

AGING: A NATURAL HISTORY
by Robert E. Ricklefs and Caleb E. Finch

INVESTIGATING DISEASE PATTERNS: THE SCIENCE OF EPIDEMIOLOGY
by Paul D. Stolley and Tamar Lasky

Other Scientific American Library books now available in paperback:

POWERS OF TEN
by Philip and Phylis Morrison and the Office of Charles and Ray Eames

THE DISCOVERY OF SUBATOMIC PARTICLES
by Steven Weinberg

THE SCIENCE OF MUSICAL SOUND
by John R. Pierce

THE SECOND LAW
by P. W. Atkins

MOLECULES
by P. W. Atkins

THE NEW ARCHAEOLOGY AND THE ANCIENT MAYA
by Jeremy A. Sabloff

THE HONEY BEE
by James L. Gould and Carol Grant Gould

EYE, BRAIN, AND VISION
by David H. Hubel

PERCEPTION
by Irvin Rock

FROM QUARKS TO THE COSMOS
by Leon M. Lederman and David N. Schramm

HUMAN DIVERSITY
by Richard Lewontin

SLEEP
by J. Allan Hobson

DRUGS AND THE BRAIN
by Solomon H. Snyder

BEYOND THE THIRD DIMENSION
by Thomas F. Banchoff

If you would like to purchase additional volumes in the Scientific American Library, please send your order to:

Scientific American Library
41 Madison Avenue
New York, NY 10010